UNIVERSAL STUDIOS
MONSTERS

UNIVERSAL STUDIOS
MONSTERS
A LEGACY OF HORROR

MICHAEL MALLORY

UNIVERSE

Published by Universe Publishing, a division of Rizzoli International Publications, Inc.
300 Park Avenue South
New York, New York 10010
www.rizzoliusa.com

Publisher: Charles Miers
Associate Publisher: Jim Muschett
Managing Editor: Lynn Scrabis
Text: Michael Mallory
Foreword: Jason Blum
Design: Chris McDonnell

For NBCUniversal:
Roger Almendarez, Deb Buynak, Kristin Conte, Sam Douglas, Audrey Eig, Adora English, Brian Goldsworthy, Lauren Hoffman, Barbara Layman, Shayne Mifsud, Maddie Mitchell, Michael Moccio, Melissa Rodriguez, Tom Schroder, Megan Startz, Nancy Stebler, Mike Sund, Susan Weber

Printed in China
2021 2022 2023 2024 / 10 9 8 7 6 5 4 3 2

ISBN-13: 978-0-7893-4100-6
Library of Congress Catalog Control Number: 2021934433

All images appear courtesy of Universal Pictures / Photofest and are copyright © Universal Pictures, except when noted.
All Bela Lugosi images are used with permission from Lugosi Enterprises TM
Pages 10 and 14: Courtesy Universal City Studios, Inc.
Page 221: Photo courtesy of Bob Burns
Page 227: Photo courtesy John Wooley, © 1996 Universal City Studios, Inc.

Acknowledgments:
The author and publisher would like to extend thanks to the following individuals and organizations who contributed to the creation of this book: Jerry Beck, S. Victor Burgos, Bob Burns, Jennifer Calzacorto, Jim Harmon, Robert S. Levinson, Helen Mallory, Ron Mandelbaum, David Schecter, Mark A. Vieira, the staff of the Margaret Herrick Library at the Academy of Motion Picture Arts and Sciences, and the staff of Eddie Brandt's Saturday Matinee. Special thanks are extended to Julie Adams, Ricou Browning, Elena Verdugo, Jim Muschett, Melissa Veronesi, and my research assistant Brendan Mallory. An extra special thank you to Jason Blum, Holly Goline, Vice President in charge of Universal Monsters; Mark "Crash" McCreery, creature designer; John Murdy, Creative Director/Executive Producer of Halloween Horror Nights at Universal Studios Hollywood; Jeff Pirtle, Director, Archives & Collections, Universal Studios; Mike Aiello, Senior Director of Entertainment Creative Development at Universal Orlando; TJ Mannarino, Vice President, Entertainment Art & Design for Universal Orlando; Tristan Eaton, street muralist.

This book is dedicated to the many, many actors, directors, producers, writers, artists and technicians whose combined talents created what we know as Universal Horror.

Visit us online:
Facebook.com/RizzoliNewYork
Twitter: @Rizzoli_Books
Instagram.com/RizzoliBooks
Pinterest.com/RizzoliBooks
Youtube.com/user/RizzoliNY
Issuu.com/Rizzoli

CONTENTS

FOREWORD
BY JASON BLUM

My mother introduced me to scary movies at a young age. In college, I studied the films of Alfred Hitchcock, from the high-brow, formally daring films like *Psycho* and *Vertigo* to the disreputable movies like *The Birds* and *Marnie* and *Rope*. You don't know why or how movies hit you when you're young. But there was something about the combination of grimy illicitness and sure-footed control that appealed to a disruptive kid who wanted to be liked—and wanted to be independent.

Much has been made of the way a horror film can reflect and comment on society's discontents and psyche. But when I was a kid, I was only aware of the way that horror films reflected the havoc and insecurity of my own psyche. It was an effect I would never forget.

A century ago, the movie business was in a similarly immature state. The studios, run by a group of immigrants and outsiders, were trying to convince the public that movies could be as reputable as the more "legitimate" forms of mass entertainment like live theater. (There is a reason so many theaters fashioned themselves as "palaces.") But Carl Laemmle, who founded Universal, cared more about earning money than respect. (He also didn't bother with theater ownership.) He knew that this new form had a peculiar power not available to literature or "legit" theater: with the right tools and the right talent, cinema could deliver *intensity*— and that the viewers would not see that intensity as mere sadism because they felt safe. It was in that spirit of business canniness and artistic insight that he launched a new genre—the monster movie—with Lon Chaney as the Hunchback of Notre Dame in 1923.

On their way to provoking fear in (and luring nickels from) an unsuspecting public, something funny happened to the Universal monster movie: it began to reveal a new and unique power of cinema—the power not just to provoke fear of these monsters, but also to inspire empathy for them. Cinema rendered them not only frightful—but fretful as well. That

Elisabeth Moss fights for her sanity in Leigh Whannell's The Invisible Man, *from Blumhouse Productions and Universal Picture.*

is the central contradiction of the scary movie: it can gather an audience into a state of empathy and simultaneously seek to repulse it. Indeed, the "suspense" comes from hanging in between these two states in the safety of a darkened room and the community of an audience.

For over a hundred years, Universal has been the safest harbor for these misfits—not just the monsters themselves but also the filmmakers and producers who wanted nothing more than to provoke intense responses from audiences and do it without concern for the worthiness and seriousness that the rest of the industry was apt to chase. The success of the monsters owes everything to Universal's embrace of the independent outsider.

I am lucky enough to be one of those outsiders, having grown from a disruptive Hitchcock-loving kid into one of the deviant stewards of the modern horror movie. Some of the films I've produced, like Leigh Whannell's brilliant and terrifying *The Invisible Man*, or Jordan Peele's provocative and totemic *Get Out*, have passed almost immediately into respectability. But I also produced *The Purge* franchise, serious cautionary social thrillers that have nonetheless never cracked the "Fresh" ceiling on Rotten Tomatoes.

It wasn't until the 1970s, when Hitchcock's reputation was being renovated by the French, that the monster movies were rebranded as the "Universal Classic Monsters." This new designation is a reminder that, just as it's hard to make sense of history when you're in the chaotic midst of it, so too is it hard to judge horror movies until many years later.

Let this volume stand as a testament to these classic monsters— and to the complex combination of fear and sympathy they arouse in us.

Stay safe and stay scary,

Jason Blum

1
HOLLYWOOD'S HOUSE OF HORROR

The unborn and undying creation of Dr. Frankenstein, the suave but deadly Count Dracula, the cursed and bestial Wolf Man, the immortal and vengeful living Mummy, and the amphibian predator known as the Gill Man are creatures that have haunted our collective consciousness for decades. They and many other iconic characters of horror entertainment, such as the Phantom of the Opera, the Invisible Man, and the Bride of Frankenstein, have become enduring legends of Hollywood. While some of these characters preexisted in mythology or literature, the iconic forms, images, and identities that we immediately recognize in them today all emanated from one place: Universal Studios.

During Hollywood's heyday, other studios tried their hands at making horror pictures, usually spurred on by the success Universal was having with them, but invariably they would soon get it out of their systems, and then go back to doing the styles and genres that came to them naturally. For Universal, however, thrills and chills were the specialties of the day, and to that end the studio lined up a roster of monsters that have become legendary: Dracula, the Frankenstein Monster, the Wolf Man, and the Mummy, in addition to a few whose profiles have faded with time, such as Paula the Ape Woman, the Creeper, and the Spider Woman.

Universal had its own stable of stars as well, masters of the medium who were able to deliver chills to audiences without even trying. Actors such as Boris Karloff and Bela Lugosi possessed the special ability to look straight through the camera and peer into the hearts of the movie-goers seated in theaters around the world and convince them that the impossible was happening before their eyes. Karloff and Lugosi remain so recognizable, and have been so imitated over the years, that we now assume they can be summed up by a series of vocal and visual manner-isms, but that is not the case. One has to compare the performances of these two actors in film after film to realize just how versatile and skilled they were.

Universal Studios' expansive backlot still boasts many of the precise spots where the classic horror films were shot: the Court of Miracles seen in *The Hunchback of Notre Dame*; the stone arch through which the Frankenstein Monster passed in *Bride of Frankenstein*; the house from which the Monster flung a villager in *The Ghost of Frankenstein*; the shop operated by the Conliffe family from *The Wolf Man*; the train station at which both Wolf von Frankenstein and the suspicious-looking luggage of Count "Alucard" arrived in *Son of Frankenstein* and *Son of Dracula*, respectively; and of course the village courtyard that has been the scene of many happy Tyrolean festivals, and just as many gathering places for torch-wielding mobs. Another film set not on public display is a portion of the Paris Opera House from *The Phantom of the Opera*, constructed in 1924 and still standing on Stage 28—"The Phantom Stage"—85 years later. It is the oldest interior film set in the world.

Those who visit Universal Studios today experience the enduring vision of a tiny, jovial entrepreneur, with an ever-present smile and a gambler's instinct, named Carl Laemmle. Like so many of the early film moguls, Laemmle was a Jewish European immigrant, born in 1867 in Laupheim, Germany. In 1884 the Laemmle family immigrated to the United States, where young Carl first entered the haberdashery business, but shortly after the turn of the century he became captivated by the then-modern marvel of motion pictures.

The very earliest motion picture theaters were called nickelodeons, a name that reflected their ticket price. These were usually small storefronts containing upwards of 200 folding chairs, all pointed toward a screen, on which would be projected the one-reel fare of the day. The first nickelodeon in America was opened in Pittsburgh in June 1905, and Carl Laemmle was not far behind that, opening his White Front Theatre in Chicago the following February. It would become the first link of a nation-wide chain of nickelodeons called the Laemmle Film Service.

In building his successful chain, Laemmle became a target for the monopolistic organization called the Motion Picture Patents Company (MPPC), which strictly enforced the East Coast film industry's stranglehold on distribution. After a barrage of lawsuits, Laemmle retaliated by deciding to produce his own films outside of the MPPC's jurisdiction, thus forming the Independent Motion Picture Company (IMPC) in 1909. Its first production was an adaptation of Henry Wadsworth Longfellow's epic poem "The Song of Hiawatha."

Laemmle soon migrated west in part to try and outrun the reach of the Eastern trusts, but also because Southern California had been identified as a movie-making Mecca, complete with every kind of topography one could wish, and more than 300 days of sunshine to illuminate the productions shot on outdoor stages. On June 8, 1912, Laemmle merged IMPC and four other film production entities into Universal Film Manu-fact-uring Company. The company operated out of the former Bison Studio in the town of Edendale, just north of downtown Los Angeles (now the area of L.A. called Echo Park), and the Nestor Studio in Hollywood, a small town eight miles west of downtown that had then just been annexed into the city.

The front gate of Universal Studios, 1915, complete with a banner proclaiming Carl Laemmle "King of the Movies" (in those days, a "movie" meant someone working in the film industry rather than a motion picture).

"Uncle" Carl Laemmle, the founder of Universal Pictures.

Two years later, Laemmle purchased a 230-acre ranch in the San Fernando Valley right at the spot where the treaty between Mexico and the United States that allowed for California statehood had been signed. The area was then wilderness, but that was exactly what the self-made mogul wanted: a place on which to build an entire moviemaking city, one where people could not only work, but live. When Universal City officially opened on March 15, 1915, even Buffalo Bill Cody showed up for the proceedings. Before long the City boasted some 500 residents—including a group of American Indians who lived in tepees—and a private zoo. The avuncular Laemmle (he was widely known as "Uncle Carl") even invited the general public, charging 25 cents a head to watch movies being made, thereby creating the world's first studio tour.

Uncle Carl cheerfully pioneered another staple of the motion-picture industry: nepotism. He was renowned for putting so many relatives on the company payroll that poet Ogden Nash commented: "Uncle Carl Laemmle has a very large faemmle." One relative, though, would turn out to have a major impact on Universal: Laemmle's son Julius, who later changed his name to Carl Laemmle Jr.

Orson Welles famously described a movie studio as "the biggest train set a boy ever had." That analogy could have applied equally well to Carl Laemmle Jr. Born in 1908, he joined Universal as a production supervisor while still in his teens. For his 21st birthday Junior, as he was generally known, was literally given the keys to the kingdom: he was put in charge of the studio's production output, the position held some years earlier by Hollywood's "boy genius" Irving Thalberg. While Uncle Carl's name would still be in the credits of every picture, either as "Presenter" or identified as the President of the company (which was misspelled as "Present" in the credits of *Dracula*), it was his son, a diminutive dandy with a movie star smile, who was calling the shots.

Actor Leon Ames, who debuted in the 1932 film *Murders in the Rue Morgue*, described Junior Laemmle as "a kid, a strange little fellow." Many agreed that he did not quite possess the genius, maturity, or business sense of Thalberg. Even his father came to have his doubts about his son's abilities. Yet it was Carl Jr. who had the vision that turned Universal Studios into the world's number one purveyor of horror films.

Armed with the success of 1931's *Dracula*, Junior began lining up other horror projects, beginning with *Frankenstein* and following it with *Murders in the Rue Morgue, The Mummy, The Old Dark House, The Invisible Man, The Black Cat, The Raven,* and *Werewolf of London*. While Uncle Carl personally preferred less gruesome fare, such as Westerns, he could not deny the impact his studio was having with its horror pictures.

The end of the Laemmles' tenure at Universal coincided exactly with the end of the studio's first horror cycle in 1936, though the two occurrences had little to do with each other. Financial difficulties had forced Uncle Carl to put up his controlling interest in Universal as collateral against a production loan, and this time the gamble did not pay off: he lost control of the studio. The last film completed under the Laemmle regime was *Dracula's Daughter*, after which Uncle Carl retired, living happily for another three years. Junior, meanwhile, dabbled in production at another studio, but by 1937 he was out of the film business. For the next

Buffalo Bill Cody attended the opening of Universal on March 15, 1915.

*Uncle Carl Laemmle celebrated his
67th birthday in 1934, surrounded
by Universal staff and contractees,
including cowboy star Ken Maynard
(in 10-gallon hat) and Boris Karloff
beside him.*

*Uncle Carl Laemmle and some of
his "faemmle."*

The Universal backlot in the mid-1920s. The furthermost structure, in the center, is the façade of Notre Dame Cathedral built for The Hunchback of Notre Dame.

"Little Europe" on the Universal backlot, where so many horror pictures were filmed.

Carl Laemmle Jr., then Universal production head, at work.

*Bela Lugosi and Boris Karloff toast
themselves as two of the studio's
biggest stars in 1932.*

40 years he lived in comfort in Los Angeles, becoming increasingly reclusive, and passed away in 1979.

The new owners of Universal were Charles Rogers and J. Cheever Cowdin, the executives of the Standard Capital Corporation, who immediately instituted what they called "The New Universal." The first thing swept out the door were horror films. Even the mighty Karloff, who a couple years earlier had been Universal's biggest attraction, was back to playing character roles in straight dramas, such as 1937's *Night Key*.

A year later, though, something unexpected happened: *Dracula* and *Frankenstein* were rereleased together as a double feature in order to generate some quick capital, and the smash success of the horror program surprised everybody. The studio's new head of production, Cliff Work, wondered if maybe the New Universal needed to reclaim a little bit of the glory of the Old Universal. *Son of Frankenstein* was put into production in late 1938, and its success spurred what has become known as the second horror cycle. Both Karloff and Lugosi would be part of this cycle, but its primary attraction would be a new horror man with a familiar name: Lon Chaney Jr., the son of the great silent star.

Universal's second horror cycle, propelled by producers George Waggner, Ben Pivar, and Paul Malvern; writers Curt Siodmak, Eric Taylor, and Brenda Weisberg; directors Erle C. Kenton, Reginald Le Borg, and Harold Young; and many others, coincided roughly with the duration World War II and provided fantastic escape from the realities of it. It also introduced a plethora of new characters, most notably the Wolf Man, and launched an era of sequels, many of them inexpensively produced, which proved to be hugely popular.

When Universal merged with International Pictures in 1946, bcoming Universal-International, the second horror cycle came to an end. Whereas wartime audiences needed escapism, postwar moviegoers were more in the mood for realism. Monsters would not seriously rear their ugly heads at Universal until the mid-1950s, when producer William Alland and director Jack Arnold would take over the science fiction/monster unit. The Gill Man, star of *The Creature From the Black Lagoon*, would become the last great monster in the Universal pantheon, and spawn a short-lived cycle of scientific creature-based horror films, such as *Tarantula*, *The Mole People*, and *Monster on the Campus*.

More than 60, 70, and even 80 years after they were originally made, the horror films of Universal Studios are as popular as ever, a testament to the scores of actors, writers, directors, producers, composers, designers, special effects and makeup artists, and cameramen who made them. The likes of Dracula, Frankenstein's Monster, and the Wolf Man are among the most easily recognizable fictional characters on the planet. Born out of 19th-century literary traditions, the films made by Universal in the middle of the 20th century seem well assured of lasting far into the 21st century, and beyond.

It is a true legacy of horror.

Along with his father, Junior Laemmle said goodbye to Universal in 1936.

*Cinematographer Robert Newhard
and director Wallace Worsley on
the set of* The Hunchback of Notre
Dame. *The recording set-up must
be for radio, since the picture
was silent.*

2
SILENT NIGHTMARES

The beginnings of the horror film predate not only color and sound, but also the establishment of Hollywood itself. The films of late-19th-century French magician and film pioneer Georges Méliès featured supernatural themes and characters, often used for comedic effect. But it was Germany that truly gave life to the genre of the horror film as we know it. Such eerie masterpieces as *The Cabinet of Dr. Caligari* (1919), *Nosferatu* (1922), and *Waxworks* (1924) not only defined the genre, they greatly influenced Hollywood filmmaking of the 1930s. This was because many of the filmmakers who helped develop Universal's horror style, which was steeped in expressionism, were the same German pioneers who had established the film industry of their native country. In later years, after many German émigrés found a home at Universal City, after having fled the rise of Nazi power, it is little wonder they focused on telling stories about the rise of madmen and monsters.

One of the primary requirements of a silent motion picture is to compensate for its lack of sound by offering exciting, dramatic visuals. In their silent horror classics, Universal accomplished that with stunning success.

THE HUNCHBACK OF NOTRE DAME (1923)

Universal's first genre classic was *The Hunchback of Notre Dame* starring Lon Chaney. Directed by Wallace Worsley, a popular silent filmmaker who is now largely forgotten, it was also one of Hollywood's first epic spectacles. Even when seen today, the sheer size of the crowd scenes are impressive (particularly for today's audiences, who are aware and accepting of the technique of digital crowd creation). While it is technically not a horror film, in that there are no supernatural or otherworldly elements involved, it features the first great American horror icon, the

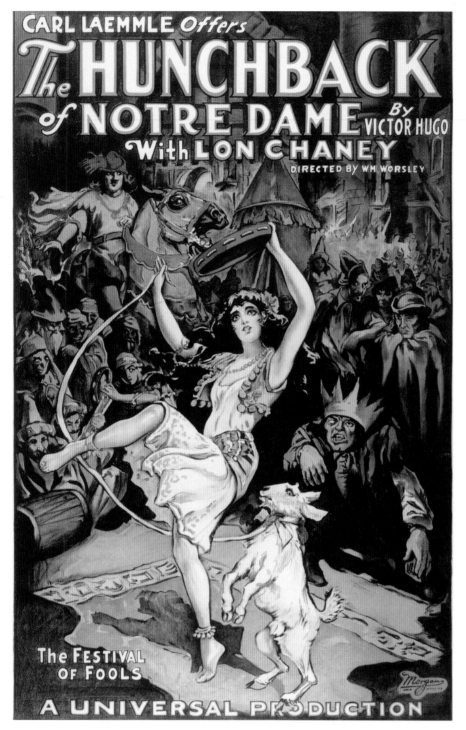

Quasimodo is crowned King of the Fools by the crowd of peasant revelers.

Trade press promotion for The Hunchback of Notre Dame.

Quasimodo (Lon Chaney) abducts Esmeralda (Patsy Ruth Miller) at the behest of Jehan (Brandon Hurst), who lurks in the background.

Quasimodo chained to the wheel, about to be whipped. For this shot Chaney wore a tight-fitting, hair-covered rubber body suit over the leather hump.

grotesquely misshapen bell ringer of the Cathedral of Notre Dame of Paris, Quasimodo.

Like the 1831 Victor Hugo novel upon which it is based, the film is set specifically in 1482. Quasimodo (Lon Chaney) is deaf, half-blind, and gravely malformed, and is allowed room and board at the cathedral, as well as the protection of the pious archbishop Dom Claude (Nigel de Brulier), in return for ringing the tower bells. Also haunting the gothic corridors is Dom Claude's brother Jehan (Brandon Hurst), a lying, grasping, selfish man with an uncanny ability to create misery all around him. Jehan forces the reluctant, but helpless, Quasimodo to act as his servant.

Entranced by a young gypsy dancer named Esmeralda (Patsy Ruth Miller), who is the ward of Clopin (Ernest Torrence), the rebellious "King of the Beggars," Jehan instructs Quasimodo to abduct her. The hunchback attempts this but is prevented and captured by the dashing Captain of the Guard, Phoebus (Norman Kerry), who falls for Esmeralda's beauty (as does just about everyone else). Quasimodo is arrested, tried, and sentenced to a public whipping. Only Esmeralda shows him any compassion, offering him water.

Sometime later, after Esmeralda has been sentenced to hang for the attempted murder of Phoebus, which was really committed by Jehan, Quasimodo repays her kindness by carrying her inside the cathedral, which offers sanctuary from the King's "justice." Esmeralda is safe, though her treatment by the crown is the spark that Clopin needs to light the fuse of revolt, which has long been simmering within the peasant class. His minions storm the cathedral to take her back, but Quasimodo only sees them as attackers and fights back from the rooftop of Notre Dame, while the city's Guard, led by the recovering Phoebus, fight them on the ground. During the chaos, Jehan makes one last attempt to capture Esmeralda, but he is killed by the enraged Quasimodo. Mortally wounded in his fight with Jehan, the hunchback drags himself to the bell tower and rings his own death knell, while Phoebus and Esmeralda are reunited.

The Hunchback of Notre Dame provided a good showcase for Universal's medieval backlot section, which included a painstakingly reproduced western façade of Notre Dame de Paris. To replicate the towers of the cathedral in long shot, glass paintings were employed.

Lon Chaney's doglike performance as Quasimodo propelled him into superstardom, and it stands as his most fully realized portrayal. To create the look of the hunchback, Chaney sculpted new features over his face with Plasto, a soft, sticky wax used by morticians to repair the faces of bodies for viewing. A wire device inside his mouth further misshaped his jaw, while a set of snaggled false teeth made of a hard substance called gutta percha and a fright wig completed the effect. His body was distorted through use of a leather hump (which probably weighed no more than 20 pounds, not the 70 often reported), shoulder padding, and a special harness that kept him in a crouched position. As grotesque as the makeup is, it is also completely believable and was surprisingly flexible, allowing Chaney to swing, scuttle, and leap across the cathedral front like a monkey (though the actor was doubled in a dangerous rope slide down the face of Notre Dame by professional strongman Joe Bonomo).

Lon Chaney wearing what is perhaps his greatest makeup—as Quasimodo.

Released in September 1923, *The Hunchback of Notre Dame* grossed $3 million, an amazing amount for the silent era. If it contained more spectacle than dramatic momentum, at least it was true spectacle.

THE PHANTOM OF THE OPERA (1925)

Based on the novel by French journalist Gaston Leroux, which was first serialized in 1909 and 1910, *The Phantom of the Opera* provided Lon Chaney with his other signature role, and through it he offered one of the most horrifying makeups ever to appear on screen.

Even though the shadowy presence known as the Phantom is well known to those who work at the Paris Opera House, the Opera's new managers scoff at the legend...until they spot a mysterious figure in Box Five, who suddenly disappears. They become convinced when letters begin to arrive instructing them not to use an established soprano, Madame Carlotta (Virginia Pearson), in the lead role of their upcoming opera, but instead cast the young and talented Christine Daäe (Mary Philbin), whom the Phantom has been secretly mentoring. When they refuse, tragedy occurs: the enormous crystal chandelier in the theater falls during a performance, crushing the patrons below.

On top of that, Christine has disappeared, much to the distress of her fiancé Raoul de Chagny (Norman Kerry). She has willingly gone with the Phantom—whom she has previously known only through his mysterious voice behind the walls—to his underground lair five storeys below the opera house. The masked figure confesses his love to her, but warns her that she must never see his face. Defying this warning, she pulls off the mask and reveals his hideous, skull-like visage. Heartbroken that she has seen his true nature, the Phantom allows Christine to return to the surface, on the condition that she never sees Raoul again.

Christine breaks her vow immediately, and during the Opera's Grand Masque Ball, the Phantom arrives disguised as the Red Death and overhears Christine beg Raoul to take her away from Paris and the "monster" who lives underneath the opera house. Consumed with the desire for vengeance, the Phantom daringly abducts Christine during a performance, but this time Raoul and Inspector Ledoux of the Secret Police (Arthur Edmund Carewe) track him to his lair. Ledoux has identified the Phantom as a brilliant but insane escapee from Devil's Island named Erik. During their pursuit they nearly succumb to a series of elaborate death traps the Phantom has prepared, and are rescued only after Christine agrees to marry the horrific Erik!

Meanwhile, a mob is forming in reaction to the discovery of a stagehand killed during Christine's abduction. They plunge into the dark underworld of the opera house and flush the Phantom up to the surface. After a wild coach ride, Erik is pursued on foot through the city by the mob (at one point they chase him past the backlot façade of Notre Dame). Finally cornering the madman, the mob beats him to death and throws his body into the Seine and Christine and Raoul are reunited.

The Phantom of the Opera was filmed on an extravagant million-dollar budget, which allowed for the elaborate Grand Masque Ball and opera sequences to be filmed in the then-new Technicolor process, but it suffered through a troubled production and a chaotic post-production. There was so much friction between Lon Chaney and director Rupert

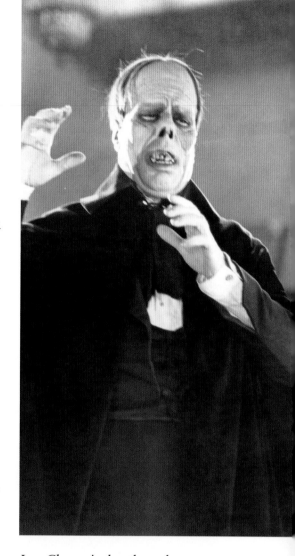

Lon Chaney's ghastly makeup as Erik, the Phantom, utilized painters' highlight and shadow tricks as well as tape and putty.

Poster for The Phantom of the Opera, *which boasted a cast of more than 5,000.*

Julian—who was then considered the studio's top director, having taken over Erich von Stroheim's problematic 1923 film *Merry-Go-Round*—that the two finally stopped speaking, forcing cinematographer Charles Van Enger to act as communicative go-between.

The film's original ending showed the Phantom dying of a broken heart in his lair after being rejected by Christine, but preview audiences found that confusing. Fearing an expensive flop, Universal replaced Julian with Edward Sedgwick—who was an odd choice given his preference for comedy—to film new scenes, including the climactic chase through the streets of Paris. After more failed previews, the studio went back and rendered out everything except the spectacle, the Technicolor, and Chaney (though the chase scene remained). What emerged was a two-hour version that opened September 6, 1925 (though this version no longer exists; most surviving prints are based on a 1930 partial-talkie reissue).

More than 80 years later, the revelation of the Phantom's face still carries a powerful jolt. To elongate and thin out his face, Chaney wore a bald cap draped with lank hair and glued his ears close to his head. To create the image of a skull he accentuated his cheekbones with putty, and pulled up his nose by gluing a strip of material called fishskin to the tip, yanking it up and fastening the other end onto his forehead. Enlarging his nostrils with wire and ringing them with black greasepaint made it appear that he had no nose, just as painting his lower eyelids white and then putting a layer of black underneath made his eyes look twice normal size. A red gaping mouth and a set of hideous, snaggled false teeth completed the ghastly effect. To heighten the shock of the Phantom's face, Universal forbade any photos of the unmasked Erik to be published prior to the film's release.

Why the Phantom is so hideous was never explained in the film. In Leroux's book, Erik is simply a freak of nature (and an architectural genius who helped to build the Paris Opera House), though the allusion to Devil's Island in the film implies that Erik might be leprous!

Unlike *The Hunchback of Notre Dame*, *The Phantom of the Opera* contains no trick or matte shots. Five tiers of theater boxes were built on a steel frame to replicate the interior of the Paris Opera House. Even the falling chandelier was real, though for safety's sake, it was filmed being *pulled up* to the ceiling, and then the film was reversed to make it look like it was falling. The film also introduced an image that would become as much a staple of Universal Horror as sparking lab equipment: the angry, torch-wielding mob.

In 1943 Universal produced a full Technicolor remake titled *Phantom of the Opera* (no *The*) using the same opera house sets, but a heavily altered storyline. In that version the Phantom is Erique Claudin (Claude Rains), the lead violinist of the Opera orchestra (and, it is strongly hinted, Christine's father) who goes into hiding after having his face burnt off with acid. This time the revelation of the Phantom's face was teased to the very end instead of occurring midway through, and Universal's makeup wizard Jack P. Pierce provided a very realistic, if somewhat less than horrific, burn scar on half of Rains' face. Legend has it that Pierce wanted to completely ravage the actor's face, making him unrecognizable, but either the studio front office or Rains himself objected, fearing it would be too ghastly.

Lon Chaney as Erik the Red Death, in the Grand Ball Masque sequence from The Phantom of the Opera. *This sequence was filmed in an early Technicolor process.*

Claude Rains played a velvet-voiced Opera Ghost in the 1943 Technicolor remake, Phantom of the Opera.

*Director Rupert Julian (in the chair) and his
crew appear to be waiting for Lon Chaney as
the Phantom to come up from the underground
stream on the set of* The Phantom of the Opera.

4159-30

The Phantom torments the
horrified Christine (Mary
Philbin) in his secret abode
(note how Chaney's head-
piece and the tilt of his
nose both seem to be
slipping).

Erik the Phantom "welcomes"
the hero Raoul (Norman
Kerry) and heroine Christine
(Mary Philbin) into his death-
trap-laden secret lair under
the Paris Opera.

The rather shady-looking lawyer Crosby (Tully Marshall) counsels innocent Annabelle West (Laura La Plante) in The Cat and the Canary.

"The Cat" goes for Crosby (Tully Marshall) from a secret passageway in The Cat and the Canary.

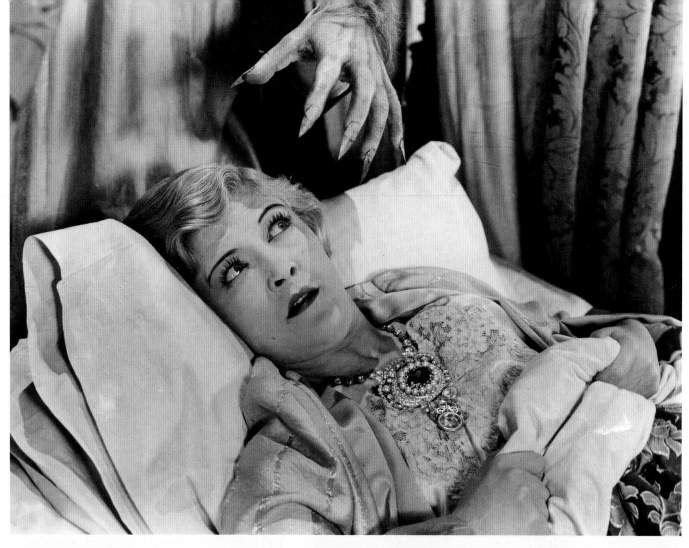

THE CAT AND THE CANARY (1927)

Films of the 1920s tended to draw their inspiration either from classic literature or popular Broadway plays. *The Cat and the Canary* falls into the latter category. Directed by German-born Paul Leni, one of the founders of film expressionism, the movie was based on a play by John Willard, which was a hit on Broadway in the 1922 season. Essentially a comedic murder mystery with as many haunted house trappings as can be stuffed into one film, *The Cat and the Canary* is the palimpsest for virtually every old dark house thriller made thereafter.

Twenty years after the death of loony old Cyrus West, his heirs are reassembled in his allegedly haunted mansion for the reading of his will. They are all shocked to learn that young, charming Annabelle West (Laura La Plante), the most distant relative with the name of West, is the sole heir for the entire estate. But Annabelle only gets the money if she is declared to be sane by a physician. If not, the entire estate goes to another heir, whose identity is revealed in a sealed envelope in the possession of the sinister lawyer, Roger Crosby (Tully Marshall).

The stage is now set for an evening of horror that includes a dead body tumbling out of a closet, an escaped lunatic somewhere on the premises, the appearance of a mysterious doctor, cut telephone lines, moving shadows, secret passageways, and clawed, hairy hands that appear from out of walls. It is an elaborate cat-and-mouse game with Annabelle as the "canary" surrounded by greedy, hungry "cats," and culminates with the appearance of a ghastly cloaked figure with one bulging eye, a protruding nose, and tusks, who is revealed to be the secondary heir in disguise, trying to drive the young heroine out of her mind.

Despite its stage origins, *The Cat and the Canary* never looks or feels like a filmed stage play. The camerawork by Gilbert Warrenton, under Leni's direction, is very fluid and in some scenes subjective, and there are interesting double exposure effects, including the brief superimposition of a grimacing skull next to a character who panics upon hearing the word *death*. Even the film's dialogue cards are made to underscore the comic horror of the proceedings: several of them are animated so that the words shiver and shake. Best of all is the painting of old Cyrus West that hangs in the library, which is *so* exaggeratedly ghastly that it elicits laughs.

Universal remade *The Cat and the Canary* as a talkie in 1930 under the title *The Cat Creeps*, and also produced a 1946 film with that title, though that one had nothing to do with the original old dark house story.

THE MAN WHO LAUGHS (1928)

Adapted from another novel by Victor Hugo, *The Man Who Laughs* is, like *The Hunchback of Notre Dame*, not so much a horror film as a period melodrama with gruesome elements. It was directed by Paul Leni, but is completely different from *The Cat and the Canary* in any stylistic sense, and was released as "A Carl Laemmle Special Production," which signified it was produced on a large budget with lavish sets and a cast of thousands.

The plot is quite complex: during the final days of the reign of James II of England, a rebellious nobleman named Lord Clancharlie is captured and sentenced to death by the King. As additional punishment, he is told by the King's vindictive jester Barkiphedro (Brandon Hurst) that his young son was taken and given to the Comprachios, a band of gypsy child traffickers who sadistically carve permanent smiles into their young victims' faces. A few years later, the boy is abandoned by the fleeing Comprachios and forced to make his way through a blizzard. He comes upon the body of a dead woman clutching a still-living baby and takes the infant with him, making his way to the trailer of a playwright and circus owner named Ursus (Cesare Gravina). After Ursus takes them in, he realizes the baby is blind.

Years pass and the boy grows up to become the renowned clown Gwynplaine (Conrad Veidt, who had also played Lord Clancharlie), the star of Ursus' traveling circus. Because of his permanent grin Gwynplaine is known as "The Laughing Man." The baby he rescued has grown into a beautiful woman called Dea (Mary Philbin), who idolizes Gwynplaine. Gwynplaine loves her back, but he will not let her touch his face out of fear that she will be repelled if she feels his deformed mouth.

Barkiphedro, who has connived his way into the noble class, recognizes Gwynplaine as the lost son of the Lord Clancharlie. He launches into a campaign of Machiavellian mischief that includes informing the Duchess Josiana (Olga Baclanova), a Jacobean party girl living on Lord Clancharlie's estate, that the true heir has been found. After seeing a performance of Gwynplaine's, Josiana (who does not realize that he is the heir) is strangely captivated by him, and summons him to her private chambers. Gwynplaine goes, rationalizing that if such a beautiful woman can love him despite his looks, he can abandon his fear that Dea would be repulsed by him. Josiana begins to seduce him, but right in the middle of things she receives the missive informing her of Gwynplaine's significance, and the horrific irony of this makes her laugh, which Gwynplaine interprets as rejection.

Due to Barkiphedro's machinations, Gwynplaine and Dea are separated. Because of his title, Gwynplaine is accepted into Parliament, where the Queen orders him to marry Josiana! This is too much, and like his father before him, Gwynplaine rebels against the throne, escaping the palace in search of his beloved Dea. After a dangerous pursuit by Barkiphedro, who is killed in the process, the lovers are united at last.

The Man Who Laughs was Universal's last big silent spectacle (or "Jewel," in the studio's jargon, which branded the films for theater owners). Even though the action is set in Jacobean London, its expressionistic interiors and use of the Little Europe backlot section make it appear more Germanic than English. Director Leni's decision to cast mostly unusual, often downright ugly faces as bit players and extras makes the film resemble a Bruegel painting come to life.

The role of Gwynplaine would have been a natural for Lon Chaney, but Chaney had since left Universal. The part went instead to German actor Conrad Veidt, who had played the somnambulist zombie in *The Cabinet of Dr. Caligari*. Given Veidt's sharp, devilish features and pale, ice cold eyes, it is surprising that he did not become a Hollywood horror star on a par with Lugosi and Karloff. But during the sound era he leaned more toward playing urbane Continental villains and Nazis in dramas and war films. Veidt died of a sudden heart attack in 1943, only 50 years old.

Creating the damaged face of Gwynplaine was the first major assignment at Universal for makeup wizard Jack P. Pierce, who would go

German actor Conrad Veidt as the ghastly, but still sympathetic, Gwynplaine in The Man Who Laughs.

Gwynplaine (Conrad Veidt) hides his affliction from his love, Dea (Mary Philbin) in The Man Who Laughs. *Veidt's makeup, including the swept-back wig, was the visual inspiration for the comic book villain The Joker several years later.*

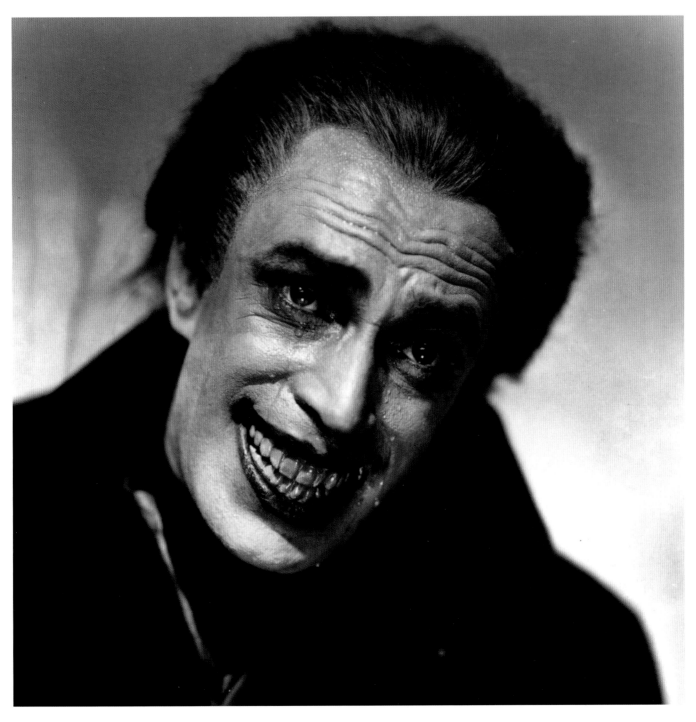

on to create the looks for all the studio's monsters. While the effect is startling, it was achieved quite simply, chiefly through a set of huge false teeth that stretched Veidt's mouth into a wide, red-lipped smile (this makeup would become the visual inspiration for the comic book villain The Joker).

As startling as Veidt's makeup is, it is the performance of Olga Baclanova that is most remarkable today. Unhindered by Hollywood's Production Code that was launched early in the sound era, Baclanova, a Russian-born actress who had a bumpy transition to talkies, presents a character of unbridled sexuality. She even has a brief nude scene.

By the time *The Man Who Laughs* reached theaters in November 1928, Universal's had already released its first all-talkie, *Melody of Love*. It was a sign that times were changing in the film industry. For Universal Horror, however, it was just the beginning.

The rebellious Lord Clancharlie (Conrad Veidt), the father of Gwynplaine, is tortured to death in The Man Who Laughs.

Gwynplaine (Conrad Veidt) is briefly accepted into the English peerage, while the evil Barkiphedro (Brandon Hurst) poses as his menial, from The Man Who Laughs.

Josiana (Olga Baclanova) rises from her bath in The Man Who Laughs. *This scene in the film contains nudity, which was not unheard of in the silent era, but which Hollywood's new Production Code would eliminate in the 1930s.*

Conrad Veidt, Mary Philbin, and director Paul Leni (right) greet visitor Erich von Stroheim (center) on the set of The Man Who Laughs.

The real face of The Man of a
Thousand Faces: a studio
portrait of Lon Chaney
from the early 1920s.

3 SPOTLIGHT:
LON CHANEY

A popular catchphrase was well known to filmgoers of the late 1920s:
Don't step on it; it might be Lon Chaney! So pervasive was this tribute to
the shape-shifting ability of Hollywood's legendary "Man of a Thousand
Faces" that many today believe he never appeared on film wearing his own
face. This, of course, is not the case.

One of Hollywood's first superstars, Lon Chaney often essayed
realistic roles that required minimal or no makeup, often in crime dramas.
For his favorite role, that of the tough Sergeant O'Hara in 1926's *Tell It to
the Marines*, Chaney boasted that he wore no makeup of any kind. But it
was his roles in extreme makeup, notably Erik in *The Phantom of the
Opera* and Quasimodo in *The Hunchback of Notre Dame*, that have
become legendary because of their startling natures.

If anything, Chaney was film's first method actor. He threw himself
into his roles, both physically and emotionally, often to the detriment of
his health: the wax wart he wore over his right eye in *The Hunchback of
Notre Dame*, for instance, affected his vision thereafter. It was not simply
ugly faces that Chaney portrayed, but tortured souls that transcended the
makeup, drawing upon an advanced gift for pantomime and body language
that was a genuine asset for silent film.

That was a gift that was practiced virtually from birth. Leonidas
(*not* Alonzo, as is often reported) Chaney was born in 1883 in Colorado
Springs, Colorado, to parents who could neither speak nor hear, making
pantomime a factor of communication at home. Not surprisingly, he
developed an early interest in acting, and at 18 joined his brother John's
theatrical company. For the next several years Chaney toured the "hard
knocks circuit," acting, singing, dancing, and doing comedy in everything
from stock companies to burlesque. When necessary, he painted scenery
and stage managed, and proudly carried a membership card in the stage-
hands union to the day he died.

Chaney landed at Universal Studios in 1913, when the paint was
barely dry on the studio walls. Over the next five years he made scores of

*Chaney as the Phantom: note the
highlighted lower eyelids and
shadowed mouth, which made
each feature appear larger.*

Teeth were always a key part of any of Lon Chaney's character makeups.

two-reelers as an actor, writer, and director. As an actor he quickly gained attention for both his intense performing style and his uncanny ability to transform himself physically. No matter what kind of character or what ethnicity a casting director might ask for, Chaney was ready to reproduce it out of his fishing tackle box stuffed with greasepaint, putty, glue, and hair.

His big break came through playing a con man posing as a cripple in 1919's *The Miracle Man.* Director George Loane Tucker had auditioned contortionists, but found none to his liking, so asked Chaney to give it a try. The actor managed to wrap his legs around themselves in such a convincing fashion, that his scene of being "cured" by jarring them loose stunned Tucker, and later audiences, though Chaney would eventually confess to the pain it caused. "Tucker didn't speak [as he watched the performance] and the sweat rolled off me," Chaney told journalist Ruth Waterbury. "Finally I heard a single whispered word from him. 'God,' Tucker said. I wanted to say that too, but not for the same reason." But the die was set, and Chaney would go on to even more startling (and painful) roles.

A major part of Chaney's mystique was that he eschewed publicity. "Between pictures, there is no Lon Chaney," he told members of the press, and on those rare occasions when he did grant an interview, he could easily become impatient or argumentative. Instead of playing the Hollywood game, Chaney far preferred spending time in his secluded hunting cabin in the High Sierras or staying at home with his second wife Hazel. (Chaney's first marriage to singer Cleva Creighton was a tumultuous one that disintegrated completely when she dramatically attempted suicide inside the theater in which he was playing; Chaney divorced Cleva and took custody of his son Creighton, who as an adult changed his name to Lon Jr.)

Chaney's reputation in Hollywood was that of a tough nut. Producer and friend Irving Thalberg eulogized him as "a diamond-in-the-rough, for he could be very hard." But he was also known for his generosity and helpfulness to newcomers, including a young struggling actor named Boris Karloff. Joan Crawford, who would make the bizarre 1927 thriller *The Unknown* with Chaney, would later say that it was his sheer intensity and dedication to a role that revealed to her what real acting was all about.

When talking pictures were introduced, Chaney was reluctant to take the plunge into sound, not because he felt his voice was insufficient, but for personal reasons: he felt that silent films were the only kind of performance art that his deaf parents could enjoy as well as anyone else, and with sound, that equity was taken away from them. But he finally acquiesced for a 1930 remake of *The Unholy Three,* for which he wore his own face throughout (albeit under a rather obvious toupee), but used five different voices!

Had he lived, Chaney might have segued into a career as "The Man of a Thousand Voices," but *The Unholy Three* would be his last film. Shortly after wrapping it, Chaney was diagnosed with throat cancer. He was only 47 years old when he died on August 26, 1930, though the effect of years' worth of painfully twisting and wrenching his face and body for his art left him looking far older.

Lon Chaney may have behaved like a common man, but he had an uncommon gift for revealing extraordinary characters.

*Bela Lugosi in the role that made
him a star and launched Universal
Horror in the sound era:* Dracula.

4

DRACULA

Prior to 1931, *vampire* had an entirely different meaning for moviegoers.

A *vamp*, at least in terms of Hollywood, was a sultry, seductive woman who was able to twist a man around her little finger, drawing willpower out of him as though it were a tangible fluid. Movie vamps were exotic silent movie sirens, such as Theda Bara or Olga Baclanova. With the release of *Dracula*, however, a vampire in a Hollywood movie would henceforth most likely be a man, and the draining of life force would not be metaphoric. He really drank blood and retreated to an earth-filled coffin every dawn.

Universal's *Dracula* was not the first screen adaptation of Bram Stoker's 1897 novel—an unlicensed German adaptation called *Nosferatu* was produced in 1922—but it became the most indelible.

DRACULA (1931)

The film of *Dracula* opens with a scene involving what would become a familiar image within Universal Horror, a gathering of middle-European villagers from an undetermined time period. An English real estate agent named Renfield (Dwight Frye) stops in the Transylvanian village en route to Castle Dracula. Despite the frightened warnings of the villagers, he makes his way to the castle, where he meets Count Dracula (Bela Lugosi, of course), who seems polite enough, if a bit strange: Dracula communes with wolves and walks through cobwebs without breaking them. Renfield, who is there to finalize the paperwork for Dracula's purchase of an abandoned abbey in the English coastal town of Whitby, tries not to notice. For his troubles, Renfield is bitten by Dracula and becomes his slave, acquiring an insatiable appetite for flies and spiders.

With Renfield in tow, Dracula travels to his new home in England on board the ship *Vesta*, which by the time it docks in Whitby harbor, is a ghost ship. The only living figure on board is the hopelessly insane

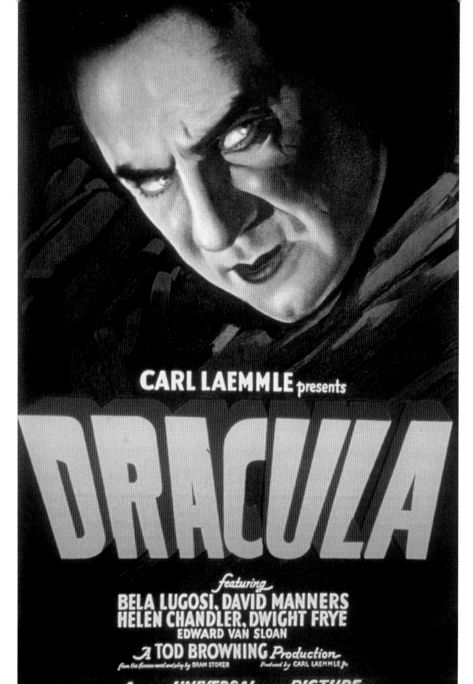

Bela Lugosi, David Manners (John Harker), Helen Chandler (Mina Harker), Dwight Frye (Renfield), and Edward Van Sloan (Van Helsing) help promote Dracula.

Renfield, who is quickly committed to the nearby asylum run by Dr. Jack Seward (Herbert Bunton). Dracula (who when not killing the crew has spent the voyage inside a box in the cargo hold), meanwhile, ingratiates himself with Seward, his daughter Mina (Helen Chandler), her fiancé John Harker (David Manners), and her friend Lucy Weston (Frances Dade). Lucy seems fascinated by Dracula, who makes her his first English victim.

Dr. Seward calls in a specialist, Dr. Van Helsing (Edward Van Sloan), to find out what killed Lucy and why her body is bloodless. Van Helsing knows only too well: it is the *nosferatu*—the undead—though Seward remains hard to convince. Only when Mina falls strangely ill and complains of nightmares in which a ghastly creature comes for her, does he give credence to Van Helsing's theory of vampires. But even Van Helsing does not realize that the charming, courtly, monocle-sporting Transylvanian count is the bloodsucker he is tracking until he notices that Dracula casts no reflection in mirrors. Both Mina and Renfield, during one of the latter's periodic spells of regretful sanity, confirm the doctor's suspicions.

Van Helsing tries to protect Mina by putting wolfbane, a plant that repels vampires, in her bedroom. But that night Dracula hypnotizes Mina's maid into removing the sprigs of wolfbane, then abducts Mina and takes her back to Carfax Abbey. Renfield escapes from the asylum and races to Dracula's side, followed by Dr. Van Helsing and John. Enraged that Renfield has led them to the castle, Dracula kills the lunatic and then tries to flee. He gets as far as the crypt, where his coffin is hidden. Van Helsing stakes the vampire, and upon his death, Mina is released from her spell.

That is where the film ends in today's prints, but the original version of *Dracula* featured an epilogue, in which Edward Van Sloan addressed the audience directly, wishing them pleasant dreams, and then bidding: "Just pull yourself together and remember that, after all, *there are such things.*" While a similar goodnight ploy had been used for the stage adaptation of *Dracula*, its purpose in the film was to inform the audience that there would be no trick ending, no jokey revelation that everything they had just watched was an elaborate hoax, which to date had been the norm. *Dracula* was the first American film to unapologetically present the supernatural at face value, a significance that is often overlooked.

Dracula's script is credited to writer Garrett Fort, though Louis Stevens, Louis Bromfield, and Dudley Murphy all had a hand in it. There are several examples of archly ironic dialogue, including the famous, "I never drink…*wine,*" and Dracula's offhand comment to Renfield that the journey to England will require only "three, uh, *boxes.*" (Incidentally, in Stoker's original novel, it is Harker who brings the realty papers to Dracula, not Renfield, who in the book is already committed to Dr. Seward's asylum.)

Today it is virtually impossible to imagine *Dracula* without Bela Lugosi, which is why it is shocking to learn that the Hungarian actor's name was at the *bottom* of the consideration list. It has long been reported that *Dracula* was planned as a vehicle for Lon Chaney, and that his untimely death in August 1930 squelched those plans. In truth, Chaney was never officially attached to the project. Carl Laemmle Jr. was *hoping* to lure him back to Universal, hiring Chaney's favorite director, Tod Browning, to sweeten the deal, but whether Chaney would have accepted Universal's offer had he not become ill with throat cancer, no one can

Bela Lugosi insisted on applying his own makeup for Dracula, *except for the widow's peak hairpiece mandated by Jack P. Pierce.*

Renfield (Dwight Frye) is warned by the Transylvanian innkeeper (Michael Visaroff) not to go to Castle Dracula in Dracula. *If only he'd listened.*

Geraldine Dvorak, Dorothy Tree, and Cornelia Thaw as the Count's "wives" in Dracula. *The castle catacombs set would be used in many subsequent Universal films.*

This scene showing Dracula at his most elegant—complete with top hat, cane, and a monocle around his neck— was shared by both the English and Spanish versions of Dracula.

Dracula (Bela Lugosi) tries to exert his powers over Professor Van Helsing (Edward Van Sloan) in Dracula. *Lugosi's hands were virtually characters unto themselves.*

Dracula director Tod Browning and Bela Lugosi greet Horace Liveright (center), who produced the Broadway production of Dracula on the set of the film. The man at right is screenwriter Dudley Murphy.

Bela Lugosi and Helen Chandler chat with director Tod Browning on the set of Dracula. Note the cigar in Lugosi's hand, something he was rarely without.

This promotional poster for Dracula makes Bela Lugosi look more like Raymond Huntley, the British actor who created the role on the stage in England.

answer. The fact that Browning seemed to lose interest in *Dracula* during the filming, at times turning the direction over to cinematographer Karl Freund, has been interpreted as possible depression over Chaney's untimely death (though Browning did manage to include one of his signature images in Dracula: gliding, placid vampire women, slightly stooped and with their hands cupped to their abdomens, looking like medieval crypt effigies come to life).

Had Chaney lived and agreed to take on *Dracula*, there is no question that the image of the Count would have been totally different than the suave, formally attired nobleman presented by Lugosi. Chaney invariably relied on the descriptions in the source novels to devise his makeups, so his Dracula would most likely have followed Stoker's description to the letter: white-haired, pointy-eared, red-lipped, and mustachioed, and far more loathsome than seductive.

Conrad Veidt was among the first actors considered for the role and he remains the only one who could have come close to rivaling Lugosi's interpretation. Two actors who were sometimes touted as "the next Lon Chaney" were also on the list: John Wray, who had appeared in Universal's 1930 hit *All Quiet on the Western Front*, and Paul Muni, who possessed a Chaney-like ability to disappear within his roles. Comedic tough guy Chester Morris was also considered, but more from the standpoint of his being a Universal contractee than being suitable for the role, which he was blatantly not.

Having played the role on Broadway to great acclaim, Bela Lugosi went after the part in a big way, even accepting a low-ball salary offer for it: $500 a week on a two-picture deal. Lugosi, who was generally not known for his comic zingers, would later quip that he got the part only after Uncle Carl couldn't turn up a relative who could play it!

Dracula would make Bela Lugosi a star and it would make Universal a fortune; and the era of horror movies was officially born. Without Lugosi...who knows?

DRÁCULA (THE SPANISH VERSION - 1931)

In the early talkie era, the technology to dub a film into foreign languages did not exist, so studios simply made the film over again in different languages. Comedians such as Laurel and Hardy or Buster Keaton, who were more important to their pictures than the storylines, appeared in each version themselves, reading their lines in each language phonetically off of blackboards. They were surrounded by foreign-speaking supporting casts (Boris Karloff, who spoke French, appeared in the French language version of Laurel and Hardy's 1931 feature *Pardon Us*). In the case of Universal's Spanish language production of *Drácula*, however, it was not so much the recognition of a lucrative foreign market that launched the production, as it was a love affair.

Among the roster of starlets at Universal City in 1930 (a list that included young Bette Davis) was a beautiful Mexican actress named Lupita Tovar, with whom Universal executive Paul Kohner was madly stricken. When Senorita Tovar expressed a desire to return to Mexico City to further her career, the lovesick Kohner grew desperate to find a way to keep her close. As a ploy, he convinced Uncle Carl that he could produce Spanish versions of the studio's hit films...adding that there was a *terrific*

Carlos Villarias (billed as "Carlos Villar") as Dracula in the Spanish language version of Drácula. *Compare this photo with Bela Lugosi in a similar pose on page 42.*

Dracula (Carlos Villarias) recoils from the cross, wielded by Professor Van Helsing (Eduardo Arozamena) in the Spanish Drácula.

Dracula (Carlos Villarias) plays host to Renfield (Enrique Tovar Avalos) in the Spanish Drácula.

Eva (Lupita Tovar) is menaced by Dracula (Carlos Villarias) in the Spanish language version of Drácula, *which would never have been made had not Universal production executive Paul Kohner been madly in love with Senorita Tovar.*

young Spanish-speaking actress already on the lot! Thus Lupita Tovar was cast as "Anita," the Annabelle West role, in *La Voluntad del muerto*, the 1930 Spanish version of *The Cat Creeps*, and then as "Eva," the equivalent to Mina, in *Drácula*.

American director George Melford (who spoke no Spanish) was assigned the project, and filming was done in the evenings on the same sets, after Browning's crew had gone home. The Spanish *Drácula* utilized the same script as the English version (though perhaps adhered to it more closely, since it runs 28 minutes longer) and in terms of camera work, atmosphere, staging, and special effects, particularly the fog-shrouded, spectrally lit scenes of Conde Drácula's rising from his coffin, it was more sophisticated. So were the costumes: Lupita Tovar's low-cut, sheer gown in the scenes after Eva has been vampirized would *never* have made it past the U.S. censors. We also actually see the puncture wounds in the women's neck in this version.

What Medford's remake did not have was Bela Lugosi. Except for one brief cribbed shot of the Hungarian outside the concert hall and a shot of Lugosi's hands reaching out of the coffin, the Count was played by Cordoba-born actor Carlos Villarías (billed as "Carlos Villar"), whose facial resemblance to Lugosi was persuasive, particularly when decked out in the widow's peak toupee that Jack Pierce insisted Lugosi wear. But that is where the likeness ended. While certainly competent, Villarías possessed none of the Hungarian's magnetism or regal Continental bearing. Whereas Lugosi's hands were characters unto themselves, twisting into seemingly impossible contortions that more resembled the actions of a flame, Villarías's gestures were clawlike. The scene involving three vampire women seen early in the film was likewise spliced in from the American version, but later, when they attack Renfield, different actresses wearing entirely different makeups and costumes take the roles.

If nothing else, the Spanish *Drácula* achieved its primary objective, which was to keep Lupita Tovar in Los Angeles. She and Kohner were married in 1932 and their union was one of the longest and happiest in Hollywood history, ending only with his death in 1988.

DRACULA'S DAUGHTER (1936)
Dracula's Daughter picks up exactly where the original left off, with Professor Van Helsing (Edward Van Sloan) down in the crypt, just having staked Dracula, while Renfield's body lies in a heap nearby (though the Harkers are nowhere to be seen). Discovered there by the police, Van Helsing is ultimately charged with murder, and accepts help with his case from a former pupil, a prominent psychiatrist named Jeffrey Garth (Otto Kruger). Complicating matters is the disappearance of Dracula's body from the Whitby police station. It has been stolen by a mysterious artist named Countess Maria Zaleska (Gloria Holden), who is actually the Count's daughter, and who cremates her father, hoping it will release her from her curse of darkness.

Encountering Garth at a dinner party, Countess Zaleska reveals to him that she suffers from an "obsession." The psychiatrist tells her that all obsessions can be overcome by confronting them. To test the confrontation method, Zaleska asks her creepy servant Sandor (Irving Pichel) to procure a young streetwalker named Lili (Nan Grey) and bring her to the

Countess Zaleska (Gloria Holden) cremates the body of her father, Count Dracula (a manikin standing in for Bela Lugosi, not too convincingly) in Dracula's Daughter.

Gloria Holden as the daughter of Dracula with her creepy manservant Sandor (actor and director Irving Pichel) in Dracula's Daughter.

Countess Zaleska (Gloria Holden, right) has her way with a streetwalker (Nan Grey) in Dracula's Daughter. *This scene carries an erotic charge that is renowned today, but totally flew past the censors of 1936.*

Dracula's Daughter (Gloria Holden) seeks the help of psychiatrist Jeffrey Garth (Otto Kruger) in Dracula's Daughter.

Countess's art studio, ostensibly to model. But the Countess's obsession is too great, and she bites the girl, who ultimately dies.

The Countess now has designs on Garth and abducts his secretary Janet (Margueritte Churchill) as a hostage to lure him to her ancestral home. When Garth arrives at the castle (with the police not far behind), Zaleska offers him a choice: if he will become her immortal mate, she will spare Janet. Garth is forced to agree, but before Zaleska can consummate their deal, Sandor, who has been expecting the gift of immortality for himself, jealously shoots her through the heart with an arrow, and then is felled by the men of Scotland Yard, who arrive just in time.

Dracula's Daughter was the result of Carl Laemmle Jr.'s having purchased the rights to "Dracula's Guest," a short story by Bram Stoker that was really an excised chapter from the original novel. Junior first persuaded director James Whale, who had recently completed *Bride of Frankenstein*, to take it on. But the initial script, which was written by Whale's frequent collaborator R. C. Sherriff, was rejected outright because of its horrific and sexual implications. Having nothing in common with "Dracula's Guest," that script depicted Dracula alive in the Middle Ages, plundering the land and abducting its women, one of whom would become his adoptive daughter. A demonic figure would turn him into a vampire as revenge, after which the film would shift to the story of the daughter, in modern times.

Bela Lugosi was contracted to reprise his signature role, but problems with the script continued. Ultimately, Whale was taken off the project, and the studio went back to square one. Garrett Fort was brought back to concoct a new storyline, one that did not involve Dracula at all, save for a quick glimpse of his dead body, which was played by a well-dressed manikin (though Lugosi was paid off to the tune of $4,000...$500 more than he'd earned for starring in *Dracula*!).

The new director, Lambert Hillyer, whose forte was Westerns, made *Dracula's Daughter* an appealingly atmospheric exercise in suggested horror. Today the film is best known for its surprising hint of lesbianism, which was hardly a safe or popular topic of films of the 1930s. Countess Zaleska's advances on Lili, and later on Janet, carried a pronounced erotic charge that the Breen Office, Hollywood's bastion of censorship, totally missed.

Despite giving a compelling performance in the lead role, exotic-looking Gloria Holden did not get much of a career boost from *Dracula's Daughter*. The London-born actress continued to work in Hollywood into the late 1950s, but never became a star. She died in 1991 at the age of 83.

SON OF DRACULA (1943)
The film's title *Son of Dracula* immediately confuses the issue as to whether the central character is indeed Dracula, traveling in cognito, or simply a descendent of the original. The opening credits read, "Lon Chaney as Count Dracula," which seems conclusive, yet within the film itself he is referred to throughout as "Count Alucard" (spell it backwards).

The picture finds the mysterious Count traveling to a Tennessee plantation at the request of Kay Caldwell (Louise Allbritton), a morbid young woman with a taste for the occult and a habit of collecting strange people, including an ancient voodoo crone named Queen Zimba (Adeline

Poster for Son of Dracula. *Whether "Count Alucard" was really Dracula's son or Dracula himself is never quite explained in the film.*

Count Alucard (Lon Chaney Jr.) puts the plot of Kay Caldwell into action by killing her father, Colonel Caldwell (George Irving) in Son of Dracula.

Voodoo crone Queen Zimba (Adeline DeWalt Reynolds) receives an ill omen on the wing, and tries to convince Kay Caldwell (Louise Allbritton) in one of Son of Dracula's *most atmospheric scenes.*

DeWalt Reynolds). Kay's fiancé Frank (Robert Paige) puts up with a lot from her, but he draws the line at the sudden intrusion into her life of a strange European nobleman called Alucard, who Frank believes is a phony (if only he knew). Kay, however, has an ulterior motive in seducing the Count: she wants to gain immortality through him, and then pass that on to Frank, whom she still loves, so that they can live forever...after Frank destroys the vampire. Her plans do not quite pan out, due to Frank's refusal to play along, and by the picture's downbeat end only he, Kay's sister Claire (Evelyn Ankers), vampire expert Professor Lazlo (J. Edward Bromberg), and sensible Dr. Brewster (Frank Craven) are left standing.

Son of Dracula was directed by Robert Siodmak, whose brother Curt Siodmak was a major contributor to Universal Horror. Robert became renowned as a master of postwar film noir, and *Son of Dracula* is perhaps the first example of "horror *noir*." The visual trappings of noir are all there—the darkness and the expressionistic shadows—but so is the soul of noir, the classic femme fatale, in the person of Kay Caldwell. Her cold, single-minded scheme to spend eternity with Frank, which starts by having her own father murdered, makes the machinations of Cora from *The Postman Always Rings Twice* look like a hopscotch game.

Son of Dracula exists outside of the ongoing Dracula continuity line as revealed through the other films of the series, in which Dracula never leaves Europe. For the first time on film, Dracula is actually shown transforming into a bat. Unfortunately, director Siodmak's staging of the first transformation scene contains a classic boo-boo: the transformation takes place in front of a mirror, and Dracula is clearly shown to cast a reflection. What is not reflected, though, is the actual special effects transformation; instead there is a jump cut between the puppet bat and Chaney. The vampire is also seen changing back and forth into wisps of smoke, which is quite effective.

The controversy among fans over casting Lon Chaney Jr. as Dracula has raged for more than 60 years. Even though his status as Universal's premiere horror man of the time made him the obvious choice for the part (particularly since Lugosi was then too old for the romantic angle), his casting was still a leap of faith since nothing on Chaney's resume to date argued that he had the equipment to play the aloof European nobleman. But Chaney managed to pull it off by reigning in his emotional acting style in order to present a character of icy, controlled menace, who is condescendingly polite to all around him, while exuding a tangible sense of danger (at least until the end, when Alucard loses control and frantically orders Frank to extinguish the blaze he set in his coffin).

The rest of the cast is equally unusual for a horror film: Robert Paige and Louise Allbritton were more commonly seen in comedies, and Frank Craven was more at home in *Our Town* than in Dracula's mansion. But everything came together to make *Son of Dracula* one of the second horror cycle's finest hours (and 18 minutes).

HOUSE OF DRACULA (1945)
Dracula, in the rakish and suavely seductive form of John Carradine, had put in a brief appearance in 1944's *House of Frankenstein*, the first of Universal's multimonster spectaculars. While he was reduced to a skeleton

The only time the Count is married on screen: Dracula/Alucard (Lon Chaney Jr.) and Kay (Louise Allbritton) visit the Justice of the Peace (Robert Dudley) in Son of Dracula.

Alucard (Lon Chaney Jr.) doesn't take too kindly to having his coffin destroyed by Frank (Robert Paige) in Son of Dracula.

ALL NEW...
ALL TOGETHER!

FRANKENSTEIN'S
MONSTER

WOLF MAN

DRACULA

MAD DOCTOR

HUNCHBACK

UNIVERSAL PRESENTS

HOUSE of DRACULA

with
LON CHANEY MARTHA O'DRISCOLL
JOHN CARRADINE LIONEL ATWILL
ONSLOW STEVENS · GLENN STRANGE
JANE ADAMS · LUDWIG STOSSEL

Original Screenplay by Edward T. Lowe   Directed by ERLE C. KENTON   Produced by PAUL MALVERN   Executive Producer JOE GERSHENSON   45/378

The monster lineup was the same as in the earlier House of Frankenstein, *though in* House of Dracula, *the hunchback was an otherwise beautiful young woman, played by "Poni" Adams.*

in that one, he not only came back the next year, he was heralded in the title of *House of Dracula.*

The film begins with the arrival of a mysterious man who calls himself "Baron Latos" (Carradine) to the home and sanitarium of Dr. Edelmann (Onslow Stevens), a scientist with a theological bent who is renowned for enacting cures on seemingly hopeless patients. Latos is, of course, Dracula, as he readily confesses to the doctor. He also confesses that he no longer wants to be a vampire, and asks Edelmann to cure him. So confident is he of the arrangement that he has taken the liberty of moving his coffin into Edelmann's basement.

Intrigued, Edelmann examines Dracula's blood and discovers it contains a strange parasite. He decides that immediate transfusions will help him, using himself as the donor. While this is going on, Larry Talbot (Lon Chaney Jr.) appears at Edelmann's door, wanting either to be cured of his lycanthropy or to die. Edelmann discovers Talbot is suffering from a pressure on the brain, which secretes hormones that result in his physical transformations into the Wolf Man. The doctor could help him, if he only had enough of a certain kind of mold he is cultivating, which makes bone malleable and alleviates surgery.

Talbot, however, refuses to endure the agony of another full moon and tries to kill himself by leaping into the sea. That evening Edelmann goes to rescue him, and in the process finds a hidden cave near the shore that contains the dormant form of the Frankenstein Monster (Glenn Strange) and the bones of Dr. Niemann (who was the mad doctor of *House of Frankenstein*). Talbot, now in Wolf Man form, is there, too, but once he transforms back, he is given new hope for a cure because Edelmann realizes that the cave has the perfect temperature to hasten the growth of his mold, meaning he can operate sooner.

The Monster is retrieved and brought to Edelmann's lab, but the doctor is now having trouble with Dracula, whose bloodlust has not been conquered. In fact the "Baron" has cast his spell over Edelmann's nurse, Miliza (Martha O'Driscoll). During their next transfusion, Dracula turns the tables on Edelmann, reversing the blood flow so that *his* parasitic blood goes into the doctor, causing him to develop a Jekyll-and-Hyde duality. The vampiric side of him decides to revitalize the Monster to do his bidding. But in his sane phase, Edelmann realizes that he has exposed his household to danger by allowing Dracula in. While the vampire rests, Edelmann drags the vampire's coffin into a ray of sunlight and destroys him. As far as the villagers in Visaria are concerned, it hardly matters: at night, Dr. Edelmann takes over where Dracula left off.

Talbot, though, has spotted Edelmann's nocturnal comings and goings, and realizes he's a murderer, but he says nothing, since the doctor represents his last chance for a normal life. Edelmann, now back in Jekyll mode, confesses to Talbot that he has become a slave to Dracula. He will try to carry out the operations on Talbot and his hunchbacked female assistant Nina (Jane "Poni" Adams), but also asks Talbot to kill him if the curse takes him over completely.

Edelmann stays sane long enough to operate on Talbot and it is a success: Talbot faces the full moon free of lycanthropy. But then the doctor's Hyde side completely takes over. He kills the loyal Nina and revives the Monster. Talbot confronts Edelmann and, realizing his soul is

John Carradine first appeared as Dracula in 1944's House of Frankenstein. *Looking more like a roue than a bloodsucker in this publicity shot from the film, he also seems more interested in starlet Anne Gwynne than in the script.*

Dracula (John Carradine) moves into the home of Dr. Edelmann (Onslow Stevens) in House of Dracula.

John Carradine was a suitably eerie Count in House of Dracula.

Dr. Edelmann (Onslow Stevens), fully in vampiric "Mr. Hyde" mode, takes his fury out on loyal assistant Nina (Jane "Poni" Adams) in House of Dracula.

lost, shoots him. At the instant of death, Edelmann's sanity returns and approves of Talbot's act. However, the Monster, who has been given new life by the doctor, is enraged. He breaks free of his bonds and destroys the lab. The now normal Talbot and Nurse Miliza escape the burning sanitarium to walk into the dawn together.

The last serious film of Universal's Frankenstein/Dracula/Wolf Man saga, *House of Dracula* is structured more like *Casablanca* than any earlier horror film: just as everybody comes to Rick's in that wartime romantic drama, every monster comes to Edelmann's. While the appearance of the Frankenstein Monster follows the storyline of the preceding film—there he went down in a bog of quicksand, and here he's dropped into the cave, but is still covered in muck—there is no effort to explain how both Talbot and Dracula returned to life after their earlier demises.

Cadaverous John Carradine makes an unnerving, if not quite terrifying, vampire, though the real star of *House of Dracula* is Onslow Stevens, an actor with a smooth, resonant voice similar to that of Orson Welles, and the talent to pull off the Jekyll-and-Hyde part convincingly. Stevens had a long, if largely unheralded, career in Hollywood, but tragically ended up as the victim of a real-life mystery: his death in a nursing home in 1977 was ruled to be the result of foul play. Dr. Edelmann is the role for which he is best remembered.

Towering, brawny contractee Glenn Strange usually played cowboys, which was somewhat ironic since he was part Cherokee. It was Jack Pierce who first thought that he might make a good replacement Monster for *House of Frankenstein*. While in that film Strange did little more than inhabit a costume, in *House of Dracula* he has more of a role to work with. The climactic sequence of the Monster rampaging through the lab, though, was economically snipped from the end of *The Ghost of Frankenstein* (1942) and shows both Lon Chaney Jr. and stuntman Eddie Parker as the Monster. Glenn Strange was a familiar face on television's *Gunsmoke* right up until his death in 1973 at age 74.

Released in December of 1945, *House of Dracula* effectively signaled the end of Universal's second horror cycle. By then such films had served their purpose, offering audiences an hour's worth of escape into a Neverland version of Europe, where 19th-century gypsies co-exist with leading ladies in contemporary fashions, where the countryside is untouched by the horrors of war, and where the monsters are recognizable by their neck bolts, not their arm bands.

5 SPOTLIGHT:
BELA LUGOSI

Unquestionably one of the most magnetic figures ever to appear on screen, Bela Lugosi was also one of the least lucky. This may seem like a peculiar statement in lieu of his enormous personal success in the role of Dracula, and his iconic status more than 50 years after his death, but Lugosi's stardom came at a price. Even his big Hollywood break carried an unexpectedly high cost.

The man who defined the image and characteristics of the vampire for generations to come was born Béla (pronounced BAY-la) Ferenc Dezső Blaskó in Lugos, Hungary, an area that is now part of Romania, in 1882. His parents were well-off enough to provide for a good education for their fourth child, whose ambitions leaned toward the theater. By the beginning of the 20th century he was a member of the Hungarian Royal National Theater, where he played roles ranging from Romeo to Jesus Christ.

After serving in World War I (and harboring injuries from it), Lugosi resumed his stage career and also entered the new medium of film, where he was sometimes billed under the name Arisztid Olt. In the late 1910s, the political situation in Hungary was such that it suddenly became advisable for the left-leaning actor to flee, first to Germany, where he resumed his film career, and then to the United States. When Lugosi, whose name now reflected his place of birth, arrived in America in 1920 he did not know a word of English. That did not stop him from conquering Broadway within only a few years, learning his lines in the plays phonetically, which, according to critics of the time, gave his performances a certain unclassifyable distinction. In between Broadway gigs, Lugosi journeyed to Hollywood where, in the silent era, his accent mattered not a bit. He picked up a few small roles, including a bit in the 1924 Lon Chaney film *He Who Gets Slapped*.

Three years later he landed the role that was to dictate the course of his life and career, Dracula, in the Broadway production of Hamilton Deane's adaptation of Bram Stoker's novel. By then Lugosi had acquired a reasonable fluency in English, but still retained his thick Hungarian accent and distinctive delivery, which would prove to be perfect for the role of the undead Transylvanian Count. *Dracula* opened on Broadway on October 5, 1927, and became a commercial hit, running well into 1928 and continuing on in touring companies.

Lugosi returned to Hollywood where he found work in supporting

Lugosi in the 1941 comedy/mystery version of The Black Cat. *By 1940, Lugosi's star had waned enough to place him firmly in the supporting character actor category.*

Lugosi (right) with the cigar he was almost never seen without off-screen, along with Glenn Strange as the Frankenstein Monster and dialogue director Norman Abbott (the nephew of comic Bud Abbott), on the set of Abbott and Costello Meet Frankenstein.

Lugosi almost unrecognizable as Ygor in Son of Frankenstein, *which many consider to be his finest screen performance.*

roles, often as a Valentino-ish heavy or red herring. When word came that Universal had bought the rights to *Dracula*, Lugosi went on a successful campaign to land the lead role. His portrayal of the vampire king brought out all the sensuality and romance of evil, and overnight he was Universal's number one horror star.

Plans to cast Lugosi as the Monster in *Frankenstein* did not pan out, which at the time was fine with him. But his loss of the role that eventually propelled Boris Karloff to the position of Hollywood's top boogeyman had an effect on the Hungarian actor: from that point on he never turned down a role, any role, in any picture, a career strategy that ultimately led down the path to Hollywood's "Poverty Row."

Still, Lugosi strove valliantly to be considered a straight character actor, even taking his appeal directly to casting directors. In the inaugural 1937 edition of the *Players Director*, a casting book published by the Motion Picture Academy, Lugosi's listing (accompanied by a photo of the actor made up as an Oriental) contained the message: "Dracula" led producers to consider Lugosi preeminent solely in the horror field. THIS IS AN ERROR.

Despite the plea, the actor's sojourns outside of the horror or thiller arenas were rare. A supporting role as the Russian commisar in the glossy 1939 romantic comedy *Ninotchka* looked like a break, but Hollywood remained unconvinced, preferring to give any Hungarian-accented straight roles to fellow countryman Paul Lukas. Even within the horror genre, Lugosi's picture-stealing turn as the evil shepherd Ygor in *Son of Frankenstein* represented an increasingly rare opportunity to strut his stuff. In the minds of many, Lugosi was, and would forever be, Dracula, a role with which he would develop a love-hate relationship; while he would have liked to have left it behind, he also bristled at seeing other actors play the role.

An intense, proud, rather shy man, whose shyness was sometimes mistaken for aloofness, Lugosi soldiered on, taking any acting work offered, including personal appearances, until he hit bottom: the quixotic, grade-Z, 1950s productions of Ed Wood Jr. By that point the five-time-married actor was mercilessly addicted to morphine, an affliction that was the result of a medical snafu a decade earlier. Lugosi publicly committed himself to a sanitarium in order to kick the habit. While today entering rehab is almost de rigueur for any celebrity, in the 1950s it was an incredibly courageous and risky admission for a public figure to make. Bela Lugosi died in 1956, aged 73. He was buried in his Dracula cape, the final melding of actor with role.

Some have argued that Lugosi's inability to master the English language was the cause of his problems. Others believe that Lugosi's bravura acting style was fine for early talkies, but was no longer a good fit with Hollywood's postwar era of realism, though his completely naturalistic but still frightening reprise of Dracula in 1948's *Abbott and Costello Meet Frankenstein* belies that theory. Doubtlessly, a contributing factor was Lugosi's willingness to take questionable parts in increasingly unworthy films, just to keep working. But the larger truth is that Bela Lugosi simply could not catch a break after his initial thrust into stardom, proving that even for a talented actor with charisma to burn, Hollywood can be as harsh a place to navigate as the wilds of Transylvania.

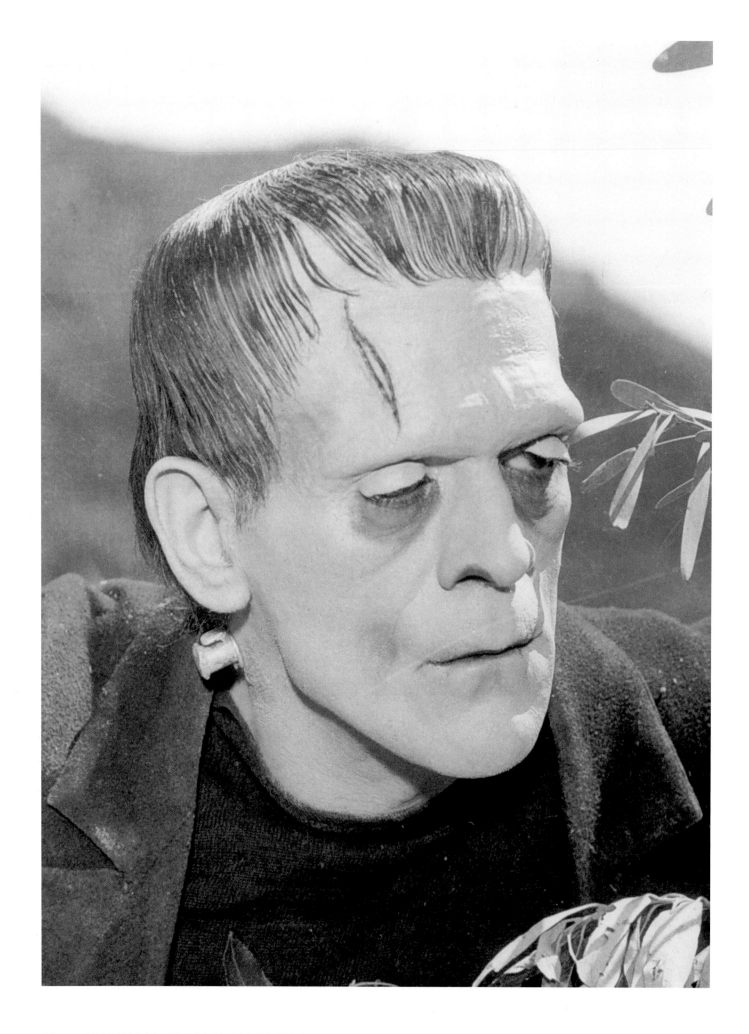

Karloff as the Monster from Frankenstein: *the end result of weeks of makeup experimentation.*

6 FRANKENSTEIN'S MONSTER

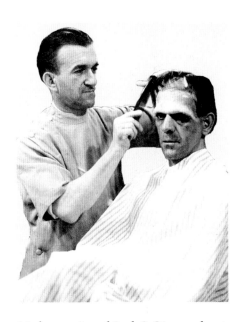

Makeup wizard Jack P. Pierce about halfway through the application process on Boris Karloff for Frankenstein.

He is the undisputed king of Universal's classic monsters, a towering, brutal, but often child-like creature who was built and imbued with life by Dr. Henry Frankenstein, and kept alive by his children and their successors. He has no official name, though with time he became known simply as *Frankenstein*. Technically, he is properly called *the Frankenstein Monster* or simply *Frankenstein's Monster*.

Based (at least in name) on the 1818 novel *Frankenstein, or the Modern Prometheus*, by Mary Wollstonecraft Shelley, Universal's original film of *Frankenstein* gave an indelible shape and face to the man-made being, which had previously been little more than a concept. Since then, the Frankenstein Monster has been the heart and soul of Universal Horror.

FRANKENSTEIN (1931)

The story of the development and creation of the film *Frankenstein* has become the stuff of Hollywood legend, rife with contradictions and a myth or two. But just like its central character, the resultant film was created by piecing together parts from various sources.

Universal bought the rights to a stage adaptation of *Frankenstein* by Peggy Webling, who had been part of the theatrical company of Hamilton Deane, the driving force behind the stage version of *Dracula*. It was by no means the first theatrical treatment of the story; that had been written by Richard Brinsley Peake and was staged in 1823, a mere five years after the novel was published.

French-born writer/director Robert Florey, who developed an early screenplay with Garrett Fort, desperately wanted to direct the picture. He filmed a test for it on June 16–17, 1931, on sets leftover from *Dracula*. This long, elaborate test featured Edward Van Sloan, Dwight Frye, and Bela Lugosi...as the *Monster*...and seems to have been an attempt to prove to producer Carl Laemmle Jr. that Florey could handle the picture. If so, it failed to convince anyone.

Dwight Frye as the sadistic hunchback Fritz in Frankenstein, *the role that sealed his fate in Hollywood.*

Uncle Carl Laemmle was so skittish over studio secretaries being terrified by the sight of Boris Karloff in full Monster makeup for Frankenstein *that he ordered the actor to walk back and forth to the set wearing a veil. His guide is makeup artist Jack P. Pierce.*

Initially believing that he was being sought out for the role of Dr. Frankenstein, Lugosi was not happy to learn he was instead expected to play a grunting, growling ogre (in the book, the Monster sounds more like captain of his college debate team). He groused his way through the screen test, for which he was slathered with clay-colored greasepaint and given a huge wig, complaining that he was reduced to playing "a scarecrow." When shown the test, Carl Laemmle Jr. rejected it outright; in fact, he reportedly burst out laughing while watching it. While subsequent generations of monster fans have hoped that this legendary footage would someday turn up in a vault, it was most likely destroyed by the studio.

For his part, Lugosi had no regrets about letting the role slip away, at least not at first. Robert Florey, however, was crushed when *Frankenstein* was officially assigned to director James Whale, whose success with Universal's *Waterloo Bridge* had rocketed him to the studio's A-list. For the rest of his life, Florey would claim that the project had been stolen away from him.

Armed with a retooled script by Francis Edwards Faragoh, Whale began prepping and casting the picture. Even though Lugosi was unwilling to play the Monster, he remained contractually obligated to the studio, which diluted his power to refuse the part. But Whale was already looking elsewhere. Several actors were interviewed, including young John Carradine, who bailed when he learned of the nature of the part. Nobody satisfied Whale, and the director was getting desperate until he came upon the gaunt, haunted face of a 43-year-old British expatriate named Boris Karloff.

There are several different versions of how Karloff, who had been struggling in Hollywood for about 15 years, caught Whale's eye. It was not because of his size: Karloff was reasonably tall—5'11"—but lean to the point of boniness (then again, so was Carradine). The most convincing story that has been put forth is that Whale's domestic partner David Lewis recommended him, having seen him a year earlier in the Los Angeles production of a stage play called *The Criminal Code*, in which the actor made quite a splash in the role of a murderous convict. Once hired, Karloff immediately began putting in late nights in Jack Pierce's makeup room, as various makeups were tested.

For the approved version of the Monster, Karloff's brows and forehead were built up with cotton and a thick, sealing liquid called collodion, which Pierce also used to make the scars. A layer of cheesecloth was put over the cotton to simulate pores in the skin. A green-gray greasepaint covered everything, which cast the pallor of death on film, while purple was used for shadows. A stringy wig was draped on top of Karloff's enlarged head. The actor's contributions to the makeup consisted of requesting a layer of wax on the eyelids, which made his eyes look dead, and removing a dental bridge, which made his face more sunken. This indentation was further exaggerated with shadow, a detail that metamorphosed into the Monster's strange "beauty mark" on subsequent actors in the role. Thirteen-pound boots with two-and-a-half-inch soles elevated his height (though nowhere near the seven-and-a-half feet that the studio publicity department claimed), and a black suit was fashioned with shortened sleeves to make him appear, in Karloff's words, "gigantic and gawky, like a big boy who had outgrown his rompers."

The Monster (Boris Karloff) finds a friend in Little Maria (Marilyn Harris) in Frankenstein. *Far from being frightened by Karloff in full makeup, the seven-year-old actress wanted to ride with him to the location at Lake Sherwood, about 40 miles from Hollywood.*

The expressionistic lab of Dr. Frankenstein, with John Boles, Mae Clark, and Edward Van Sloan watching on the left, Colin Clive and Dwight Frye in the middle, and a swathed Boris Karloff on the table being raised in the air.

The accidental drowning of Little Maria (Marilyn Harris) by the Monster was for years censored out of theatrical prints of Frankenstein. *Here her body is carried through the village by her grief-stricken father, Ludwig (Michael Mark).*

The makeup took about three-and-a-half hours to put on and two hours to remove, and was deemed so disturbing by Uncle Carl that he ordered Karloff to wear a veil over his face while walking to and from the set, so as not to cause any pregnant secretaries to miscarry! This nervousness on Laemmle's part carried over to the film itself, which opens with Edward Van Sloan stepping in front of the camera to talk directly to the audience, this time to warn them that they may be horrified by what they see, and that the squeamish should leave the theater at once.

What follows is the story of zealous scientist Henry Frankenstein (Colin Clive) who ignores his family and fiancé Elizabeth (Mae Clarke) in order to hole himself up in a tower laboratory and conduct experiments on the creation of life. Assisted by a sadistic hunchback named Fritz (Dwight Frye), he creates a being who is stitched together from parts of corpses, but when it comes time for the brain, he inadvertently puts in one removed from a known criminal.

When Dr. Frankenstein's new "Adam"—whose "birth" is witnessed by Elizabeth, her old boyfriend Victor Moritz (John Boles), and Frankenstein's former teacher Dr. Waldman (Edward Van Sloan)—turns out to be a monster, Frankenstein tries to wash his hands of it. But the Monster turns murderous, killing both his tormenter Fritz and Dr. Waldman, who had tried to dissect him. The Monster also inadvertently kills Little Maria (Marilyn Harris), a young village girl who is friendly to him.

Now on the loose, the Monster turns up at Château Frankenstein on Henry and Elizabeth's wedding day and wreaks havoc in the house and town, which causes a mob to form in order to hunt him down. Leading part of the mob, Henry confronts his creation in the woods, and is dragged to the top of a windmill where he is thrown off and nearly killed. Meanwhile, the angry, terrified villagers set fire to the mill, presumably destroying the Monster.

The original ending of *Frankenstein* had Henry Frankenstein dying at the hands of his creation. But even as the film was being shot, Universal could see the prospects of a sequel, so the ending was rewritten to have Henry survive the fall. A new coda showing him recovering in his bedroom with Elizabeth at his side was filmed, though neither Colin Clive nor Mae Clarke was available for this final shot. Hollywood legend has it that future B-movie cowboy star Robert Livingston, his face turned away from the camera, filled in for Clive.

Seen today, *Frankenstein* displays little of the creakiness from which most early talkies suffer. The creation scene—ablaze with the sights and sounds of all manner of strange, sparking equipment created by electrical engineer Kenneth Strickfadden—set the prototype for all subsequent laboratory sequences. British actor Colin Clive, ostensibly the star, delivered a characteristically intense performance, but the enduring revelation is Boris Karloff, who was billed in the opening credits as "?" Never once is the viewer reminded that the Monster is simply an actor buried in makeup. Karloff is thoroughly believable as a creature brought into the world like an unwanted child. "Whale and I both saw the character as an innocent one and I tried to play it that way," Karloff later said.

As visually shocking as the film was in 1931—the scene showing the Monster accidentally drowning Little Maria was removed as being *too* horrifying, though its absence inadvertently left the impression that something even nastier might have happened to her first—it was \blasphemy that really outraged the censors of the time. Only recently has Henry Frankenstein's frenzied line, delivered at the moment of creation, been restored to the film: "Now I know what it feels like to be God!"

BRIDE OF FRANKENSTEIN (1935)

A sequel under the title *The Return of Frankenstein* had been floated two years after the original. In 1934 all the pieces fell into place, including the return of director James Whale, and stars Boris Karloff and Colin Clive. Because of his enormous success in *Frankenstein,* the actor formerly known as "?" had for press purposes become "KARLOFF"—no first name required. He may have been the one who sold the tickets, but *Bride of Frankenstein* was definitely James Whale's film, giving full reign to his vision, personality, and quirky—sometimes perverse—sense of humor.

The film opens with a gathering of Mary Shelley (Elsa Lanchester), her husband Percy (Douglas Walton), and Lord Byron (Gavin Gordon), the same people who, in 1816, had staged a ghost story contest that resulted in Mary Shelley composing *Frankenstein.* Byron is marveling at demure young Mary's ability to chill the blood, and begs her to continue the story, which she does, picking it up exactly where *Frankenstein* left off, with the burning windmill and the rescue of Henry Frankenstein (nothing of which, of course, is actually in Mary Shelley's book). A group of villagers are at the mill to make sure the Monster has died. They get a very rude awakening, as the burnt creature emerges from the mill and goes on the rampage once more.

Back home at Château Frankenstein, the injured Henry is being tended by Elizabeth (brunette British Valerie Hobson replacing blonde American Mae Clarke), and hoping the nightmare is over. No such luck; showing up at their door is the bizarre Dr. Septimus Pretorius (Ernest Thesiger), a former philosophy professor who was kicked out of University for "knowing too much." He wants Henry to assist him with his own experiment in life and death. Pretorius counters Henry's obvious reluctance with emotional blackmail, reminding him that *he* is ultimately responsible for all the murders committed by the Monster.

Despite Elizabeth's impending sense of doom, Henry is drawn into the demented world of Pretorius, who somehow grows his creations from cells rather than stitching them together from dead limbs. He proposes they create a mate for the Monster (who is still at large) in order to bring in a "new world of gods and monsters." While seeking bones for the new creature in a crypt, Pretorius runs into the Monster and learns that his mind has been expanded through interaction with a kindly blind hermit (O. P. Heggie). The Monster can now speak and, to a certain degree, reason. Realizing he has a potentially powerful ally in the Monster, Pretorius tells him of their plans, and enlists him to kidnap Elizabeth in order to keep Henry working on the new project.

During a violent thunderstorm, which powers the equipment in the lab, "The Bride" (Elsa Lanchester, whose billing for this part remained "?" in both the opening and closing credits) is brought to life, and the Monster is understandably delighted with her. She, on the other hand, rejects him outright. Heartbroken, the Monster grabs a lever on the wall of the lab that Pretorius warns "will blow us all to atoms." After instructing

Elsa Lanchester as the Monster's would-be mate from Bride of Frankenstein. *The character's trademark hairdo was created by taking Lanchester's real hair and combing it up over a wire beehive.*

By Bride of Frankenstein *(to which this poster adds a* The*), Boris Karloff had become simply "Karloff."*

The Monster receives humanity lessons from the blind beggar (O. P. Heggie) in a classic sequence from Bride of Frankenstein.

Elsa Lanchester as a demure Mary Shelley in the prologue of Bride of Frankenstein. *That isn't a vampire attacking her hand, it's Mary's husband Percy (Douglas Walton). Lord Byron (Gavin Gordon) is on the right.*

Ernest Thesiger as the deranged Dr. Pretorius, showing off his home-grown creatures, in Bride of Frankenstein.

Elsa Lanchester touches up her makeup before a shot in Bride of Frankenstein.

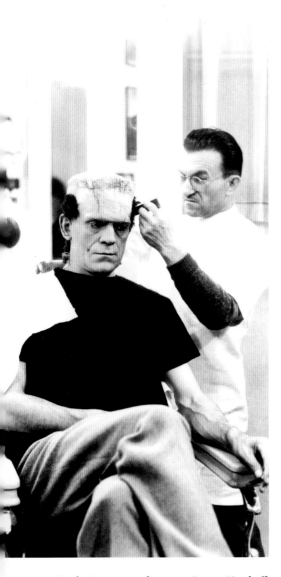

Jack Pierce working on Boris Karloff for Bride of Frankenstein. *This time the headpiece was made of rubber instead of built-up strips of cotton and collodion.*

Henry and Elizabeth to flee, the Monster turns on Pretorius, his one-time ally, and intones: "We belong dead." With a final, tearful gaze at his would-be mate, the Monster pulls the lever and atomizes the lab.

The script for *Bride of Frankenstein* was credited to William Hurlbut, though no less than nine writers worked on it, including John L. Balderston and R. C. Sherriff. The hand of Whale, however, is eminently apparent, particularly in the juxtaposition of pure comedy with horror. After deboning a corpse in the crypt, a grave robber named Karl (Dwight Frye) turns to his fellow ghoul and cracks, "If there's much more like this, whatcha say, pal, we give ourselves up and let 'em hang us?" There is also puckish humor in the sight of the Monster guzzling wine and then burping, and in the first glimpse of the Bride: the row of safety pins securing the wrappings on her forehead is a perfect parody of the Monster's metal clamps. Yet another bizarre joke is that lever on the laboratory wall, which the Monster knows is deadly: why would an other-wise brilliant scientist install a device in a laboratory whose raison d'être was to blow the place to smithereens? (Another such lever would feature in the climax of *Frankenstein Meets the Wolf Man.*) Perhaps the wildest of all is the reaction of actress Una O'Connor—the prototype for all of the shrill, hooting, cockney harridans that would come to populate the realm of Universal Horror—to the approach of the Monster; O'Connor's double-take and comic wail would not be out of place on *I Love Lucy.*

The script originally called for Henry Frankenstein to atone for his crimes by being blown up at the end along with Pretorius, but once again, the end was rewritten to keep him alive. Despite this, Colin Clive is clearly visible in the explosion scene.

Karloff's Monster makeup was modified from the original film. A rubber head-piece was used instead of cotton and collodion ridges, and Jack Pierce created burn scars on the Monster's face and arms. His character is altered as well: if the Monster in *Frankenstein* was a childlike innocent, here he is portrayed as a nightmarish teenager. Not only does he pick up smoking and drinking habits, but he shows a newfound interest in women, talks back to his "parent," and suffers from falling in with a bad influence, namely Dr. Pretorius. Pretorius, as played by Ernest Thesiger, a highly respected British stage actor, and champion needlepointist in real life, is so waspish and effeminate that Henry's protest that he cannot go back with the professor because he is about to be married can be taken on more than one level, no doubt intentionally so. It is another of Whale's little jokes that would fly by most of the audience (and the Breen Office).

The rich musical score by Franz Waxman has become one of the legendary scores of Hollywood, and showed how far sophisticated film-making techniques had become in the four short years since *Frankenstein*, which except for a brief bump during the credits, had no music at all. So convinced was Universal that it had a sure-fire hit in *Bride of Frankenstein* that it bumped up its April 29 release date by a week, bucking what was then called "the Lenten lull" for movie attendance.

SON OF FRANKENSTEIN (1939)

The first horror film to be produced under the aegis of "The New Universal," *Son of Frankenstein* pulled out all the stops. Not only was Boris Karloff back as the Monster, but Basil Rathbone, then at the peak of his

Lionel Atwill as the officious, one-armed Inspector Krogh in Son of Frankenstein, *one of the most effective (parodied) performances of Universal Horror.*

Bela Lugosi as Ygor and Boris Karloff as the Monster are both barely recognizable in Son of Frankenstein.

An example of the nightmarish, expressionistic sets from Son of Frankenstein.

stardom, was cast in the title role, the son of the Baron Frankenstein who had created the Monster (though the Baron is now referred to as *Heinrich*, not *Henry*), while Bela Lugosi took on a part so radically different from Dracula that some moviegoers had a hard time recognizing him. Early plans called for the film to be shot in Technicolor, and tests were made, showing a bright green Monster clad in a brown, fleecy sweater. But it was decided that color was more of a distraction than an asset (though the sweater, which Karloff hated, remained, despite the fact that it was only there as a concession to color).

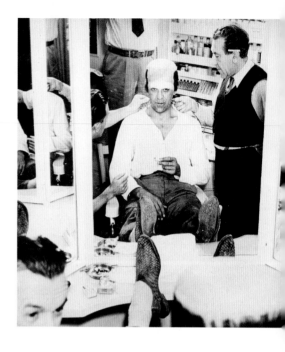

Jack P. Pierce (glimpsed in fore-ground left) and his assistant prepare Boris Karloff for the day's shooting in Son of Frankenstein.

The film begins with Wolf von Frankenstein (Rathbone) en route to the European village of Frankenstein, having left his comfy job in an American university in order to inherit his father's castle. Once there he learns that his family name carries a lot of baggage (though not so much as to encourage the residents to change the name of the town, apparently). Among those unhappy to see him is Inspector Krogh (Lionel Atwill), a would-be military general with a wooden arm, who warns Wolf to leave for his own good. Wolf bristles at any talk of his father's Monster, which he believes is mythical, but Krogh sets him straight: when the Inspector was a boy, the Monster attacked him and tore his arm out by the roots, killing any chance of a military career.

The chastened Wolf, his wife Elsa (Josephine Hutchinson), and their young son Peter (Donnie Dunagan) move into the dark, dank, creepy castle. In the nearby lab—which is built over a bubbling sulfur pit—Wolf soon encounters Ygor (Bela Lugosi), a demented shepherd who was tried and hanged for grave robbing ("so they *said*") but who did not die, despite his neck having broken. There is another unexpected resident of the castle: the Monster, who is virtually comatose. Before his illness, Ygor used the Monster to murder the jurors who condemned him to hang. At first Wolf is horrified, but upon the realization that the Monster is virtually inde-structible, he becomes fascinated, so much so that he restores the creature to wellness, hoping it will vindicate his father.

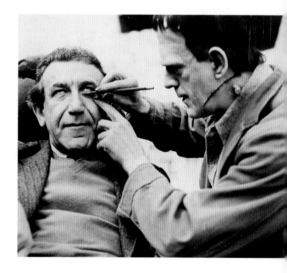

Boris Karloff turns the tables on Jack Pierce's makeup assistant on the set of Son of Frankenstein *(though he appears to be using a writing pencil, not a makeup pencil).*

Unfortunately, once the Monster is well he continues Ygor's campaign of murder. This alerts Krogh, who accuses Wolf of continuing his father's work. Wolf *has* continued his father's work, but he denies any complicity. Later, Wolf confronts Ygor and shoots him in self-defense. The Monster finds Ygor's body and is distraught over the death of his one friend, howling in anguish. Then he concocts a devious plan of revenge: he sneaks through the castle's secret passageways, abducts Wolf's son, and threatens to fling him into the sulfur pit. Wolf, aided by Krogh (who this time has his *false* arm ripped out by the Monster), manages to save his son by kicking the Monster into the pit instead. Deciding he has had enough of the village of Frankenstein, Wolf gathers up his family, deeds the castle to the village, and gets out of town.

This was producer/director Rowland V. Lee's only excursion into the horror film (one cannot count his 1939 historical melodrama *Tower of London*, which co-starred Karloff, Rathbone, and Vincent Price, as true horror, despite that cast). The result was not only the longest film in the Frankenstein series, at 99 minutes, but also the most visually expressionis-tic, with some of art director Jack Otterson's interiors looking like they were constructed of nothing but shadows.

Basil Rathbone, who was billed above both Karloff and Lugosi, was

A farewell to arm (it was artificial anyway) for Krogh (Lionel Atwill), who threatens the Monster (Boris Karloff), who in turn is threatening young Peter Frankenstein (Donnie Dunagan). Child actor Dunagan's brief career would conclude with voicing the young Bambi *in the Disney classic.*

Basil Rathbone (left) and Bela Lugosi (right) help Boris Karloff celebrate his 51st birthday on the set of Son of Frankenstein. *Karloff's only child was born that same day—November 23, 1938.*

known to loathe horror films, which is perhaps why his performance as Wolf is so shrill and uncharacteristically hammy. Bela Lugosi, for a change, fared much better, taking what had originally been a small part and turning it into a major presence in the film. Speaking in a guttural growl that reflects his broken neck, Lugosi's Ygor is as evil and devious as the script demanded, but also surprisingly and perversely funny. Seeing what the actor was up to early in the filming, the delighted Rowland Lee responded by building up the part of Ygor day-by-day on the set, to the point where Lugosi walks away with the picture.

Ever the purist where his Monster was concerned, Boris Karloff concluded after *Son of Frankenstein* that "there was not much left of the character of the monster to be developed." Except for an appearance at a Hollywood charity baseball game in 1940, an unused dream sequence cameo in the 1947 film *The Secret Life of Walter Mitty* (to which the actor may have agreed simply to give work to the just-laid-off makeup wizard Jack Pierce), and a 1962 episode of television's *Route 66*, Karloff never wore the Monster makeup again. What *did* delight Karloff during the filming of *Son of Frankenstein* was the birth of his only child, Sara Jane, on November 23, 1938, his 51st birthday. Frankenstein may have had a son, but the Monster had a daughter.

Lon Chaney Jr. as the Monster in The Ghost of Frankenstein. *Chaney's interpretation was more brutal and less soulful than Karloff's.*

THE GHOST OF FRANKENSTEIN (1942)

The Ghost of Frankenstein continues the adventures of the Monster and Ygor (again Bela Lugosi), the latter having survived Wolf von Frankenstein's bullets. Ygor is holding vigil beside the lump of hardened sulfur that contains the body of the Monster. Down in the village of Frankenstein, the townspeople are restless; they view the castle as the last visible vestige of the "curse of Frankenstein" that has blighted the town. Forming a mob, they storm the castle and blow it up, but instead of ridding the village of its curse, the explosions reactivate it by breaking open the sulfur block and releasing the Monster (Lon Chaney Jr.).

Delighted by the Monster's resurrection, Ygor takes him to see his "brother," Dr. Ludwig Frankenstein (Sir Cedric Hardwicke), Heinrich's other son, who is a psychologist and brain surgeon running a sanitarium in the village of Vasaria. Aided by the haughty Dr. Theodor Bohmer (Lionel Atwill), who was once Ludwig's teacher but who now, thanks to an unfortunate (and undisclosed) medical indiscretion, has been reduced to the position of assistant, Frankenstein has just successfully removed and replaced a brain in a living patient.

Ludwig has lived in Vasaria secure in the knowledge that his family heritage remains a dark secret. Even his beautiful daughter Elsa (Evelyn Ankers), who is in love with the town's prosecutor, Erik Ernst (Ralph Bellamy), knows nothing about his connection with the Monster. But the arrival of Ygor and the Monster change that, particularly when the Monster innocently tries to help a small, fearless girl named Cloestine (Janet Ann Gallow). When the young girl wants to retrieve her ball, which has been kicked onto a rooftop by the town bully, the Monster steps in to help her and kills two interfering villagers in the process.

Ygor manages to get the Monster to Dr. Frankenstein's sanitarium, but Ludwig wants nothing to do with him, knowing that the *real* curse has been on the Frankenstein family. He comes around, however, after being

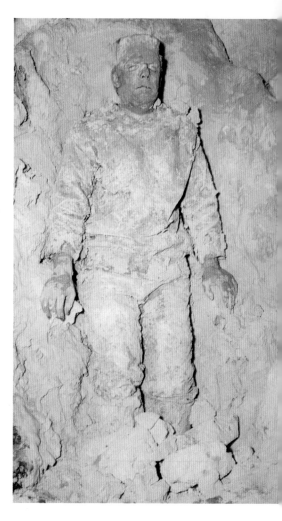

Lon Chaney Jr. as the Monster, just about to emerge from the dried sulfur pit in The Ghost of Frankenstein.

In an echo of the original Monster's meeting with Little Maria, the Monster in The Ghost of Frankenstein *becomes infatuated with a little girl named Cloestine (Janet Ann Gallow). Ralph Bellamy is on the right.*

Poster for The Ghost of Frankenstein. *The ghost in question was the specter of the original Dr. Frankenstein, played by Cedric Hardwicke, who appears to his son (also Hardwicke).*

Evelyn Ankers, Cedric Hardwicke (as Ludwig, the second son of Dr. Frankenstein), Lon Chaney Jr., and Janet Ann Gallow try to work through their differences in The Ghost of Frankenstein.

Blinded and enraged, the Monster (Lon Chaney Jr.) takes his anger out on Dr. Bohmer (Lionel Atwill) in The Ghost of Frankenstein.

visited by the titular ghost of his father, who tells him the problem is all in the creature's brain. Replace the brain, the ghost of Frankenstein says, and you reform the Monster. Ludwig wants to transplant the brain of a lab associate named Dr. Kettering who the Monster has already killed, but to the shock of all, the Monster has a different idea: he wants *Cloestine's* brain, and kidnaps the girl so the transplant can take place.

The disappearance of Cloestine has roiled the villagers, who believe Ludwig is sheltering the Monster. Forming a mob, they go to storm the sanitarium, but Erik heads them off, arriving there first to investigate. Instead of hiding the Monster from view, Ludwig proudly shows him off to Erik, explaining that the brain of Dr. Kettering has been put into his skull, making him harmless. But the doctor is in for a nasty shock: preying up on Dr. Bohmer's gargantuan ego, Ygor had earlier convinced him to take charge of the operation by putting *Ygor's* brain, not Kettering's, in the Monster's head!

The once placid face of the Monster now forms an evil leer as he begins to speak with Ygor's voice, describing grandiose plans to take over the world. To his horror, Ludwig realizes that he has created a worse monster than either his father or brother had. But at the height of his raving, the Monster himself receives a shock: he suddenly goes blind! Dr. Bohmer carelessly failed to take into account that Ygor had a different blood type from the Monster, causing the brain's sensory nerves to malfunction.

Enraged, the Monster throws Dr. Bohmer into a machine, electrocuting him, and then tears apart the laboratory, starting a fire. Ludwig is trapped inside to atone for his sins, but Elsa and Erik escape. After returning Cloestine to her worried parents, they watch the conflagration destroy the sanitarium from afar.

Tall and burly Lon Chaney Jr. was a natural to step into the heavy boots vacated by Boris Karloff, and he was by now used to suffering the rigors of three- and four-hour monster makeups, but he did not do so gladly. For *Ghost of Frankenstein*, Chaney had it worse than ever before: not only was there the usual Monster makeup, but in his early scenes, the actor was sprayed with a layer of mud to replicate a coating of sulfur, and then he endured additional burn makeup for the conflagration scene. Making the situation even worse was that Chaney was allergic to the kind of rubber from which his Monster headpiece was fabricated, and it irritated his forehead to the point of bleeding.

The Ghost of Frankenstein marked the last appearance of Ygor (who seems to have seen his dentist since *Son of Frankenstein*) though his name, or variations of it, has gone on to become the generic name for any mad doctor's hunchbacked lab assistant.

More importantly for the ongoing saga, *The Ghost of Frankenstein*, which was written by W. Scott Darling and directed by Erle C. Kenton, would be the last film to feature the Monster as the central figure of the movie. *Frankenstein Meets the Wolf Man, House of Frankenstein,* and *House of Dracula* would all be graced by a monstrous appearance, but each one focused more on the Wolf Man, who was Universal's top monster of the 1940s.

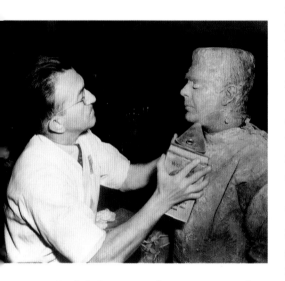

Jack P. Pierce applies a coating of mud to Lon Chaney Jr. to simulate his encasement in sulfur in The Ghost of Frankenstein. *This would be Chaney's only official appearance as the Monster.*

7 SPOTLIGHT:
BORIS KARLOFF

Sometime in the late 1920s, a struggling, middle-aged actor named Boris Karloff was walking home from an unrewarding day's work at the movie studio, wondering with every step if he was ever going to achieve real success in the film business. A car horn tooted behind him and Karloff turned to see Lon Chaney, then one of Hollywood's biggest stars, in the driver's seat. Karloff and Chaney already knew each other, so Chaney offered the Britisher a ride and some advice, which he never forgot. "The secret of success in Hollywood lies in being different from everyone else," Chaney said. "Find something no one else can or will do and they'll begin to take notice of you."

A few years later, Boris Karloff did indeed find it, and as a result rocketed to stardom after having spent more than two decades trodding the boards in regional stock theaters all over Canada and the United States and laboring in the bit-part talent pool in Hollywood.

Given his stage name, journalists of the time, and even some directors, assumed Boris Karloff was a Russian transplant. He was really a British transplant, born William Henry Pratt in the Dulwich section of London in 1887. Karloff was the youngest member of a large Anglo-Indian brood whose family business was civil service (his great aunt was Anna Leonowens, whose experiences as a royal governess in Siam would be musicalized as *The King and I*). It was expected that young "Billy" would follow suit and become a diplomat after graduation from King's College, but he had other ideas. His favorite brother, George Marlow Pratt, had been an actor for a brief time, and from an early age Billy Pratt dreamed of following him in that profession. In May of 1909, he sailed to Canada to pursue his goal, and in the process conjured up the name "Boris Karloff" for his professional billing, later joking, "After all, one can't be an actor and be called 'Pratt'!" He would claim that "Karloff" was his grandmother's family name, though there is no evidence to support this.

After touring Canada for a decade, Karloff made his way to California, eventually settling in Los Angeles to try and take advantage of the burgeoning film industry. For years he took any acting job available and

Karloff, made up as Ardath Bey, studies his script for The Mummy.

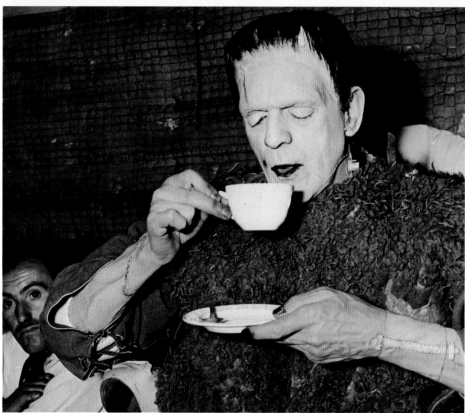

There were always tea breaks on Karloff sets. This shot is from Son of Frankenstein.

supplemented his income as a truck driver and laborer. When the talkies overtook Hollywood in the late 1920s, he found himself a bit more in demand because his rich, classically accented voice recorded well, despite his lisp. Ironically, when his long-awaited big break finally came, it had nothing to do with his voice. Following Chaney's dictum, Karloff did what several actors had already refused to do: endure a grueling and painful makeup ordeal in order to play an inarticulate brute. It was, however, the *way* Karloff played the inarticulate brute that made all the difference.

The monster success (so to speak) of *Frankenstein* meant that the years of hardship were over for the actor, though they were not forgotten. Throughout his career, Karloff would manage his money as carefully as possible, just in case his success faded as rapidly as it had arrived. Even after achieving stardom he augmented his studio income by selling produce grown on his rustic two-acre estate in Coldwater Canyon. He did not have to worry; Universal had wasted no time putting him into a string of horror films including *The Old Dark House*, *The Mummy*, *The Black Cat*, *The Raven*, and *Bride of Frankenstein*, billing him as "Karloff" or "Karloff the Uncanny." These roles the actor interspersed with less monstrous, but usually villainous, parts in films for other studios, such as *House of Rothschild*, with the great (but now forgotten) actor George Arliss, and John Ford's *The Lost Patrol*, both released in 1934. For the rest of his life, even as his body weakened with age and his health diminished, Karloff was never out of demand for films, Broadway, radio, television, even for commercials and recordings.

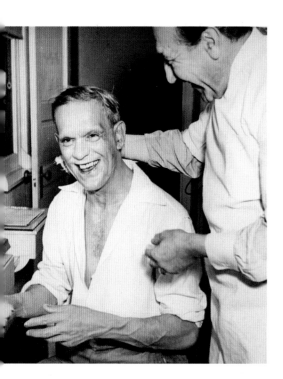

Karloff with Jack P. Pierce's makeup assistant. Given the glee on the actor's face, it probably means the makeup is coming off, not going on.

On a personal level, Karloff was the polar opposite of any of the horrific roles in which he excelled. By all accounts he was a gentle, cultured man who was fond of both children and animals, addicted to breaking for four o'clock tea, and passionately devoted to cricket, gardening, and the writings of Joseph Conrad. In 1933, only a year after achieving his hard-won stardom, Karloff joined a small group of fellow actors to form the Screen Actors Guild (SAG), which was not a popular proposition with the studios at that time. He would serve on the union's board for more than 20 years and was known to be uncompromising in his insistence that studios complied with SAG rules.

At the same time, Karloff was a rather mysterious man who kept much of his personal history to himself. He was married and divorced multiple times; even a couple of his wives did not know exactly how many! (For the record, six marriages, five divorces, with his final one to Evelyn Helmore being the lasting one.) He never publicly revealed his East Indian heritage, instead putting forth the story that his dark coloration was the result of time spent in the California sun. He never relinquished his British citizenship and never legally changed his name, signing contracts and all legal documents as "William H. Pratt, a.k.a. Boris Karloff."

Most surprisingly of all, given his great success as an actor, Karloff was a genuinely modest man who always expressed gratitude toward the role of the Frankenstein Monster. He would forever tell people that it was a stroke of luck that he landed the part, adding, "Any actor who played it was destined for success."

When Boris Karloff died at home in England in 1969, at age 81, it was virtually in the fashion that he frequently stated was his goal: to go "with his boots on."

Henry Hull as the werewolf from Werewolf of London. *Makeup artist Jack P. Pierce wanted more hair; Hull wanted more dignity. Hull won.*

8

THE WOLF MAN

Even a man who is pure of heart,
And says his prayers by night;
May become a wolf when the wolfbane blooms,
And the autumn moon is bright.

That ancient gypsy saying is one of the most familiar in all of Universal Horror, a harbinger of doom for any unfortunate soul who finds himself bearing the curse of lycanthropy. Surprisingly, however, it is not really ancient and not really from Romany tradition; it was penned by screenwriter Curt Siodmak in 1941 for *The Wolf Man.*

Unlike Frankenstein's Monster, Dracula, and the Invisible Man, the Wolf Man cannot boast of literary roots; rather the character was based on legends and folklore. And while vampires, mummies, and man-made monsters had been subjects of silent films prior to the start of the first great horror film cycle, no one had ever attempted a werewolf story, despite the ubiquity of the legend.

It would be up to Universal to show how it was done.

WEREWOLF OF LONDON (1935)

Universal's first treatment of lycanthropy, *Werewolf of London*, starred none of the studio's regular horror men, but, rather, an American stage actor named Henry Hull, who resembled Boris Karloff slightly and possessed a distinctive, resonant voice and a florid acting style. Hull played Dr. Wilfrid Glendon, a dedicated, if somewhat priggish, London doctor who on expedition in the mountains of Tibet, hikes to a legendary hidden valley where grows the rare and mysterious mariphasa luna lumina plant, whose blossoms photosynthesize in moonlight, not sunlight. In the process of tracking down the plant, Glendon is attacked by a strange half-seen creature that ferociously bites him.

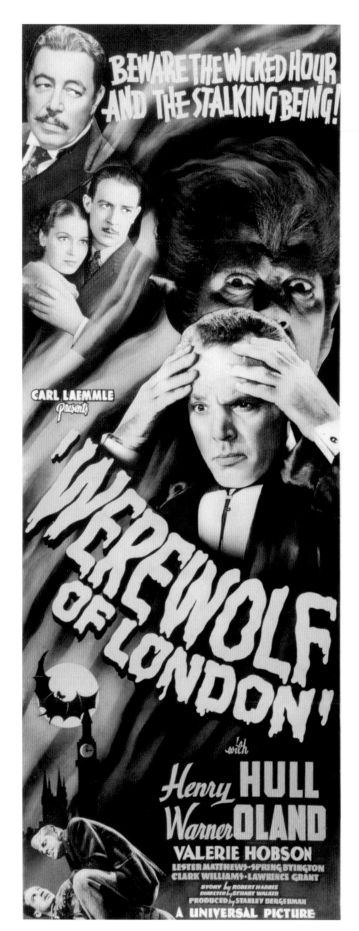

Dr. Glendon (Henry Hull, left) learns from the mysterious Dr. Yogami (Warner Oland) that the bites he suffered in Tibet might lead to bigger problems in Werewolf of London.

The comically drunken Mrs. Whack (Ethel Griffies, left) and Mrs. Moncaster (Zeffie Tilbury) in Werewolf of London *were attempts to duplicate the sort of cockney eccentrics with which James Whale filled his films.*

Universal's first treatment of lycanthropy was Werewolf of London.

*Dr. Yogami (Warner Oland), himself
a werewolf, dies at the roots of the
precious mariphasa plant in
Werewolf of London.*

*Glendon (Henry Hull) in full
wolf mode and on the prowl in
Werewolf of London.*

Back in London, he tries to get the plant to bloom using a special moon ray lamp, all the while ignoring his beautiful young wife Lisa (Valerie Hobson), who is being comforted by a childhood friend Paul Ames (Lester Matthews), an aeronaut recently returned from America. Also lurking about the lab is the mysterious Dr. Yogami (Warner Oland), who, although Glendon does not realize it, is the human side of the creature that bit him in Tibet. Yogami tells Glendon that the mariphasa plant acts as an antidote to werewolfism, adding that there are, at that moment, two werewolves at large in London.

When the skeptical Glendon begins to grow hair and fangs he is convinced, but he then learns that Yogami has stolen the mature buds from his mariphasa plant, leaving him helpless. Glendon attempts to hide out in a cheap boarding house, but it cannot hold him. He goes on a murderous rampage, but tries to distance himself physically from Lisa, for her safety. Facing Yogami in a final battle over the last mariphasa bloom, Glendon kills the older werewolf, but then goes after Lisa. Instead of fleeing in terror, she appeals to his human side, buying enough time for the police to arrive and shoot him.

Werewolf of London was the sole horror film for director Stuart Walker, who created a very convincing London atmosphere on the backlot, and with screenwriter John Coltin, presented something of a compendium of motifs from James Whale's earlier horror films. The obsessed scientist–beautiful wife–old boyfriend triangle is there (and even though they are playing childhood friends, Valerie Hobson was only 17 during filming, while Lester Matthews was 35), as are the cockney policemen, and the shrill, comedic female characters in the persons of "Mrs. Whack" and "Mrs. Moncaster," the boarding house hooting harridans.

Jack Pierce had originally planned to completely immerse Hull's face in putty, paint, and hair, for an effect similar to that later seen in *The Wolf Man*, but Hull objected, accepting only a minimal (though still highly effective) lupine disguise. Glendon's first transformation to werewolf was accomplished by having him walk past a series of pillars, emerging from behind each one with a more extreme makeup. Later, the change begins in full view of the camera, with shadows and lines appearing on his face as if by magic. This was done using a common cinematic trick in which shadows were painted on the face in red, then filmed through a red filter, which bleached them out. When the filter was removed, the shadows appeared as though by magic.

In its review of *Werewolf of London, Variety* dubbed Henry Hull the new Lon Chaney, but it was a short-lived pronouncement. Lacking Chaney's ability to elicit sympathy, Hull would find his true métier playing cranky, eccentric codgers, often in Westerns.

THE WOLF MAN (1941)

Universal's second version of the werewolf legend was the one that proved to have legs, hairy though they were. More than any other film, *The Wolf Man* would launch the studio's second horror cycle and create a new iconic character, one that would become the most popular of the 1940s: the doomed, but undying, Lawrence Stewart Talbot, a.k.a. the Wolf Man.

The film's fairy tale tone is announced by the very first shot: that of a book opening to a passage on lycanthropy, an image reminiscent of the beginning of a Disney film. The action begins with young Larry Talbot (Lon Chaney Jr.) returning to his ancestral home in Llanwelly, Wales, after having spent nearly two decades in America. His relationship with his father, Sir John Talbot (Claude Rains), the local landowner, has been rocky since Larry's elder brother was made heir to the estate. But with his brother now dead, Larry returns to try and patch things up.

Working fast to ingratiate himself with the village, Larry asks beautiful Gwen Conliffe (Evelyn Ankers) to accompany him to a nearby gypsy carnival, and she agrees, but only in the company of a friend, Jenny (Fay Helm). At the carnival, Jenny has her palm read by the gypsy fortuneteller Bela (Bela Lugosi), who sees in her hand the sign of the pentagram. Bela is really a werewolf who soon attacks Jenny. Wielding the silver-headed cane he bought from Gwen's shop, Larry rushes to Jenny's rescue and bludgeons to death what he believes to be a wolf, but he is bitten during the struggle. Soon he takes Bela's place, transforming into the Wolf Man and randomly killing victims in the village, deaths which are ascribed to a normal wolf. He tries to explain to his father what is happening, but Sir John refuses to believe him. Only Bela's mother Maleva (Maria Ouspenskaya) understands.

To force his son to deal with his fears, bull-headed Sir John ties Larry to a chair in Talbot Manor while the village is hunting for the wolf. Knowing he is powerless to fight his affliction, Larry begs his father to carry his silver cane with him on the hunt, just in case. When the moon rises, Larry becomes the Wolf Man; he breaks free and rushes out into the foggy woods, where he attacks Gwen. Sir John finds the creature and beats it to death with the silver cane, only to have the wolf turn back into his son before his horrified eyes.

The Wolf Man stands as one of Universal's all time best, but had director George Waggner filmed Curt Siodmak's original screenplay as written, it would have been a very different film. Titled *Destiny*, the script was more of a psychological thriller than a straightforward horror film, with the audience actually seeing the Wolf Man only once in a scene near the end, shot through Larry's point of view, in which he sees himself reflected in water.

What's more, in the original version, Larry was no relation to Sir John Talbot. He was Larry *Gill*, an American technician, in Wales to install Sir John's telescope. Despite the fact that the very American Chaney seems like an unlikely offspring of the very British Rains, making him the scion of the family adds an interesting level to the character. Within the context of the film, we observe Larry having communication problems with his father, while he starts to feel a newfound sense of power that he doesn't know how to control, and he starts to sprout hair in strange places to boot. Add to that the attention Larry is showing to girls, namely Gwen, and you have a perfect metaphor for male adolescence. Whether intended or not, this level of interpretation (which echoes the Monster's child/teen nature) would have been lost had Sir John and Larry not been father and son.

One sequence that was filmed as written but later cut was one in which Larry agrees to wrestle a bear at the gypsy carnival and ends up pummeling the animal half to death, as a result of his growing bestial side. The shooting of the scene elicited a lot of press attention, including one write-up that stated, "A 500-pound ursus negrus Americanus tangled with

In a sequence cut from The Wolf Man, *Larry Talbot (Lon Chaney Jr.) wrestles a bear at a gypsy carnival… and wins! The scene was removed because it made Larry look too bestial.*

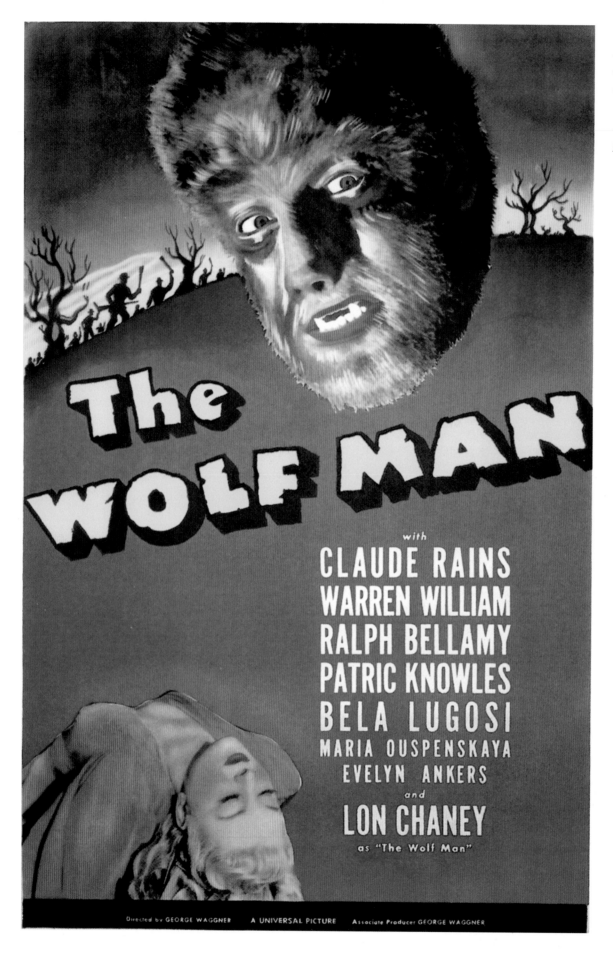

The Wolf
Man *featured
one of the best
casts of any
Universal
Horror
picture.*

American-raised Larry Talbot (Lon Chaney Jr.) adjusts the telescope of his father, Sir John (Claude Rains), in The Wolf Man. *In the original script, the two characters were not related, and the reason Larry was at Talbot Manor was to work on the telescope.*

Larry Talbot (Lon Chaney Jr.) with the gypsy Maleva (Maria Ouspenskaya), the only person who understands his curse.

Colorized lobby card for The Wolf Man, *showing Lon Chaney Jr. and Evelyn Ankers. In real life the frequent co-stars could not stand each other: Chaney called her "Shankers" and she called him "The Mad Ghoul."*

"The way you walked was thorny, through no fault of your own." Maleva (Maria Ouspenskaya) gives lupine Larry Talbot (Lon Chaney Jr.) the gypsy benediction in The Wolf Man. *Of course, Larry would walk again, his way becoming even thornier.*

Jack P. Pierce finally got to realize his dream werewolf makeup on Lon Chaney Jr. in The Wolf Man.

a homo sapiens Hollywoodus, 200, and the latter won a decision." But at the last minute it was decided that the scene made Larry (as opposed to the Wolf Man) look unsympathetic and it was edited out.

Finally allowed free reign to create the wolf of his dreams, Jack Pierce spent three to four hours turning Chaney into a beast, using yak hair, a rubber snout, dark greasepaint, and clawed, hairy gloves and slippers. The actual transformation scene would take most of an entire day to film. After Pierce applied one stage of makeup, Chaney would hit his pose and be filmed, after which that makeup would be removed and the next stage put on, during which time the shot film would be developed and used as a guide to line Chaney up for the next shot. When the 20-or-so stages of makeup were joined together through lap dissolves, it appeared that the Wolf Man emerged in a matter of seconds.

Despite the ordeal, Chaney had a fondness for his hirsute "baby." "He was *mine*," the actor averred, proud that while all the other classic monsters had been played by different actors over the years, no one but him ever appeared as the cursed Larry Talbot.

FRANKENSTEIN MEETS THE WOLF MAN (1943)

Frankenstein may get top billing (and inadvertently solidify the confusion between creator and creature), but *Frankenstein Meets the Wolf Man* is really the Wolf Man's film. Ostensibly a joint sequel to both *The Wolf Man* and *The Ghost of Frankenstein*, it more faithfully continues the Larry Talbot saga, never explaining how the Monster, who when last seen was being burnt to death, ended up encased in a wall of ice.

The film opens in one of the most atmospheric graveyard sets in any Universal film. Two grave robbers break into the Talbot family crypt, having heard the rumor that Larry was buried with money in his pockets. Unfortunately, they didn't hear the *other* rumor regarding Larry. They open his coffin right as the full moon rises and restores him to life and murderous power.

Not long afterwards, Larry is found unconscious by a bobby in Cardiff, miles away from Llanwelly, suffering from a head wound. He is taken to Queen's Hospital, where Dr. Frank Mannering (Patric Knowles) operates on him, saving his life. Recovering miraculously quickly, Larry tells a story about being a murderer, which attracts the interest of Inspector Owen (Dennis Hoey). Larry escapes from the hospital and seeks out the gypsy Maleva (Maria Ouspenskaya), the mother of the werewolf who bit him, to ask her to guide him to a conclusive death. She agrees to take him to Dr. Frankenstein, who can help him.

The two journey to the village of Vasaria (whose residents are now *very* aware of the Frankenstein family heritage, thanks to the action covered in *Ghost of Frankenstein*), only to learn that Dr. Frankenstein is dead. Larry seeks out his records in the ruins of his castle, but instead finds the Monster (Bela Lugosi), whom he releases from a wall of ice. Larry hopes *he* knows the location of the missing journals, but when the secret hiding place is found, there are no notes. There is however, a photo of Dr. Frankenstein's daughter Elsa so Larry decides to seek her out for help

On the pretense that he wants to buy what's left of the castle, Larry meets Elsa (Ilona Massey) and escorts her to Vasaria's gala harvest celebration, the Festival of New Wine, where he tries to convince her to help him.

Frankenstein Meets the Wolf
Man *was the first Frankenstein
film in which a Dr. Frankenstein
does not appear, lending credence
to the notion that the Monster
himself is called "Frankenstein."*

The Wolf Man makeup was perfected, as were the transformation scenes, in Frankenstein Meets the Wolf Man.

Bela Lugosi as the Monster and Lon Chaney Jr. as the Wolf Man duke it out for the publicity department. The actual battle royal at the end of Frankenstein Meets the Wolf Man was performed by stuntmen Gil Perkins and Eddie Parker.

But two unexpected guests show up at the Festival: Dr. Mannering, who tracked Talbot across Europe from the newspaper accounts of wolfish killings, and the Monster, who galumphs into the middle of the celebration. Talbot manages to get the Monster back to the castle, but the next day Mannering and Elsa come looking for him. Elsa retrieves the journals, and upon reviewing them, Mannering realizes he can destroy both the Monster and Talbot by reversing the original process and drawing off their life forces.

Like so many doctors before him, Mannering cannot bring himself to kill the Monster. Instead he restores it to power, after which the creature breaks free, just as Talbot transforms into the Wolf Man. They conduct a titanic fight, from which Mannering and Elsa barely manage to escape. Meanwhile, a crazed, fearful villager has dynamited the nearby dam, which crumbles, releasing a cascade of water that destroys the castle and washes away the fighting creatures.

Frankenstein Meets the Wolf Man represented a feast for horror buffs: *two* monsters for the price of one. In a publicity gimmick, Chaney was initially slated to play *both* monsters, the idea being that through split screen and the use of doubles, the illusion could be maintained. At the last minute, though, cost and logistical considerations forced the studio to abandon that plan. Since the Wolf Man was Chaney's "baby," another actor had to be found to play the Monster. It had to be a true actor, too, not just an anonymous stunt guy, since the script called for dialogue from the Monster, who was given speech but robbed of sight as the results of the brain transplant from *The Ghost of Frankenstein*.

The solution to the problem was half-obvious, half-ridiculous: Bela Lugosi, whose voice had been dubbed over Lon Chaney Jr.'s line readings in *Ghost*, could play the Monster. Even though Lugosi had disdained the role 11 years earlier, he had become less choosy about the roles he accepted. With the added incentive of dialogue, Lugosi was persuaded to take the part and endure the makeup, which now included that post-Karloff "beauty mark," which was in nearly the same place as Ilona Massey's natural one.

It seemed like a good idea at the time. What no one stopped to consider was that Lugosi was 60 years old and not physically up to the demands of the role. Stuntmen Gil Perkins and Eddie Parker were hastily enlisted to fill in for Lugosi in any scene that required heavy lifting (and Ilona Massey was not petite), plus a few that didn't. The Monster's introductory scene, in which he is pulled from the ice block by Talbot, featured Gil Perkins in full-face close-up, not Lugosi. The substitution of stuntmen seemed to work fine, but then a funny thing happened on the way to the movie theater: all of the Monster's dialogue was edited out, in addition to any reference to his blindness, leaving only Lugosi's groping gestures to insufficiently communicate the lack of sight.

Why was the role so drastically altered in post-production? Years later, screenwriter Curt Siodmak put the blame solely on Lugosi, describing his performance as "Hungarian funny," and claiming that preview audiences laughed at the Monster's dialogue. Yet no one reported hilarity ensuing from the end of *Ghost of Frankenstein* where Lugosi spoke for Chaney's Monster. It is more likely that the dialogue itself was the problem; hearing the Monster rant about immortal life and world domination might

Larry Talbot (Lon Chaney Jr.) stumbles upon the body of the Monster (Bela Lugosi) encased in ice in Frankenstein Meets the Wolf Man. *That's Lugosi behind the ice in this still, but in the film it's stuntman Gil Perkins playing the Monster in this sequence.*

An excised scene from Frankenstein Meets the Wolf Man *which involved dialogue between the Monster (Bela Lugosi) and Larry Talbot (Lon Chaney Jr.)*

Stuntman Gil Perkins, doubling for Bela Lugosi, carries away Ilona Massey in Frankenstein Meets the Wolf Man.

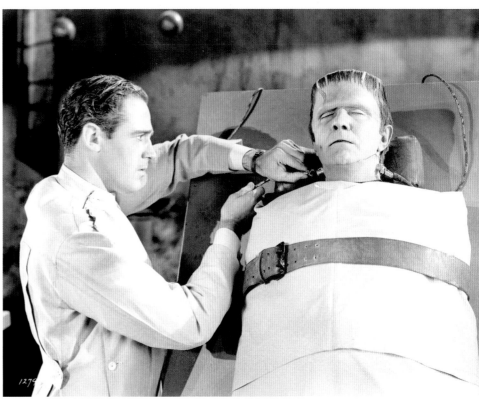

Dr. Mannering (Patric Knowles) preps the Monster (Bela Lugosi) for rejuvenation in Frankenstein Meets the Wolf Man.

have made him too much of a Hitler surrogate for comfort for wartime audiences. Whatever the reason, the Monster was once more mute, though Lugosi's lips can be seen moving wordlessly in a couple scenes (and for the record, the excised dialogue explained how the Monster wound up in the ice; he escaped the fire and fell into a stream, which froze.)

Frankenstein Meets the Wolf Man has also become renowned for the Festival of New Wine sequence, which is highlighted by the song "Faro-La, Faro-Li," belted out by Russian bass Adia Kuzentzoff, a kind of gypsy calypso written by Curt Siodmak and Hans J. Salter. While Universal Horror is not known for its musical numbers, this one is an absolute gem.

HOUSE OF FRANKENSTEIN (1944)

If one monster is good, and two are even better, than why not *three*? Now add to the mix a mad doctor surrogate, and yes, a hunchbacked servant, and the result is *House of Frankenstein*, Universal's first so-called monster rally, featuring the Frankenstein Monster, the Wolf Man, and Dracula. The original plans called for the Mummy to join the party, but that contrivance would have been too much.

Having sat out the series since 1939, Boris Karloff returned as Dr. Gustav Niemann, a devotee of the original Dr. Frankenstein, who has been incarcerated for 15 years in the Neustadt Prison for the Criminally Insane for the crime of grave robbing. In that time he has continued his scientific theorizing, and has concluded that Dr. Frankenstein was *almost* right when it came to transplanting brains. His "pupil" is the faithful but dangerously strong hunchback Daniel (J. Carrol Naish, whose performance established the prototype for all hunchbacked assistants who utter, "Yes, Master!").

When a bolt of lightning strikes the crumbling prison and collapses its walls, Niemann and Daniel escape to freedom. They take cover in the show wagon of Professor Bruno Lampini (George Zucco), who operates a traveling Chamber of Horrors, the star attraction of which is the skeleton of Dracula. Seeing an opportunity to revenge himself against the people who testified against him and sent him to prison, he instructs Daniel to kill Lampini and his driver, and then they take their places.

Their first stop is Reigelburg, where one of Niemann's accusers, Herr Hussmann (Sig Rumann), is now the Burgomaster. Accidentally raising Dracula (John Carradine) from the dead, Niemann strikes a deal with him, using him as an instrument of revenge against Hussman, whom the vampire bites and kills. When Dracula abducts Hussman's niece Rita (Anne Gwynne), he is chased by the police, and sacrificed by Niemann, who jettisons his coffin out in the open. Trying to return to it, Dracula is killed by the rising sun, leaving Niemann and Daniel free to move onto their next revenge spot, Visaria (which was spelled *Vasaria* in the two previous Frankenstein films). There the two encounter a gypsy encampment where an attractive young gypsy dancer named Ilonka (Elena Verdugo) plies her trade. After saving the girl from a brutal beating, Daniel begs Niemann to bring the girl with them. Ilonka flirts with the lovesick Daniel until she sees his twisted back, but she remains kind to him (the playing of this scene is highly reminiscent of one from *The Hunchback of Notre Dame*, with Lon Chaney and Patsy Ruth Miller).

They proceed on to the ruins of Castle Frankenstein, where Niemann searches for Dr. Frankenstein's records. In an ice cavern below

Lon Chaney Jr. remembered to wear his hairy gloves in this scene from House of Frankenstein. *For one scene, he would forget.*

A desperate Larry Talbot (Lon Chaney Jr., right) tries to force Dr. Edelmann (Boris Karloff) to attend to his problems instead of the Monster's (Glenn Strange) in House of Frankenstein.

The Wolf Man (Lon Chaney Jr.) attacks the gypsy dancer Ilonka (Elena Verdugo), who loves the man inside, in House of Frankenstein.

THE DEVIL'S BROOD!

All the Screen's Titans of Terror—Together in the Greatest of All **SCREEN SENSATIONS!**

FRANKENSTEIN'S
MONSTER!
WOLF MAN!
DRACULA!
HUNCHBACK!
MAD DOCTOR!

Starring **BORIS KARLOFF** **LON CHANEY** *with* **JOHN CARRADINE** **J. CARROL NAISH**

ANNE GWYNNE   PETER COE   ELENA VERDUGO   LIONEL ATWILL

The Devil's Brood *was the working title for* House of Frankenstein.

The Monster (Glenn Strange) drags the unconscious form of Dr. Niemann (here stuntman Carey Loftin doubling Boris Karloff) away from the ubiquitous angry mob in House of Frankenstein.

the structure, they discover the frozen forms of the Monster (Glenn Strange) and the Wolf Man (Lon Chaney Jr.), who Niemann thaws out, hoping one of them will know the location of the hidden records. Once he has the records, Niemann completes his revenge, finds the two remaining men whose testimony put him away, and abducts them, planning to put their brains into the bodies of the monsters.

Blinded by his revenge, Niemann is ignorant of a growing triangle between Ilonka, Talbot, and Daniel, which is exacerbated by his reneging on his promises to give the hunchback a new body and rid Talbot of his curse. When Ilonka dies of wounds received from the transformed Wolf Man (but not before she kills him with a silver bullet, out of love), Daniel snaps and strangles Niemann, which incenses the Monster, who breaks free. After throwing Daniel from the top of the castle, the Monster takes up Niemann and tries to escape, but is chased by torch-bearing villagers into a quicksand bog, into which the Monster and the doctor sink.

The working title for *House of Frankenstein* was *The Devil's Brood*, and despite its high monster content, it is anchored by the characters of Dr. Niemann and Daniel. Essentially Dr. Frankenstein under a different name, Niemann at one point in the film reveals that, while he never actually met the good doctor, his brother was Frankenstein's lab assistant. Could his brother have been Fritz? Karl? *Ygor*?

House of Frankenstein was Glenn Strange's first appearance as the Monster; for the rest of his life he would praise Boris Karloff for coaching him in the role (though for the most part, the Monster in the film is immobile). Coaching aside, Karloff was seen more than heard on the picture's set. "He was sort of a loner," recalls Elena Verdugo, "but there was an aura about him, a silent, powerful feeling when you were around him."

Verdugo, whose 19th birthday was celebrated on the set, found Lon Chaney Jr. much chattier. "We'd go out the stage door and sit in the prop box, and he'd have a beer and I'd have a Coke, and he was perfectly charming," she says. That was once she had gotten used to his visage. In the scene where the Wolf Man transforms and rushes past Ilonka, crashing through a window, Verdugo—who had never seen Chaney in makeup or in action—let out such a bloodcurdling shriek that the professional "screamer" who had been hired to dub her was sent home. "They said, 'We don't have to use her!'" the actress recalls. Director Erle C. Kenton apparently sent home the on-set continuity person too, since nobody noticed that Chaney was not wearing his hairy Wolf Man gloves for the shot.

Karloff, incidentally, made one contribution to the picture that did not involve his character, Dr. Niemann. When Daniel falls from the roof of the castle, having been thrown through the window by the Monster, the accompanying scream is actually Karloff's voice. The Universal sound department had taken his anguished howl from *Son of Frankenstein*, when the Monster finds the body of Ygor, and added it to its stock sound library. In addition to Daniel's death fall, Karloff's scream can also be heard accompanying Ted de Corsia's fatal plunge in 1948's *The Naked City*.

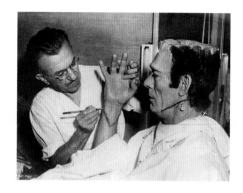

Jack P. Pierce fine-tunes Glenn Strange's Monster makeup for House of Frankenstein.

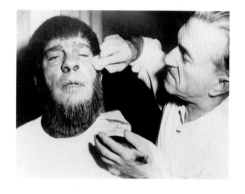

Jack P. Pierce working on a mid-transformation Wolf Man stage on Lon Chaney Jr. from House of Dracula *(note the putty blocking out Chaney's moustache).*

She-Wolf of London *featured no real werewolves at all, but rather, a diabolical killer. Lloyd Corrigan is the victim here.*

She-Wolf of London was the end of the road for Universal's lycanthropy cycle.

SHE-WOLF OF LONDON (1946)

Even though the term "werewolf" is frequently invoked, *She-Wolf of London* is not a continuation of the Wolf Man saga. Nor is it about actual werewolves.

When a man is savagely attacked in a London park, Scotland Yard Inspector Latham (Lloyd Corrigan) believes a werewolf might be involved. Then more murders are chalked up to the "werewolf killer," who leaves the footprints of a woman. All this greatly upsets young heiress Phyllis Allenby (June Lockhart), who fears that she suffers from the "Allenby Curse," which is lycanthropy. The last of the Allenbys, she lives in a foreboding mansion with Martha Winthrop (Sara Hayden) and her daughter Carol (Jan Wiley), treating Martha as her aunt and Carol as her cousin, even though they are not actually related—in fact, the cold and controlling Martha used to work as housekeeper for the Allenby family.

As Phyllis declines both physically and mentally, to the distress of her fiancé Barry Landfield (Don Porter), she becomes more and more convinced of her guilt, particularly after a masked woman is spotted leaving the mansion on the evenings of the murders. But it is all a plot on the part of Martha to drive Phyllis insane, take possession of the Allenby estate, and snare rich, handsome Barry for her own daughter...a plot that fails.

Directed by Jean Yarbrough and produced very cheaply and quickly in the last three weeks of 1945, *She-Wolf of London* really isn't a horror movie at all, but, rather, a gruesome mystery in which the killings are accomplished in a manner similar to those in the 1944 Sherlock Holmes entry *The Scarlet Claw*. One note of interest for film buffs is the very brief appearance of regular Laurel-and-Hardy-foil Jimmy Finlayson as a policeman.

Released in May of 1946, *She-Wolf of London* was the last horror, or even quasi-horror picture of Universal's golden age. It would be quite some time before the old monsters came back.

9 SPOTLIGHT:
CURT SIODMAK

Novelist and screenwriter Curt Siodmak might have simply remained one of a talented but anonymous pack of scenarists at Universal in the 1940s if not for one thing: his scripting of *The Wolf Man*, complete with the *Even a man who is pure of heart...* verse that would become the mantra of Universal Horror. From that point on, Siodmak's position in the history of the horror film was secured. "Hollywood at the time didn't only typecast the actors but also the writers," Siodmak recalled 30 years later.

Kurt (later Curt) Siodmak (pronounced "see-ODD-mack") was born in Dresden, Germany, in 1902, and trained as a mathematician and engineer. In the mid-1920s he drifted into newspaper work, through which he made the acquaintance of director Fritz Lang, who cast Siodmak in a bit part in his epic silent science fiction drama *Metropolis*. Siodmak himself began writing screenplays and became allied with a group of young European filmmakers who would come to have enormous influence over American films: Billy Wilder, Fred Zinneman, Edgar G. Ulmer, cinematographer Eugene Schufftan, and Siodmak's brother Robert.

By the early 1930s Siodmak had become a successful novelist, but he quickly fled Germany under the growing threat of Hitler's Nazi Party. He first went to England, where he resumed his screenwriting career, and then in 1937 resettled in America. His entrée at Universal came in 1939 courtesy of Viennese director Joe May, whom Siodmak had known back in Germany, and who hired him to write the script for *The Invisible Man Returns*.

Siodmak would quickly become one of the studio's most reliable writers, contributing either the story or screenplay—occasionally both—for *Black Friday, The Invisible Woman, The Wolf Man, Invisible Agent, Frankenstein Meets the Wolf Man, Son of Dracula, The Climax*, and *House of Frankenstein*.

After his 1942 novel *Donovan's Brain* became a bestseller, Siodmak became better known as a science fiction writer, though he continued writing and directing movies into the 1960s, including Universal-International's *Curucu, Beast of the Amazon*. Among his non-Universal credits are 1946's *The Beast With Five Fingers* and 1951's *Bride of the Gorilla*, a variation of the werewolf mythology, this time with an ape. In later years, he became a popular lecturer at universities, often speaking on science fiction topics, and regaling anyone interested about his years in the "trenches" of Hollywood, always from the standpoint of the writer's lot. "When [*The Wolf Man*] made its first million, the producer got a $10,000 bonus, the director a diamond ring for his wife, and I got fired, since I wanted $25 more for my next job," he would later write (and even though the record implies he was soon rehired, it was a good story).

Later in life Siodmak claimed that he was in the horror field strictly for the money, though he would express amused pride that such contributions as his Wolf Man verse and his Dracula *nom de fang* "Count Alucard" would eventually be regarded as bits of genuine European folklore.

Curt Siodmak died in 2000 at the age of 98, thinking and writing right up to the end.

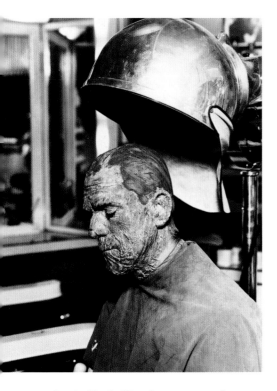

The makeup in this shot of Boris Karloff as Imhotep in The Mummy *differs slightly from the version seen in the film, mostly in the hair. This might be from a makeup test.*

Boris Karloff in the process of being mummified.

10

THE MUMMY

Given Boris Karloff's sudden rise to stardom as a result of *Frankenstein*, the race was on at Universal to find material that would enhance his image as "Karloff the Uncanny." Many ideas never made it past announcement stage, though once such, called *Cagliostro*, did. It was written by scenarist Nina Wilcox Putnam and Universal's story editor Richard Schayer and told the story of a man who had lived through millennia (though the writers seemed to confuse the 18th-century con man Allesandro di Cagliostro with his contemporary, the Comte de Saint-Germaine, another charlatan who actually did make claims of immortality). That basic premise became *The Mummy*, with the deathless European wanderer going under wraps to become an undying high priest of Egypt. With the discovery in 1923 of the tomb of Pharaoh Tut-Ankh-Amen still fresh in people's minds, the shift gave the story a contemporary context.

Unlike other classic Universal monsters, the identity of the Mummy would change over the years, though his backstory would remain essentially the same: one who loved not too wisely, but downright blasphemously.

THE MUMMY (1932)

The action of *The Mummy* begins in 1921 in Egypt. An expedition led by Sir Joseph Whemple (Arthur Byron) unearths the mummy of Im-Ho-Tep (Karloff), high priest of the Temple of Karnak, who was buried alive as punishment for sacrilege. The ancient, cursed Scroll of Thoth, which when read aloud has the power to revive the dead, was buried with him (in Egyptian mythology, Thoth is the powerful Ibis-headed deity who gave the world science, religion, and magic). Occultist Professor Muller (Edward Van Sloan), a consultant to the expedition, warns Sir Joseph to rebury the scroll for safety's sake. But an eager young Egyptologist named Norton (Bramwell Fletcher) ignores the warning, translates the scroll, and reads the curse aloud. As he does so, the eyes of the ancient, desiccated mummy open up and Im-Ho-Tep (Boris Karloff) steps out of the sarcophagus and retrieves the scroll, then shuffles into the night. Seeing the mummy come to life shatters Norton's mind.

Eleven years later, Sir Joseph's son Frank (David Manners) is leading a new expedition in the Valley of Kings, but the season is about to end and they have nothing to show for it, until a shriveled, mysterious Egyptian named Ardath Bey (Karloff, in a far less severe makeup) leads them straight to the tomb of princess Anck-es-en-Amon, lost for 3,700 years.

After the mummy of the princess is transported to the Cairo Museum, Bey—who is really a revitalized Im-Ho-Tep—holds a secret vigil over it, attempting to raise it from the dead, using the Scroll of Thoth. His calls, however, are intercepted by a young woman named Helen Grosvenor (Zita Johann), who cannot understand her compulsive attraction for the Cairo Museum, just as Frank and Professor Muller are hard pressed to understand how she can suddenly speak ancient Egyptian.

After meeting and recognizing Helen as the spitting image of Anck-es-en-Amon, Bey draws her to his home. It turns out Helen *is* Anck-es-en-Amon—at least the reincarnation of her—with whom Im-Ho-Tep was so desperately in love that after her death he stole the Scroll of Thoth in an attempt to resurrect her. He was caught and mummified alive for his sacrilege. "No man ever suffered as I did for you," he tells her, having revealed to her evidence of their past reincarnations. Bey now plans to kill Helen and then resurrect her, thus reuniting her soul with her body. But as he attempts to kill her, Helen—who has accepted that she is two different women—decides she prefers the modern one. As Bey raises his knife to slay her, she desperately prays to a statue of Isis for salvation. The statue comes to life and shoots a blast of power from an ankh that destroys the Scroll of Thoth. Bey turns back into the desiccated Im-Ho-Tep and then crumbles to dust.

Universal could not have found a more fitting person to write the script for *The Mummy* than John L. Balderston, who prior to his tenure in Hollywood had been a reporter for the *New York World*, and as such had a front-row seat for the opening of King Tut's tomb. He was, in fact, one of the first journalists to learn of the "curse" that allegedly accompanied it.

The film originally contained an extended sequence showing how Im-Ho-Tep and Anck-es-en-Amon had carried on their love affair throughout the centuries in reincarnated forms. This sequence was removed just before release, which is why an actor named Henry Victor is listed in the credits as "Saxon Warrior," yet no such character or flashback scene appears in the film. (This sequence would not have made much sense anyway in the context of the story, since Im-Ho-Tep's curse seems to preclude his soul from being available for reincarnation.)

Cinematographer Karl Freud stepped behind the camera as director for the first time (at least the first official time, having staged some scenes for *Dracula*). While visually adept, Freund seems to have been less skilled with his actors, particularly Zita Johann. The Hungarian-born actress would later characterize Freund as a sadist. "The first thing he said to me—he didn't say hello or anything—was, 'In one scene you have to play it nude from the waist up,'" she told the *New York Post* in 1989. "He wanted me to say, 'The hell I will,' so he could blame everything that went wrong

"Karloff the Uncanny" was at his uncanniest in The Mummy.

Boris Karloff as Ardath Bey in The Mummy. *Within the film it is never explained how Imhotep manages to partially reconstitute himself.*

Southern California's Red Rock Canyon stood in for Egypt in The Mummy.

The Mummy's Hand *introduced Universal's new mummy*
character, Kharis, the high priest of Karnak (later Arkam).

Actress Zita Johann doesn't appear too thrilled at director Karl Freund's hands-on attention on the set of The Mummy. *The man at right is cinematographer Charles Stumar.*

on me. But I told him, 'It's all right with me if you can get it past the censors.'" Having called Freund's bluff, Johann heard no more about it. Making only a handful more films before returning to the stage, Johann died in 1993, aged 89.

Boris Karloff's makeup for Im-Ho-Tep was the most arduous of his career, requiring *eight* hours at the hands of Jack P. Pierce. The mummy's ravaged countenance was achieved by gluing layers of cotton onto Karloff's face and painting over each layer with spirit gum, which caused the cotton to form into thick wrinkles and rivulets. After a heavy coating of yellowish-gray greasepaint, Pierce shadowed the deep wrinkles with an eyebrow pencil and added bits of sculpted decay, then plastered the actor's hair with clay, wrapped him in treated gauze, and baked everything under a heat lamp so it would flake. There were so many layers caking Karloff's face that the actor was unable to speak, even to complain about the fact that Pierce's mummy wrappings had left him without a fly opening. For Ardath Bey, Karloff wore a much thinner application of cotton and spirit gum that took only four hours.

Given all the time and trouble it took to mummify him as Im-Ho-Tep, though, it seems almost cruel that Freund only filmed small bits and pieces of the makeup and costume for the awakening scene, letting the audience's imagination fill in the rest...cruel, but undeniably effective.

THE MUMMY'S HAND (1940)

The Mummy's Hand was not a continuation of *The Mummy* as much as a reimagining of a living mummy character for a new series. It is also one of the last examples of the sort of breezy B-picture that had defined late 1930s Hollywood, mixing chills with equal parts comedy and romance, as though encouraging the audience not to take it too seriously.

The film finds archaeologist and adventurer Steve Banning (Dick Foran) and his sidekick Babe Jenson (Wallace Ford) stranded in Cairo because Steve was recently fired by Scripps Museum in Manhattan for failing to find any treasures. Their plans to return home are interrupted when Steve spots a broken vase in a street bazaar that he is convinced shows the location of the tomb of the Princess Ananka. He takes the vase to the Cairo Museum, where Dr. Petrie (Charles Trowbridge) verifies its authenticity. The museum's director, Professor Andoheb (George Zucco), however, declares it a fake, and then carelessly drops it, shattering it.

Neither Steve nor Dr. Petrie can understand Professor Andoheb's skepticism. They do not realize that Andoheb is also the current High Priest of Karnak, whose job it is to protect Ananka's tomb from infidels. Aiding him in this is Kharis the Mummy (Tom Tyler), who loved Ananka in life millennia ago, and who defied the gods after her death by stealing the forbidden tana leaves—the fluid of which can raise the dead—to bring her back. As punishment, Kharis is buried alive and cursed to watch over Ananka for all eternity, kept alive through regular administrations of tana fluid by the high priests: three leaves to keep his heart beating and nine to give him movement. *More* than nine, however, will turn him into an uncontrollable monster.

Knowing none of this, Steve launches his own expedition to find Ananka, obtaining financing from a traveling magician who calls himself The Great Solvini (Cecil Kellaway), who is touring Egypt with his daughter

Cecil Kellaway meets the title character in The Mummy's Hand.

Cowboy star Tom Tyler was chosen for The Mummy's Hand *because it was felt he looked like a young Boris Karloff, and could be matched to stock footage.*

The Mummy's Hand*'s hero Steve Banning (Dick Foran) discovers that bullets don't work on Kharis (Tom Tyler).*

For this scene in The Mummy's Hand, *Tom Tyler (who is holding leading lady Peggy Moran) is wearing a rubber Mummy mask instead of Jack P. Pierce's painstaking (and often painful) cotton-based makeup.*

Marta (Peggy Moran). Before long they discover a tomb, but it is not Ananka's: it is Kharis's. The Mummy is revived by Andoheb, who instructs the creature to kill the members of the expedition. When Kharis goes for Solvini, Marta distracts him and gets picked up and carted off to the hidden tomb of Ananka for her trouble.

Once Andoheb lays eyes on Marta, he forgets his vow of purity to the gods of Karnak (a recurring plot device for all subsequent Mummy movies), and decides to make her immortal through the tana fluid, so that the two of them can spend eternity together. Babe, however, has tracked the Mummy to the tomb, and he shoots Andoheb before he can carry out his plans. But now Kharis is making a bee-line for the tana fluid that Andoheb was brewing to immortalize Marta, and he has no intention of drinking responsibly. Having found the secret passage that connects Kharis's tomb to Ananka's, Steve arrives just in time to keep the Mummy from getting the fluid, and destroys him with fire. At the film's end, Ananka is on her way to the Scripps Museum, Steve has been rehired and he and Marta are now in love, and everyone else is en route back to Manhattan.

The Mummy's Hand was directed by Christy Cabanne, a workhorse whose career went back to the earliest days of the silents, and was scripted by Griffin Jay (who would come to specialize in Mummy films) and Maxwell Shaw. The film is rife with cheerful inconsistencies, the most obvious of which is the fact that the underground tomb of Kharis is laterally connected through a passageway to a temple that sits in plain sight atop a small mountain, and is accessible from the outside by very long flight of irregular stone steps. What's more, the exterior of the temple bears Incan iconography instead of Egyptian. This set, as well as the lavish interior of the temple, was actually built for the 1940 jungle adventure *Green Hell*, and redressed for *The Mummy's Hand*.

Former professional weightlifter Tom Tyler was more at home in Westerns and serial adventures, but he was chosen for Kharis because Universal felt his looks were close enough to Boris Karloff's that he could easily be intercut with stock footage from *The Mummy* for the flashback scenes. Tyler had to suffer through Jack Pierce's cotton-and-spirit-gum ordeal for close-ups, but in other shots his makeup consisted of a molded rubber mask. While the difference between the two is fairly easy to spot, the mask is no less effective, a point that would not go unnoticed for future Mummy films. Also for close shots, Tyler's eyes were optically blacked out, creating an eerie effect, though in medium to long shots, the whites of his eyes can clearly be seen.

Tyler's career would falter by the end of the decade as he succumbed to severe rheumatoid arthritis, and he died in 1954 at age 50. Along with the title role in the serial *The Adventures of Captain Marvel*, Kharis is chiefly what Tyler is remembered for today.

THE MUMMY'S TOMB (1942)
The Mummy's Tomb picks up the story of *The Mummy's Hand*, but 30 years later. Steve Banning (Dick Foran) is now retired and living in Mapleton, Massachusetts, with his inexplicably Scottish sister Jane (Mary Gordon), not far from his son John (John Hubbard) and John's fiancée Isobel (Elyse Knox). Steve believes Kharis the Mummy is dead. He should be so lucky.

The new look of Kharis (Lon Chaney Jr.) from The Mummy's Tomb—*a damaged left eye, arm, and leg, and a general sooty appearance—reflects the end of* The Mummy's Hand, *in which Kharis was burnt to "death."*

High Priest Andoheb (George Zucco, right) instructs his successor Mehemet Bey (Turhan Bey) on the care and feeding of Kharis in The Mummy's Tomb. *Not only can the Gods of Ancient Egypt keep someone alive for 3,000 years, they can give the formerly bald Andoheb a full head of white hair.*

Kharis (Lon Chaney Jr.) is readied for the ocean voyage from Egypt to New England by Mehemet Bey (Turhan Bey) and Andoheb (George Zucco) in The Mummy's Tomb.

Women always seem to get carried away around Kharis (Lon Chaney Jr.). In this case, it is Isobel (Elyse Knox) in The Mummy's Tomb.

Kharis "dies" by fire yet again at the end of The Mummy's Tomb.

Not only has Kharis survived, but so has Andoheb (George Zucco), who was not fatally shot and even survived the joint-crunching three-storey tumble down the temple steps (a stunt actually performed by a "double" who even in long shots looked nothing like Zucco). Now on his death-throne, Andoheb is passing on the reins of protecting Kharis (Lon Chaney Jr.) to a new High Priest of Karnak, Mehemet Bey (Turhan Bey). He instructs Bey to finish the job that he and Kharis have failed to do: kill those who desecrated Ananka's tomb. He has arranged for Mehemet to take the job of caretaker at the Mapleton Cemetery, which will be the cover for his activities. Mehemet embarks for America with Kharis safely tucked away in the ship's cargo hold.

No sooner are they in Mapleton than Mehemet sends Kharis out to murder Steve. As Kharis stalks through the town, many of the residents report seeing a strange moving shadow, and experiencing an eerie, foreboding feeling as it passes. This gives rise to press stories about "The Mapleton Monster." Steve Banning's murder, particularly the reports of gray mold on his throat, draws his old partner Babe Hanson (Wallace Ford, who in *Hand* had been Babe *Jenson*) to Mapleton, where he unsuccessfully tries to convince the police that they are dealing with a living mummy. He has better luck with the press, but before Babe can convince many, Kharis finds him and strangles him.

Mehemet Bey's murderous plans are on track until he begins to succumb to the very thing that had previously derailed Andoheb: from afar, he falls in love with Isobel, and instructs Kharis to bring her to him so he can make her immortal. But by now the sheriff has connected the dots between talk of a living mummy and that Egyptian fellow who has recently arrived to maintain the cemetery. A mob forms to confront Mehemet, who is shot when he tries to kill John Banning. Kharis, meanwhile, has taken Isobel back to the Banning house. The mob follows and sets the place on fire, immolating the Mummy.

A good deal of the footage of *The Mummy's Tomb* is stock footage from *The Mummy* and *The Mummy's Hand*, involving both Boris Karloff and Tom Tyler. Producer Ben Pivar, who oversaw Universal's horror unit during the 1940s, and director Harold Young even lifted a couple of torch-bearing-mob shots from *Frankenstein*.

The Mummy was Lon Chaney Jr.'s least favorite character and it is not hard to see why. The actor was completely encased in uncomfortable, dirty wrappings and a grotesque, one-eyed latex rubber mask to which he was allergic, and forced to shamble around with a gimpy leg and immobile arm. Unlike Karloff and Tyler, he had no scenes out of the Mummy suit and makeup, which rendered him completely unrecognizable to the audience. Chaney may have been cast in the part simply to cash in on his name, but since the "Jr." had been dropped from his billing, it was really his *father's* name fronting the picture, which must have further rankled the actor.

Still, Chaney endured the costume and the mask, and shambled to the best of his ability. His slow, painful movements convey the impression that Kharis is truly *dead* and yet still walking around. For the scene in which he comes upon Babe, Chaney radiates hatred through his one unobscured eye and even forces a silent-mouthed curse through his mummy mask. The ferocity of Kharis's attack was something of an in-joke, since Chaney frequently acknowledged the huge debt of gratitude he owed to

Wallace Ford, who had kick-started his career by casting him as Lennie in the Los Angeles production of *Of Mice and Men*.

THE MUMMY'S GHOST (1944)

Set just a few years after the action of *Tomb*, *The Mummy's Ghost* begins to alter some of the established continuity of the series, including the fact that the High Priests are now from *Arkam* not *Karnak*.

Yousef Bey (John Carradine), the latest High Priest to take over from the shriveled but seemingly indestructible Andoheb (George Zucco), is now assigned the duty of returning the body of Ananka, which remains on display at the Scripps Museum in New York, to its true resting place in Egypt. Kharis, meanwhile, is still at large in Mapleton, but he only emerges during the full moon, and if anyone happens to be brewing tana leaves. When venerable Professor Norman (Frank Reicher) brews some in the course of his research on Egyptology, Kharis breaks into his house and kills him. One of Norman's students, Tommy Hervey (Robert Lowery) is disturbed to hear of the doctor's death, but even more disturbed to learn that his Egyptian girlfriend, Amina Mansouri (Ramsey Ames), was found at Norman's house around the time of the murder.

Yousef and Kharis make their way to the Scripps Museum, but when they try to remove the body of Ananka it disintegrates, causing an enraged Kharis to destroy the exhibit room and kill a watchman. Yousef is puzzled by the destruction of the mummy, not knowing that at the very moment it crumbled, Ananka's soul entered the body of Amina, miles away.

Tommy tries to take Amina away, but she is inexplicably drawn to Kharis. Once Yousef realizes her significance, he instructs Kharis to get her and bring her back to their hideout. Overcome with her beauty, Yousef develops "Andoheb Syndrome" and prepares to mummify her so they can live together through eternity. Having figured out that Yousef is sacrificing their mission for personal gratification, Kharis turns on him and kills him, then picks up Amina and carries her into the countryside. Along with a posse from town, Tommy tracks the Mummy, who flees into a swamp. As Kharis and Amina sink into the ooze, Tommy watches the young woman he loved transform into a withered mummy.

Filmed in late summer 1943, but held for release until the next year, *The Mummy's Ghost* offers a couple new wrinkles (so to speak) to the mythology, such as restricting the Mummy's activity to cycles of the full moon, but the script by Griffin Jay, Henry Sucher, and Brenda Weisberg never explains how Kharis escaped from the burning building, nor where he has been hiding ever since. Sharp-eyed moviegoers (with good memories) may have recognized the long ramp leading to Yousef Bey's hideout, up which Kharis lugs Amina, as the mine car track from 1940's *The Invisible Man Returns*.

As much as he despised his Mummy, Lon Chaney Jr. nevertheless threw himself into the role. For the scene in which Kharis goes on the rampage at the Scripps Museum, Chaney refused to wait for the installation of breakaway candy glass on the set and was filmed driving his hand through real glass. A shard of it flew up and cut his face through the mask, and Kharis can clearly be seen bleeding from the chin throughout the rest of the sequence.

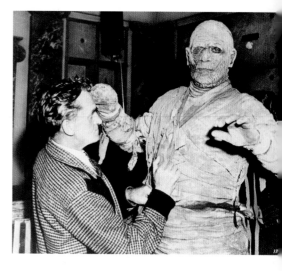

Lon Chaney Jr. gets fitted for his "mummy belt," a special harness that helped distribute the weight of the leading ladies he had to carry around as Kharis, on the set of The Mummy's Tomb.

NAMELESS!
FLESHLESS!
DEATHLESS!

The MUMMY'S GHOST

starring

LON CHANEY
as Kharis, The Mummy

with

JOHN CARRADINE
RAMSAY AMES
BARTON MacLANE
GEORGE ZUCCO
ROBERT LOWERY

In an unusual move, Universal included a picture of Lon Chaney Jr. sans makeup on the poster for The Mummy's Ghost *to reassure moviegoers that it really was him under all the wrappings and rubber.*

Kharis (Lon Chaney Jr.) goes after a museum guard (Oscar O'Shea) in The Mummy's Ghost. *The dark blotches on Chaney's mummified chin are blood stains; he cut himself going through real glass on the set.*

Director Reginald Le Borg and Lon Chaney Jr. on the set of The Mummy's Ghost.

Lon Chaney Jr. on a break from filming greets his wife Patsy and a young visitor on the set of The Mummy's Ghost.

THE MUMMY'S CURSE (1944)

The Mummy's Curse was the second Kharis film of 1944, released in December, five months after *Ghost*. It would prove to be the last. Directed by Leslie Goodwins and written by Bernard Schubert, it represents perhaps the biggest single continuity inconsistency in all of Universal Horror: in *The Mummy's Ghost,* Kharis and Ananka sank into a bog in Massachusetts, yet when they rise 25 years later, it is from a swamp in *Louisiana.*

The swamp in question is in the process of being drained by Pat Walsh (Addison Richards), a construction engineer who is running into superstition among the local Cajuns regarding the legend of the Mummy and his Princess. When disappearances and murders begin to occur within the work crew, some of the workers refuse to continue operations.

In the midst of all this come Dr. James Halsey (Dennis Moore) and Dr. Ilzor Sandaab (Peter Coe), both from the Scripps Museum, who arrive with authorization to explore and excavate the drained swamp in search of the mummies of Kharis and Ananka. For Walsh they are an annoyance, but for his secretary and niece Betty (Kay Harding), they are welcome arrivals, particularly Halsey. What not even Halsey knows, though, is that Ilzor is really the latest in the line of High Priests of Karnak, there in the guise of a scholar to recover Ananka and take her home. Helping him is his servant Raghab (Martin Kosleck), who is posing as a worker on the crew, and who has hidden the sarcophagus of Kharis up in a ruined hilltop monastery, awaiting the Mummy's resurrection.

During the excavation work, the makeshift grave of Kharis is discovered, but the Mummy has already risen. Then when no one is looking, Princess Ananka (Virginia Christine) digs herself out of the muck, clawing her way to the sunlight and staggering to a pond, where she washes off the mud as well as 3,000 years, emerging as a beautiful young woman. Seeming to have appeared out of nowhere, Ananka makes her way to Halsey's base of operations and becomes part of his team, in the process demonstrating a working knowledge of ancient Egypt that even she cannot explain. Ilzor, though, recognizes her as the Princess and later sends Kharis (Lon Chaney Jr.) out to get her.

It takes several attempts (culminating in several murders), but Kharis finally catches up with Ananka, taking her unconscious form up to the monastery, where Ilzor gives her the tana fluid—*not* to have her spend eternity with him, but rather to remummify her. Meanwhile, Raghab abducts Betty, with whom he has become infatuated, and takes *her* to the monastery, planning never to let her go. Ilzor interrupts Raghab's lascivious attack on Betty and curses him for his lapse, but the crazed servant turns on his master and kills him. While this is taking place, Halsey has discovered Kharis's distinctive footprints (step-*slide*; step-*slide*) and follows them to the monastery, where he is attacked by Raghab as well. Before Raghab can kill Halsey, Kharis intervenes and prevents him.

Raghab flees to a cell of the monastery and locks himself in, but Kharis—who throughout the film has expressed hatred for the little man—literally tears the walls down to get to him. As a result the ceiling caves in, crushing them both. In another room of the monastery, Halsey finds the mummy of Princess Ananka, whom he recognizes as the mysterious girl who had joined his expedition team.

The mummified Princess Ananka (Virginia Christine) rises from the swamp in The Mummy's Curse.

Is this the second coming of Mehemet Bey? No, it's Peter Coe in identical makeup and costume as Ilzor in The Mummy's Curse, *along with Virginia Christine and Dennis Moore.*

Kharis (Lon Chaney Jr.) dispatches the monastery caretaker (silent star William Farnum) in The Mummy's Curse.

Even with a bum leg, Kharis (Lon Chaney Jr.) could always catch up to his victims (though this one, played by Kay Harding, gets away).

(From left to right) Napoleon Simpson, Charles Stevens, Dennis Moore, Kay Harding, and Addison Richards, and extras in the background, contemplate the remummified form of Ananka (Virginia Christine) in The Mummy's Curse.

Lon Chaney Jr., director Leslie Goodwins, and Virginia Christine take a break on the set of The Mummy's Curse.

Taken on its own merits, *The Mummy's Curse* stands as the best of the Chaney Mummy series. The sequence of Ananka rising from the swamp is one of the most striking in all of Universal Horror, and Virginia Christine perfectly captures the otherworldly quality of revived Egyptian princess. An actress of unconventional beauty who rarely found herself in leading lady roles, Christine would achieve her greatest fame decades later as "Mrs. Olsen," the commercial spokeswoman for Folger's Coffee. She passed away in 1996, at age 76.

It is only when one takes *The Mummy's Curse* within the context of overall series that problems arise. Aside from the aforementioned mysterious transfer of the two mummies from New England to the bayou, there is the timeline covered by the Kharis saga. Thirty years passed between *The Mummy's Hand* and *The Mummy's Tomb*, three or four years separated *Tomb* and *The Mummy's Ghost*, and the gap between *Ghost* and *The Mummy's Curse* is set 25 years. If *The Mummy's Hand* was contemporarily set in 1940, that means the action of *Curse* has to be set in the late 1990s! Since the films were not intended to be seen altogether, nobody worried about the continuity logic.

Kharis would stalk one more time in the bandaged form of Christopher Lee, in 1959's *The Mummy*, made by Britain's Hammer Films and released by Universal. Hammer's *Mummy*, which recycled story elements and character names from *The Mummy's Tomb*, cleverly tweaked the Universal convention of the lame, shuffling Mummy who still manages to catch up to his victims by making its hero, John Banning (Peter Cushing), lame and slow, yet always able to get away from the unstoppable Kharis.

Lon Chaney Jr. in leading man mode, from the mid-1940s.

11 SPOTLIGHT:
LON CHANEY JR.

No major Hollywood figure has so confounded film historians as Lon Chaney Jr. Was he a good actor, or was he as one critic described, a "hulking, unimaginative" one? Did he have range as a performer, or could he only play monsters and brutes? Was he his father's son, or a second-rater cashing in on his father's famous name?

The availability of films on common home-use formats, and the ability to easily compare and contrast different movies, has helped to answer those questions. Most horror buffs today are in agreement: *yes,* Chaney was a good actor, and *yes,* he had a range, a surprisingly wide one, in fact (which critics of the 1940s often noted). As for cashing in on his father's name, it was not his idea. "I am most proud of the name Lon Chaney," the actor once declared. "I am *not* proud of Lon Chaney Jr., because they had to starve me to make me take this name."

Creighton Tull Chaney was born in 1906 in Oklahoma City, where his father was playing on stage. Young Chaney would have an unsettled childhood, moving from place to place with his father, his mother being out of the picture after her 1913 suicide attempt. At times he was sent to live with his grandparents, both of whom were deaf mute, which forced him to learn sign language and pantomime. Not much of one for formal schooling, Creighton liked real-life experience more—particularly if it involved a fishing pole or hunting rifle.

As he grew older, he began to show a fascination with show business, which his father did his best to squelch, publicly claiming that Creighton was too tall to be an actor (Creighton topped six feet; Lon himself stood 5'8" on good days, wearing shoes). Two years after the elder Chaney's death, Creighton took the step on his own, signing a player's contract with RKO Pictures, but refusing their request that he change his name to Lon Chaney Jr.

When that contract ran out, Chaney freelanced...and starved...and

Lon Chaney in character as "Dan McCormick" in Man Made Monster, *his first Universal hit.*

finally swallowed Hollywood's bitter pill, becoming Lon Jr. in 1935. "Any ability that I might have had is there," Chaney said years after the fact. "The name didn't change it, but it certainly changed the income." Even so, his situation did not immediately improve. A subsequent contract with Twentieth-Century Fox resulted in nothing but walk-ons. Now married for the second time, and raising two boys from his first failed marriage, Chaney was becoming desperate. His salvation came by way of the plum role of Lennie in the 1939 Los Angeles stage production *Of Mice and Men*, which became a personal triumph for the actor, and led to his being cast in the film version that same year.

Now armed with a reputation as well as a famous name, Chaney was finally making headway in Hollywood just as Universal was about to start its second horror cycle in 1941. Chaney's "pilot" as horror star for the studio was *Man Made Monster*, and from there he went on to what would become his signature role, Larry Talbot, in *The Wolf Man*. While Chaney would eventually play all the studio's top monsters, the Wolf Man remained his favorite. Looking for a moniker reminiscent of "Man of a Thousand Faces," Universal dubbed him "The Master Character Creator" and dropped the "Jr." from his billing, a decision over which Chaney was conflicted; while he had fought against taking the name Lon Jr. in the first place, dropping the *Jr.* created *too* close of a comparison with his father (interestingly, at the outset of his career, Creighton was compared not with his father, but with Clark Gable).

While he was being put through his paces as the reigning star of horror films, Chaney had a simultaneous career at Universal as a utility player, appearing in supporting roles in crime dramas, South Seas adventures, even Olsen and Johnson comedies. Alternating lead roles with supporting ones meant that Chaney was seen in *15* Universal films in 1943 and 1944 alone.

With the horror cycle winding down in 1945, Chaney was let go by the studio. He moved into a solid career as a character actor and continued to make films and television shows until illness prevented him from working in the early 1970s. Many of his films, particularly in the later years, were really not worth making, but Chaney was an actor, and an actor's job is to act.

It is no secret that for most of his life Chaney battled the bottle and frequently lost, which endangered his career. Some who knew and worked with him, including Curt Siodmak and director Reginald Le Borg, felt that Chaney was never able to resolve conflicted emotions about his father, both personally and professionally (father and son had even been estranged for a time as a result of Creighton's finding out that his mother was still alive after Lon had told him she was dead). Still, most of the actors who worked with him remembered Chaney with fondness (one notable exception was Evelyn Ankers; despite their on-screen chemistry, she and Chaney could not abide each other). An amateur chef whose chili was said to rival that of Chasen's, he would sometimes cook lunch for his co-stars in his dressing room, and was known to invite struggling young actors into his home for a good meal.

The enigma of Lon Chaney Jr. is that he was a very complex man who somehow projected simplicity on the screen. That, perhaps, is the reason his critical reputation began to suffer in later years: he had the

Lon Chaney Jr. never hid his displeasure at playing the Mummy, even from publicity photographers. With him is makeup artist Jack P. Pierce.

1310-95

Universal got their money's worth out of Lon Chaney Jr., who appeared in supporting parts in non-horror films (such as Cobra Woman, *with Maria Montez and Sabu) while starring in the studio's thrillers.*

ability to make you believe he was not acting at all, but was simply playing himself, no matter what the role, which meant that his talent and range tended to go unnoticed.

Like his father before him, Chaney died of throat cancer, succumbing to the disease in 1973 at the age of 67. Unlike his father, in whose memory Hollywood had virtually shut down for a day, he left wishes that his death not be publicized.

Claude Rains under wraps in The Invisible Man. *The nose is artificial.*

Griffin (Claude Rains) defies the cockney police (and in the world of James Whale, all policemen were cockney) and the villagers of Iping in The Invisible Man.

12

THE INVISIBLE MAN

Universal's *Invisible Man* series is unique among the studio's literary-based horror sagas. Unlike the other classic horror series, the author of its source material, H. G. Wells, who published the novel *The Invisible Man* in 1897, was still alive and very much kicking throughout the run of the five-film series. Perhaps this is why James Whale's initial film adaptation bore greater fidelity than usual to the book upon which it is based.

The series is also unconventional in that it did not cover a continuous storyline. Except for the occasional reference to an earlier personage, there was no one character that appeared in more than one of the films. The single thread of continuity was simply the presence of a man (or, in one case, a woman) who was invisible. Without a connective story arc like the ongoing saga of the Frankenstein Monster, a recurring protagonist such as the Mummy, or a returning lead actor to carry the series the way Lon Chaney Jr. did for the Wolf Man films, Universal's in-house special effects wizard John P. Fulton emerges as the true star of the *Invisible* films. Not only did Fulton dazzle the audiences, he impressed his peers, earning Academy Award nominations (but, alas, no wins) for *The Invisible Man Returns*, *The Invisible Woman*, and *Invisible Agent*.

THE INVISIBLE MAN (1933)
A strange bundled-up man trudges through the snow and heads into the Lion's Head Inn, a boisterous public house in the English village of Iping. His entrance stops all conversation, when the customers see that the man's face is completely obscured by bandages.

The strange man, Jack Griffin (Claude Rains), asks for a room, but demands privacy. He soon sets up scientific equipment in the room and tries to quietly conduct research, but the locals have a hard time ignoring him, particularly Jenny (Una O'Connor), the innkeeper's wife.

Griffin works as a research assistant employed by Dr. Cranley

(Henry Travers), whose business is chemical food preservation. Cranley's daughter Flora (Gloria Stuart) is in love with Griffin, though another research assistant named Kemp (William Harrigan) is also interested in Flora, and thus tries to use Griffin's mysterious month-long absence against him in her eyes. None of them realize that Griffin is hiding out in order to search for an antidote for the chemical monocane, which turns his body invisible.

When Iping's curiosity becomes too much, Griffin becomes petulant, and then violent. The police are summoned, and in front of them Griffin unwraps his head to reveal...nothing. Stripping completely, Griffin vanishes altogether.

Unfortunately, the serum that caused him to disappear also produces madness, and Griffin now wreaks mischief on the village. As his madness increases, the mischief turns to havoc, then to violence and murder, and ultimately delusions of world domination. When Griffin returns, barely sane, to ask Kemp for help in getting his journals out of Iping, Kemp instead calls the police on him.

As the police try to figure out ways to catch the now-rampaging invisible man, Griffin stalks and kills Kemp for his betrayal. During a snowstorm, Griffin is finally cornered in a barn, which is burned, driving him out. Shooting at the spontaneously formed footprints in the snow, the police hit Griffin. Rushed to the hospital, Griffin briefly turns visible before dying in the presence of Flora.

Boris Karloff was originally slated to play the Invisible Man, but walked out in a contract dispute with Carl Laemmle Jr. James Whale then approached Colin Clive to replace him, but Clive was not interested, so the director called upon Claude Rains, whom he had known in England. A veteran stage actor, Rains had never before appeared in a film—and he *barely* appeared in this one, actually being seen for about 20 seconds at the end.

Today the film's special effects remain startling, but in 1933 they were astonishing. The total invisibility shots were accomplished using props controlled by wires, or else a process in which Rains or a stunt double, dressed completely in black and wearing a helmet that totally encased the head, manipulated objects using sticks against a solid black velvet background. A double was often used because of the grueling nature of the costume, which necessitated breathing through a tube (all shots of Griffin bandaged were the actor himself). When filmed, only the objects would show up and appear to be floating. This footage was then combined with the previously shot scene through use of the traveling matte process, in which four separate layers of images, two positive and two negative, were overlaid and printed into a single composite picture.

The shots showing the Invisible Man partially dressed were done the same way. Rains's double, wearing whatever item of clothing was needed over the black jumpsuit, would be filmed against the black background, and only the clothing piece would show up. This footage would then be matted into the scene. For shots in which Griffin directly interacted with another character, both actors would be filmed against the velvet and then matted into the background plates. Any flaws in the process were corrected by hand on each frame of film, an estimated 64,000 of them!

A frame enlargement from The Invisible Man *shows the painstaking matte photography effect that went into turning the character transparent.*

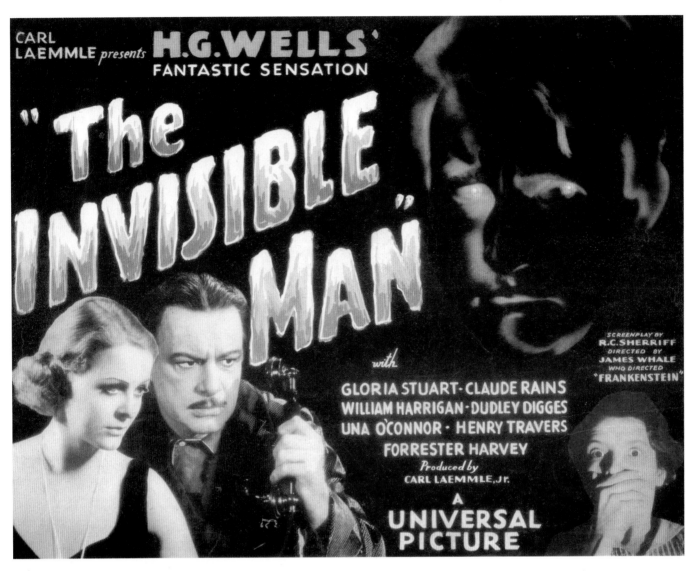

Without a major star to hype, the studio promoted both the author of the novel, H. G. Wells, and director James Whale on the poster of The Invisible Man.

Without the use of his face or even his eyes, Claude Rains, in his movie debut, relied on dramatic poses to get the character of Griffin across in The Invisible Man, *here with leading lady Gloria Stuart.*

James Whale employed many of his trademarked directorial flourishes in the film, notably the three-shot, jump-cut visual conceit he invariably used for introducing his monsters, and peppered the cast with some of his favorite actors, including shrieking Una O'Connor as the innkeeper's wife, Dwight Frye as a reporter, and John Carradine as a police informer (wearing a putty nose, for some reason).

THE INVISIBLE MAN RETURNS (1940)

The invisible man in *The Invisible Man Returns* is not *the* Invisible Man, but rather *an* invisible man: Geoffrey Radcliff (Vincent Price), who turns transparent in order to escape a death sentence for the murder of his brother. Geoffrey is innocent, of course, but vanishing is his only option for cheating the hangman and discovering the identity of the real killer. He does so through the efforts of Frank Griffin (John Sutton), who is the younger brother of Jack Griffin (who is represented in the film by a photo of Claude Rains).

Scotland Yard Inspector Sampson (Cecil Kellaway), however, knows the history of the Griffin family, so when Geoffrey disappears, he's pretty certain he has another invisible one on his hands. For his part, Geoffrey knows enough about the invisibility drug, now called "duocane" (apparently it's twice as strong as monocane), to know that it causes insanity. While Frank feverishly works on developing an antidote, Geoffrey hides out in an old cottage. He begs his fiancé Helen (Nan Grey) to put him out of his misery should he begin to lose his mind before the antidote is discovered.

Geoffrey manages to stay sane, but only just, as he conducts his investigation. It leads him to a drunken watchman named Spears (Alan Napier), who has inexplicably been made supervisor of the mine Geoffrey and his brother owned, which was managed by the Radcliff's cousin, Richard Cobb. It takes very little "haunting" to get Spears to confess that Cobb was actually the murderer of Michael Radcliffe, and that Geoffrey was set up for the killing to get both Radcliff brothers out of the way.

Now showing warning signs of madness, Geoffrey abducts Cobb (Cedric Hardwicke) and takes him to Spears's home, confronting him with the information, but Cobb kills Spears to maintain his silence. He shoots Geoffrey and then flees, but the wounded Geoffrey chases him all the way to the mine, where the two fight their way to the top of a high coal dump, from which Cobb falls, living just long enough to confess his crime.

Cold, tired and gravely wounded, Geoffrey returns to Frank's lab, desperately in need of a blood transfusion. The loyal men of the mine provide the blood, and the new blood turns out to be the antidote. Geoffrey returns to visibility, exoneration, and life with Helen.

The storyline of *The Invisible Man Returns* takes place nine years after the action of the first film, though it was shot only six years later. Vincent Price, then at the start of his film career, brought the same natural asset to his invisible role as had Claude Rains: a mellow, distinctive voice. Also like Rains, he is actually seen only at the very end of the film, turning visible via a series of dissolves, first depicting the blood veins, then the musculature, followed by a dissolve into Price himself. As to that blood, which in the film's context is offered by many different donors, there is never any mention of compatible type, which would be a major plot point

Vincent Price unwraps himself in The Invisible Man Returns.

The Invisible Man "haunts" Spears (Alan Napier, who 25 years later would play Alfred the butler on the television series Batman) in The Invisible Man Returns. *In the actual film, though, the outline of the invisible one cannot be seen.*

Vincent Price's only visible moment in The Invisible Man Returns *comes at the very end. Here he is with Nan Grey.*

The Invisible Man (who's profile in this trick shot is clearly not Vincent Price) forces a confession out of the nefarious Cobb (Cedric Hardwicke) as Spears (Alan Napier) looks on in a precarious position, in The Invisible Man Returns.

two years later in *The Ghost of Frankenstein*.

German cinema pioneer Joe May co-wrote the story (with Curt Siodmak) and directed the film, and while Universal was something of a home-away-from-increasingly-dangerous-home for European filmmakers, May was not one of the more popular expats on the lot. "He really couldn't speak any English at all," Vincent Price recalled many years later. "I had lived in Germany and been to school there, so I was able to understand him better than most. He would try to give me direction and I'd say, 'For God's sake, Joe, tell me in German, because I can get along with you much better in German than I can in English!' I don't think John Sutton understood a word he said, nor did Nan Grey. Cedric [Hardwicke] hated him, really hated him! There was an enmity between him and Joe, as I remember."

John P. Fulton was able to add a few enhancements to his invisibility effect toolbox for this film, including having Geoffrey appear in faint outline in the rain.

THE INVISIBLE WOMAN (1941)
Despite having a story once again written by Curt Siodmak and Joe May, *The Invisible Woman* has nothing to do with the official series, being instead a screwball comedy about a wacky scientist (John Barrymore) who invents an invisibility ray, which is taken by a career girl (Virginia Bruce) as a means of getting revenge on her nasty boss (Charles Lane). There is a subplot involving a dopey crime boss (Oscar Homolka) who wants to disappear to escape the police, and also complications involving the rich playboy (John Howard) who is financing the scientist, and his long suffering, accident-prone butler (Charlie Ruggles). Scripted by Robert Lees, Frederick Renaldo, and Gertrude Purcell, and directed by A. Edward Sutherland—comedy specialists, all—*The Invisible Woman* is a fast, funny

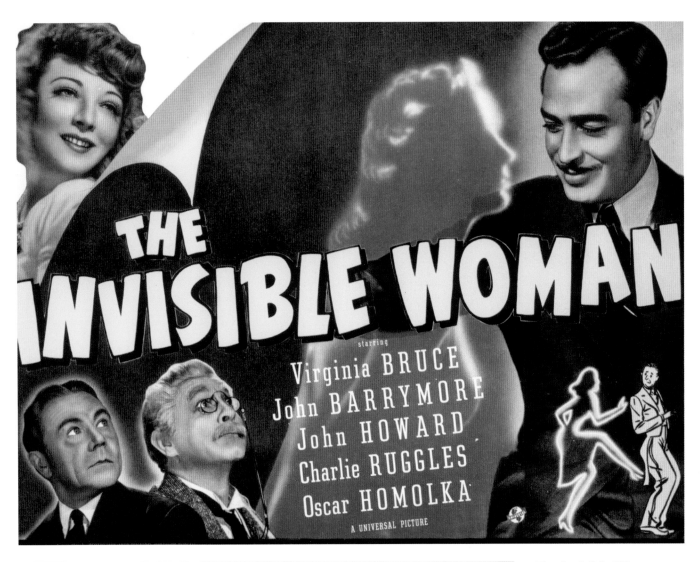

The Invisible Woman *was a departure from the main series, being a screwball farce with an invisibility angle.*

The Invisible Woman (Virginia Bruce) acts as the avenging "conscience" of her nasty boss, Charles Lane, in The Invisible Woman.

Invisible Agent *was not designed as a B-film sequel, but rather a prestige wartime moral-booster.*

romp with a remarkable cast: try to name another film that can boast John Barrymore, Maria Montez, and The Three Stooges' Shemp Howard, all in the same cast!

INVISIBLE AGENT (1942)

The fact that the opening credits for *Invisible Agent* feature a special title card solely for John P. Fulton is an indication as to whom Universal was considering to be the major contributor to the series' success. Written by Curt Siodmak and directed by Edward L. Marin, the film is an example of slick wartime propaganda.

Jon Hall plays Frank Raymond, a.k.a. Frank Griffin, whose grandfather, Frank Sr. [sic], developed the invisibility formula, but who has eschewed the family trade of science in favor of working as a printer. His shop is visited one night by a group of Axis spies including Conrad Stauffer (Cedric Hardwicke) and Baron Ikito (Peter Lorre), who demand on pain of torture his grandfather's formula, understanding that an army of invisible soldiers means instant wartime victory. Stauffer claims to be able to control the madness inherent in taking the formula. The resourceful Griffin manages to overcome the spies and escape. Shortly thereafter, though, the U.S. government likewise asks for the formula, hoping to create an invisible spy who can operate unseen (literally) behind enemy lines. Again Griffin refuses, knowing only too well how dangerous it is.

The Japanese attack on Pearl Harbor, however, changes his mind. Griffin approaches the war office and this time agrees to give them his grandfather's invisibility formula, but on one condition: that he be the one who takes it. The risk, he says, is too great to ask anyone else to do it. The government agrees, and soon the invisible agent parachutes into enemy territory, where his mission is to discover the identities of Axis agents working in America. His contact is sultry Maria Sorenson (Ilona Massey), who is vamping information out of a buffoonish Nazi wannabe named Karl Heiser (J. Edward Bromberg).

Something of an invisible bull in a china shop, Griffin initially undoes all of Maria's carefully laid plans. "Are you insane?" she demands. "No, just transparent," he replies. At first Griffin is attracted to Maria, but as his invisibility mania begins to take hold, he becomes convinced that she is a double spy. Stauffer, meanwhile, has heard enough reports of an invisible parachutist that he begins to realize what is really going on. He attempts to set a trap for Griffin, but the invisible agent escapes, managing to take Stauffer's list of American-based agents with him. He also learns that Germany is planning a direct aerial attack on New York.

He and Maria (who surprisingly proves to be an experienced pilot) manage to escape Germany in a stolen Luftwaffe plane, while Stauffer, Ikito, and Heiser, all manage to destroy one another (because of their joint failure, Ikito commits *hara kiri*). Now deeply paranoid, Griffin tries to fight Maria in the cockpit, but the altitude overcomes him, and she manages to get him into a parachute, so they can both escape the plane, which is now over England and being shot down as an enemy aircraft. Griffin awakens in the hospital, where he learns that Maria is really a British agent who was working in Germany. He turns visible for the final clinch.

Jon Hall, who appears on camera almost as much as he appears invisible, plays what Hollywood liked to depict as the average American

Frank Griffin Jr. (Jon Hall) is threatened by a collection of Axis spies led by Stauffer (Cedric Hardwicke, left) in Invisible Agent.

Transparent spy Frank Griffin Jr. confronts Stauffer (Cedric Hardwicke) in Invisible Agent. *The see-through silhouette in the chair in this tricked-up publicity still is not actor Jon Hall; ironically, it's Vincent Price!*

Peter Lorre's "Baron Ikito" is about to commit hara kiri *in* Invisible Agent. *For some reason, the Hungarian-born former star of the German cinema was often cast as Japanese in Hollywood.*

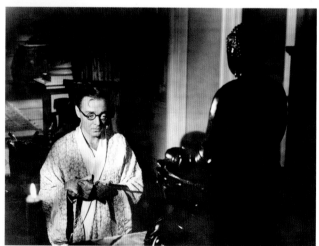

Ilona Massey knows the invisible one is there, but Cedric Hardwicke and J. Edward Bromberg don't. This time the transparent image looks like Boris Karloff! (The folks in the Universal Publicity Department must have had fun with Invisible Agent.*)*

Jon Hall became sort of visible with the aid of cold crème and a turban in Invisible Agent. *Ilona Massey is comforting him.*

soldier overseas: brave, plucky, resourceful, and convinced he's going to come out on top, no matter the adversity. As his nemeses, Cedric Hardwicke as the Oxford-educated Nazi leader is evilly urbane, and J. Edward Bromberg manages to invest a kind of pathos into the weak, overreaching Heiser. But it is Peter Lorre, making his only Universal Horror appearance, who steals every scene he's in. In his early days in Hollywood Lorre was often cast as Japanese characters (he was really Hungarian) and here he manages to squeeze some comedy out of his scripted perfidy.

The invisibility effects took another leap in sophistication, this time showing Griffin partially reveal himself on camera by painting his face with cold crème. However, for the scene of Griffin lifting Maria up in the air, an old-fashioned harness and wires were used, to the great indignation of Ilona Massey. Universal invested a comparatively high budget in *Invisible Agent*—about $320,000—but it paid off, earning more than $1 million worldwide.

THE INVISIBLE MAN'S REVENGE (1944)

Jon Hall returns as Robert Griffin in *The Invisible Man's Revenge*, but it is an entirely different character that, name aside, is of no stated relation to the family of scientists. This Robert Griffin has escaped from an asylum and turns up on the upper-class doorstep of Lady Irene Herrick (Gale Sondergaard) and Sir Jasper Herrick (Lester Matthews), who live in a manor house. Griffin's story is that he was a partner with them in a diamond-mining expedition in Tanganyika several years earlier, during which time he received a blow on the head and was left by the Herricks for dead. He disappeared, but only recently suffered another blow, which revived him from his amnesia. Now he is demanding his share of the fortune that has come from the diamonds, which he can verify by a written document. But Jasper claims to have lost most of the fortune in bad investments, and cannot pay him.

Sensing danger, Lady Irene drugs Robert, and then takes his written contract from him. She convinces her husband that Robert has become deranged, and encourages Jasper to throw him out. Robert subsequently stumbles on to the cottage of Dr. Peter Drury (John Carradine), a crackpot with delusions of greatness and a houseful of invisible animals, all created through his invisibility formula, which he is eager to try on a human. Griffin fits the bill, since invisibility is a great way to elude the police who are looking for him. Realizing he can also get even with the Herricks, Griffin goes to them and demands their entire estate, nearly driving the couple crazy in the process.

Meanwhile, Griffin is becoming more and more obsessed with the Herrick's daughter, Julie (Evelyn Ankers), who is engaged to a reporter named Mark Foster (Alan Curtis). Griffin demands that Dr. Drury restore his visibility, but learns that the process would entail an extensive blood transfusion, which would result in the donor's death. Griffin doesn't care; he forces the doctor to be the donor, and once he is visible again, he sets fire to Drury's cottage, then runs out. Foster, having been called earlier by Drury, shows up in time to pull the scientist's body from the inferno.

Griffin reappears at the manor house as "Martin Field," but the Herricks know who he is, and Foster is catching on as well. When Griffin discovers he needs constant blood to maintain visibility, he tries to take it

At least they were right about The Invisible Man's Revenge *being "ALL NEW!"...the film actually contained more comic relief than thrills.*

The mad scientist's dog is ultimately the only one who's on the trail of Griffin (Jon Hall) in The Invisible Man's Revenge.

Griffin (Jon Hall) is invisible only a small part of the time in The Invisible Man's Revenge, *but he goes see-through in order to torment former business partner Sir Jasper Herrick (Lester Matthews).*

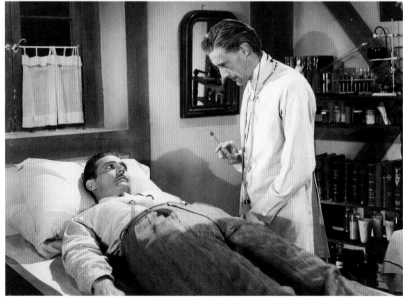

In The Invisible Man's Revenge *it's batty Dr. Drury (John Carradine, right) who develops the invisibility formula and uses it on Griffin (Jon Hall).*

Griffin (Jon Hall) proves to Dr. Drury (John Carradine) that his invisibility serum works, in The Invisible Man's Revenge.

from Foster, but the police intervene and kill him. After his death, Griffin is said to have suffered "imaginary wrongs" at the hands of the Herricks, implying that the act of betrayal that fuels the story took place only in his mind.

The fact that *The Invisible Man's Revenge* plays more like a mystery drama, right down to the twist ending, is perhaps due to the fact that it was scripted by Bertram Millhauser, whose usual province was Universal's Sherlock Holmes series. A lot of footage is given to comedian Leon Errol as Higgins, a comic relief sidekick of Griffin's, none of which has much to do with the main story. John Carradine, meanwhile, seems completely miscast as elderly, batty Dr. Drury (perhaps he felt so too and left before filming the scene of Drury being dragged from the burning cottage, in which the doctor is very visibly played by somebody else).

The Invisible Man's Revenge was the last of the primary Invisible series, and after a couple brushes with Abbott and Costello, he was never seen again at Universal…so to speak.

13 SPOTLIGHT:
UNA O'CONNOR

Historically, Hollywood tends to reward an artist's success in a particular field by making sure they stay within that field: in other words, *typecasting*. Certain actors can be typed, writers can be typed, even producers and directors can be typed. Then there are those people who are so unique that they become their own type. Such was Una O'Connor.

The name Una O'Connor may not be familiar to many moviegoers, but once seen (and heard) no one can forget her. She appeared in only two horror pictures, both for director James Whale—*The Invisible Man* and *The Bride of Frankenstein*—yet that was enough for her to become indelibly identified with Universal Horror. With her birdlike appearance, shrill voice, signature hands-in-the-air gesture of alarm, and deft comic sensibility, O'Connor had a tendency to walk away with any scene she was in. She was the prototype for the "hooting harridans" that would mark Universal Horror films for years to come (and decades later, *Monty Python's Flying Circus* would capitalize greatly on the archetype established by O'Connor, only with male comedians in drag playing the screeching fishwives).

Una O'Connor was born Agnes Teresa McGlade in Belfast, Ireland, in 1880. She adopted her stage name when she went on stage with the Abbey Theatre in Dublin. She made her way to London in the early part of the 20th century, and performed exclusively on the stage until 1929. After appearing in a handful of English films, including Alfred Hitchcock's *Murder!*, O'Connor came to Hollywood in 1932 to recreate her stage role in the film version of Noel Coward's *Cavalcade*.

James Whale tapped her to play Jenny in *The Invisible Man*, a role that required her to scream hysterically whenever she sees her mysterious guest in a state of invisibility, and practically any other time as well. Her role of Minnie in *Bride of Frankenstein* was ostensibly that of the Frankenstein's maid, but the character appeared as more of a Greek chorus

throughout the film, siding with the townspeople in their desire to see the Monster's body, and hooting and shrieking through the village like a town crier with news that the creature is still alive.

O'Connor would become a fixture in Hollywood, appearing in such non-Universal classics as *The Informer, The Adventures of Robin Hood,* and *The Bells of St. Mary's.* Her last film was 1957's *Witness for the Prosecution,* in which she again recreated a role she had played on the stage. That same year James Whale died, naming O'Connor in his will.

The actress, who never married, died in 1959 at the age of 78.

Una O'Connor as inn mistress Jenny is about to get the shock of her life (and respond accordingly) in The Invisible Man.

Prelude to a shriek: Una O'Connor and Boris Karloff in Bride of Frankenstein.

14 SPOTLIGHT:
JOHN P. FULTON

The man who made it possible for the Invisible Man to be invisible, who figured out how to show Larry Talbot transforming into the Wolf Man and Dracula transforming into a bat, who set up castle after castle for destruction, and who blew up more labs than a first-year chemistry student, was John P. Fulton, the head of Universal's special effects department from 1930 until 1946.

Fulton was born in Nebraska in 1902 to a theatrical family; his father, Fitch Fulton, was a scene painter for vaudeville shows. The family came west to California when John was 11, but it was not to get into the fledgling film industry. In fact, Fitch forbade his son from entering the entertainment industry, insisting that he learn a trade. Young John complied and studied electrical engineering, and ended up working as a surveyor for Southern California Edison in Los Angeles. But his real interest remained in moviemaking.

In 1923 Fulton talked himself into a job as assistant cameraman for silent comedian Lloyd Hamilton's production company at $25 a week. By the decade's end he had worked his way up to cinematography. Fulton's ultimate goal was to get into producing and directing, but he settled in the field of special effects photography, the techniques for which were at that time literally being made up as the industry went along. He received his training in special effects photography from Frank D. Williams, whom Fulton brought to Universal to supervise the visual effects for *The Invisible Man.*

At Universal, Fulton did everything from matte paintings and glass shots (scenery painted on sheets of glass and positioned in front of the camera), to creating and filming miniatures, to what would become his specialties: transformations and invisibility effects. His technique for miniature vehicles was to film them at high speed, which slowed down the action, making them appear fully weighted.

For *The Invisible Man* he was allowed to serve as the director for the effects shots. Due to the intricacies of positioning the performer (Claude Rains or his stand-in) to make certain that a part of the clothing was not blocked out in the matte, and because the black helmet required for the effect blocked out most sound, including Fulton's voice, it was a long and grueling process. "By take 20 of any such scene we felt ourselves merely getting well started toward getting our shot," Fulton recalled.

Fulton won two Academy Awards for his work in special effects, including one for parting the Red Sea in Cecil B. DeMille's *The Ten Commandments*. He died in 1965, having fallen ill in England while planning the special effects shots for *The Battle of Britain* (1968). He may not have achieved his personal career goals—to produce and direct films of his own—but the industry is filled with producers and directors who did not have the impact on motion pictures that John P. Fulton achieved.

15

CREATURES, CREEPERS, AND CHILLERS

UNIVERSAL'S LESSER KNOWN MINOR SERIES

Always on the lookout for new horror sensations, Universal tried a handful of lesser series. While they never quite broke into the studio's A-list of monsters, each was memorable in its own right.

PAULA, THE APE WOMAN

The saga of Paula the Ape Woman, a.k.a. "The Gorilla Girl," covers horror ground similar to that of the Wolf Man, only in reverse: rather than a normal human being who changes into a beast, the beautiful Paula Dupree was the result of a mad doctor's efforts to change a beast into a woman.

Paula was introduced in the 1943 film *Captive Wild Woman*, which is set against the backdrop of a circus. The newest exotic animal addition to the show is Cheela, a female gorilla with an almost human personality, who was captured by big game hunter Fred Mason (Milburn Stone). When overzealous endocrinologist Dr. Sigmund Walters (John Carradine) sees Cheela, he realizes this is his chance to elevate the kind of gland transplants he has been doing with small animals to an epic scale. He hires a disgruntled ex-employee of the circus to gorilla-nap Cheela, and gives her a human gland and cerebrum, which causes the ape to change into an exotic-looking woman whom he names Paula Dupree, and whose mind he controls.

Due to her strange effect over animals, Mason puts Paula (Acquanetta) in his big cat act, much to the consternation of his fiancée Beth (Evelyn Ankers), with whom the silent, glaring Paula begins a bizarre rivalry. This only intensifies after Paula begins to regress back to ape-like form. Reverting completely back to a gorilla, she kills Dr. Walters, but actually saves Fred when his big cat act goes bad and he's attacked.

Paula Dupree (Acquanetta) reverted to apish form from Captive Wild Woman.

Unfortunately, those watching fail to understand the gorilla's affection for him, and they shoot her.

Directed by Edward Dmytryk (some years before his inclusion in the "Hollywood Ten," a group of blacklisted filmmakers), *Captive Wild Woman* opens with a title card thanking legendary lion tamer Clyde Beatty for staging the animal scenes. What it does not mention is that the scenes were staged a decade earlier for Beatty's film *The Big Cage* (1933). Character actor Milburn Stone landed the leading man role of Mason because of his resemblance to Beatty, which allowed for him to be intercut with the old footage.

Acquanetta, the former fashion model who played Paula in human form, was being hyped by Universal as "The Venezuelan Volcano," even though she was not really Venezuelan. She was really of Native American heritage. Never any threat to Joan Crawford as an actress (or even Joan Leslie, for that matter), Acquanetta possessed a screen presence and a penetrating stare that was put to good use as Paula. For the character's more bestial side, Western star Ray "Crash" Corrigan donned the gorilla suit as "Cheela."

1944's *Jungle Woman* picks up the Paula story from the very end of *Captive Wild Woman*. It turns out that the gorilla was not killed after all, merely wounded. She is taken in by Dr. Carl Fletcher (J. Carrol Naish) who has purchased the late Dr. Walters sanitarium and laboratory. Cheela spontaneously turns back into Paula (Acquanetta), only now she is a verbal and more vindictive, murderous version of Paula. What's more, it is rumored that Paula *started out* as a woman in Africa, and was turned into a gorilla by a witch doctor. Maybe that's why she becomes fixated on Bob Whitney (Richard Davis), the fiancé of Fletcher's daughter, Joan (Lois Collier). When Bob rejects her, she tries to kill him and Joan by swimming like a shark to the canoe they are enjoying in the moonlight and pulling it under! Later, after stalking Joan, Paula viciously attacks Dr. Fletcher, who kills her with an injection, and afterwards finds himself before a coroner's jury to explain the death.

Assembled more than directed by Reginald Le Borg, *Jungle Woman* comprises two separate stories with largely different casts, both related in flashbacks, and framed by scenes of the coroner's inquest. The first recaps *Captive Wild Woman* using stock footage (which results in a flashback within a flashback!) plus a few new scenes featuring Milburn Stone and Evelyn Ankers; the second tells the story of the strange triangle between Paula, Bob, and Joan. The film concludes with Dr. Fletcher exonerated for the killing after the coroner's jury visits the morgue and finds that Paula's body has reverted to its simian form, meaning that Fletcher did not kill a *human*.

In the final Paula film, 1945's *The Jungle Captive*, Dr. Fletcher comes to an unfortunate end; he is killed (off-screen) by the grotesque Moloch (Rondo Hatton), the assistant to the mad endocrinology researcher Mr. Stendahl (Otto Kruger). While not actually a doctor, Stendahl is an outwardly respected scientist, admired in particular by his assistants Ann and Don (Amelita Ward and Phil Brown). Stendahl is obsessed with bringing dead animals back to life...and the biggest dead animal in town is the Ape Woman, whose body Moloch steals from the morgue for the scientist. Stendahl revives Paula, but her brain no longer

In Jungle Woman, *Paula (Acquanetta) remained in human form for most of the movie, but her actions were bestial, such as her killing of the simple-minded Willie (Edward Hyans).*

Armed and dangerous: Paula (Acquanetta) goes on a rampage in Jungle Woman.

JUNGLE CAPTIVE

with OTTO KRUGER

Amelita Ward   Phil Brown   Jerome Cowan
and

VICKY LANE   RONDO HATTON
as the Ape Woman   as Moloch, the Brute

Irish-born starlet Vicky Lane, a Vivien Leigh lookalike, took over the role of Paula for the final Ape Woman film, Jungle Captive.

The refined Ape Woman makeup used on Vicky Lane in Jungle Captive *included more hair and a chimpanzee nose and upper lip.*

Mad scientist Stendahl (Otto Kruger) has a hard time taming his patient, Paula Dupree (Vicky Lane) in Jungle Captive.

Paula the Ape Woman (Vicky Lane) takes revenge on Stendahl (Otto Kruger), thereby saving Ann Forrester (Amelita Ward, on gurney) from a horrible fate in Jungle Captive.

functions, so he plans to give her Ann's brain. The scheme fails, though, when Paula reverts to her apelike self and kills the doctor before he can operate, and then dies herself.

Directed by the unsung Harold Young, *The Jungle Captive* is the best of the Paula films. It has a linear storyline and contains no stock footage, but has more scenes than usual of Paula in her ape-ish form, which utilized a revised chimp-like makeup built around a rubber snout and upper lip appliance. There is also a good Dr. Frankenstein wannabe in Stendahl, whose personal mantra is that the advancement of science is more valuable than a few individual lives. Even the grotesque killer Moloch possesses more humanity than Mr. Stendahl.

What *The Jungle Captive* does not have is Acquanetta. Here Paula is played by 18-year-old starlet Vicky Lane, whose brief career completely fizzled out after this picture. Phil Brown, however, who played the film's hero, would achieve cult stardom more than 30 years later as Luke Skywalker's Uncle Owen in the original *Star Wars*.

Why did the Paula films fail to achieve the kind of success that Universal enjoyed with the Wolf Man series? Maybe it was because the monster's name, whether "Ape Woman" or "Gorilla Girl," never appeared in any title. Maybe with a recognizable star, such as Maria Montez, the films would have made a bigger splash. For whatever reason, Paula the Ape Woman remains a second-tier—if guiltily pleasurable—monster within the Universal Horror pantheon.

THE CREEPER

Late in its second horror cycle, Universal introduced a wholly unique "monster," the hulking, murderous figure known as the Creeper. He was unique because he was played by a man who was not required to spend hours, or even minutes, in the makeup chair: Rondo Hatton, "the Monster without Makeup."

Rondo Hatton (that really was his given name) was born in Maryland in 1894. Handsome in his youth, he served in World War I and later became a newspaper reporter. Then something began to happen to him: a glandular disorder called acromegaly started to enlarge and deform his face, hands, and body. Something even stranger resulted: film producers saw him as an interesting character face and Hatton started getting work in movies, first in 1930's *Hell Harbor*, filmed in Florida where he was living and working, and later in Hollywood.

Hatton had a bit part in Universal's 1939 crime drama *The Big Guy*, but his real break came via the 1944 Sherlock Holmes adventure *The Pearl of Death*, directed by Roy William Neill (whose only other contribution to Universal Horror was *Frankenstein Meets the Wolf Man*). Hatton played "the Hoxton Creeper," the murderous tool of master criminal Giles Conover (Miles Mander). Seen only in shadow and silhouette until the final three minutes of the film, Hatton made an enormous impact when he was finally revealed as the back-breaking human monster. He even managed to frighten Holmes (Basil Rathbone, of course).

Realizing it had a new star on the lot, Universal quickly cast Hatton as Moloch in *The Jungle Captive* and as the deaf mute servant Mario in *The Spider Woman Strikes Back*, the latter being a follow-up to *The Spider Woman*, another Holmes mystery in which actress Gale Sondergaard had

Rondo Hatton as The Brute Man. *While his face remained unaltered, the studio often padded him out to Monster proportions.*

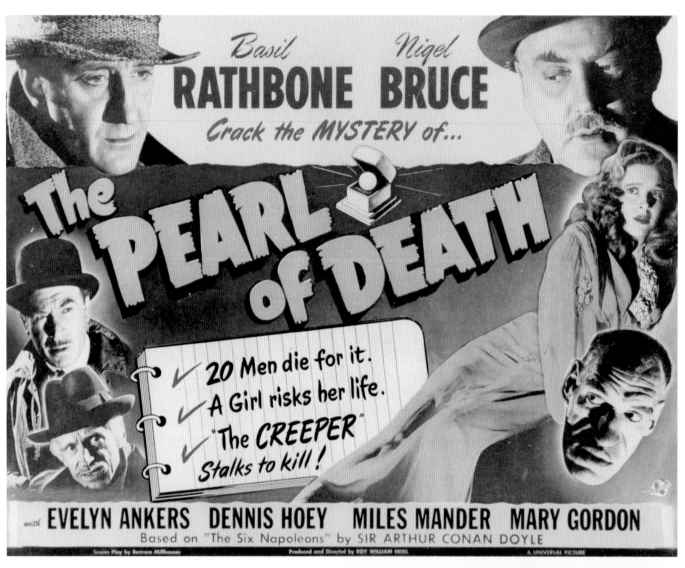

Rondo Hatton (bottom right) was promoted on this lobby card for The Pearl of Death, *but within the film itself he was kept hidden until the end.*

Rondo Hatton as "the Hoxton Creeper" dispatches master criminal "Giles Conover" (Miles Mander) in The Pearl of Death, *a Sherlock Holmes mystery.*

House of Horrors *officially "introduced"*
The Creeper, played by Rondo Hatton.

In House of Horrors *the Creeper (Rondo Hatton) becomes the muse of a mad sculptor, played by Martin Kosleck. Only one such bust appears in the film, but since it had to be destroyed the studio prop department made a spare for a second take.*

The Creeper (Rondo Hatton) is not what wealthy Virginia Scott (Jan Wiley) wants to see staring back at her in the mirror, in The Brute Man.

Rondo Hatton with Gale Sondergaard in The Spider Woman Strikes Back, *Universal's attempt to launch a horror series around a female antagonist. Sondergaard had earlier played a variation of the femme fatale in the Sherlock Holmes adventure* The Spider Woman.

played a deadly murderess. The first official Creeper film was 1946's *House of Horrors*, which carried a special title card "introducing" Rondo Hatton as the Creeper.

After being saved from drowning and befriended by the starving, despondent would-be artist Marcel De Lange (Martin Kosleck), the Creeper—a serial killer who snaps the spines of his victims—becomes the sculptor's tool for revenge, murdering the art critics who have trashed De Lange in print, particularly the snake like F. Holmes Harmon (Alan Napier), who enjoys destroying people's reputations. When Joan Medford (Virginia Bruce)—the only critic who has ever looked kindly to De Lange's Picasso-esque works—comes too close to the truth, she is also put on the list for death.

George Bricker's surprisingly witty script for *House of Horrors* owes quite a bit to the classic mystery *Laura*, particularly in its treatment of acidic critics and other New York socialite types, though its intrepid heroine, Joan Medford, is straight out of *His Girl Friday. House of Horrors* was in fact filmed under the title *Joan Medford is Missing*, which in retrospect does not make much sense, since she does not go missing until the climax, and then only momentarily.

Director Jean Yarbrough, who bounced back and forth between horror films and Abbott and Costello comedies, created a moody and atmospheric environment, and Rondo Hatton, whose torso was padded out to gorilla like portions, gives what is probably his best performance, not simply looking frightening, but acting so as well. The film also provides a good role for German actor Martin Kosleck, who spent the war years in Hollywood playing mostly Nazis or more handsome Peter Lorre–type maniacs. De Lange may be crazy as a loon, but Kosleck manages to makes his mania somewhat understandable, particularly when juxtaposed against the sliminess of the critics.

In *The Brute Man*, the last film of the series, released in 1946, the Creeper's origin was revealed. He is really Hal Moffet, a hot-headed former college football star who was disfigured as the result of a chemistry lab explosion, for which he blames his old roommate Cliff Scott (Tom Neal), and the woman they both love, Virginia Rogers (Jan Wiley). Many years later, Cliff and Virginia are married and very successful, and the Creeper visits them, having paused his murderous career long enough to fall for a young blind woman, Helen Paige (Jane "Poni" Adams), the only person who is kind to him. While trying to extort jewelry from the Scotts in order to finance an operation to restore Helen's sight, Moffet is shot by Cliff, whom he subsequently kills. But he does get away with the jewelry, which he delivers to Helen, who unsuspectingly tries to have it appraised. The police are notified and a trap is set up, using Helen as bait, to capture the Creeper.

Jean Yarbrough again directed, and while *The Brute Man* is not up to its immediate predecessor, its script by George Bricker and M. Coates Webster offers a note of sympathy for the Creeper, through its *Bride of Frankenstein*–like subplot involving the kindly blind girl. Having the Creeper captured at the end but not killed left the door open for more sequels, but fate intervened. In February of 1946, even before the film could be released, Rondo Hatton died of complications of his acromegaly at the age of 51.

Since the merger of Universal and International Pictures had resulted in a new focus for the studio that was characterized by shutting down its B-movie units, so *The Brute Man* was sold off to Poverty Row's Producers Releasing Corporation, which released it as a PRC original. The rest of the Universal B catalogue was leased to a company called Realart Pictures, which rereleased them in double features until the mid-1950s.

Despite his fearsome appearance and harsh, jackhammer voice, Rondo Hatton was by all accounts a gentle soul and a devoted husband, who was known for going out of his way to help others. "He was a pleasure to work with," Martin Kosleck recalled years later, "intelligent, sensitive and kind." Hatton may have resented the way his physical affliction was exploited by Hollywood, but that exploitation also allowed him to pay for medical treatment for his ever-worsening condition. The increasing enlargement of his lower jaw meant that he had to have constant dental attention just to be able to eat. It was a tragic affliction, yet the fashion in which Hatton faced it was little short of heroic.

While never a threat to Spencer Tracy, Rondo Hatton did prove to be irreplaceable. In the history of Hollywood, there has never been anyone like him.

THE INNER SANCTUM

All but one of Universal's "Inner Sanctum Mysteries" begin with the same shot: a distorted head floating inside a crystal ball invites the audience into a strange realm in which the human mind destroys, distorts, creates monsters, and commits murder. "Even you, without knowing, can commit murder," the head (played by David Hoffman) says. That opening is the perfect visual metaphor for the six low-budget, noirish crime dramas that constitute the series: they are mysteries that want to be horror films when they grow up.

Based on the "Inner Sanctum" book imprint from publisher Simon and Schuster, the series featured Lon Chaney Jr. as a different character in each film, but always a professional man who is accused of, or is otherwise implicated in, murder. Only the second and last entries, *Weird Woman* and *Pillow of Death*, have any kind of legitimate supernatural connection, though each one can at least boast of the trappings of horror.

First off was 1943's *Calling Dr. Death*, in which Chaney plays Dr. Mark Steele, a brilliant psychiatrist who fears his own mind might be going when circumstantial evidence in the case of his wife's murder and mutilation by acid seems to point directly to him...while he can't remember anything about it. *Calling Dr. Death* set the formula for the series, including Chaney's whispered internal ruminations, which are delivered as voice-over narration.

1944's *Weird Woman* was based on Fritz Leiber's 1943 novel *Conjure Wife*, which pits a logical, rational college professor against the powers of voodoo. Chaney plays professor and bestselling author Norman Reed, a man of rationality who believes the gulf between *science* and *séance* will never be bridged. Meanwhile his young wife Paula (Anne Gwynne), who grew up on a pagan island in the tropics that Reed had visited and studied anthropologically, firmly believes in the old gods and voodoo. (Why the studio did not cast Acquanetta in this role is anyone's guess.)

Lon Chaney Jr. played an artist who is accidentally blinded by acid in Dead Man's Eyes.

Anne Gwynne played the title role in Weird Woman.

Against this backdrop of superstition versus reason comes the bitterly evil Ilona Carr (Evelyn Ankers), who had her designs on Professor Reed before Paula came along, and afterwards goes on a campaign of psychological terrorism against Reed to try and destroy his life. Her conniving, whispering campaign results in two deaths, for which Reed and Paula are blamed. Ilona—whose perfidy is not hidden from the audience, even if the characters in the film don't catch on—comes to a bad end as a result of her actions, though whether supernatural influence was involved or not is open to interpretation.

Dead Man's Eyes (1944) concerns artist Dave Stuart (Chaney), who accidentally blinds himself by using acid instead of eyewash. When his father-in-law—who willed his eyes for an operation—turns up murdered, Dave is the chief suspect. He also acts as the film's amateur sleuth, ultimately solving the case. A straightforward mystery, *Dead Man's Eyes* was given a gruesome veneer by showing Chaney with acid scarred eyes.

The Frozen Ghost (1944) straddles three different genres: film noir crime drama, classic murder mystery, and horror film. Chaney plays Gregor the Great, a popular radio mentalist who seems to be able to kill people simply by looking at them. To escape the attention of the press, he hides out in a creepy wax museum whose owner suddenly disappears, and whose sculptor turns out to be a disgraced plastic surgeon who is now a homicidal knife-thrower! Whew! The revelation of the real criminal—and the real crime—makes *The Frozen Ghost* one of the wildest B-movie rides of all time.

J. Carrol Naish (left) and Lon Chaney Jr. dispense with the subtleties in a posed shot from Strange Confession.

Strange Confession (1945) is a reworking of the 1935 Universal thriller *The Man Who Reclaimed His Head*, which starred Claude Rains. Chaney plays Jeff Carter, a brilliant industrial chemist and family man who discovers a miracle cure that is exploited by his greedy employer. When the insufficiently tested drug results in the death of his own son, Carter loses it and finds out whether his boss really has *a head* for business. *Strange Confession* is the most serious-minded of the Inner Sanctum series.

The last Sanctum mystery was *Pillow of Death* (1945), whose title describes the murder weapon in the suffocation death of the wife of Wayne Fletcher (Chaney). Fletcher himself is the chief suspect, but he professes his innocence, even as the voice of his dead wife calls to him from beyond the grave. Punctuated by séances and spooky goings on in a graveyard, the denouement of *Pillow of Death* holds a surprise for devotees of the series. It is also the only Inner Sanctum picture without the floating head introduction.

The Inner Sanctum mysteries reflected an ongoing campaign by Lon Chaney Jr. to be accepted more as a leading man, particularly since the breed was in short supply in Hollywood during the war (and for the record, Chaney wanted to join the Marine Corps, but was deemed 4F). That said, the recurring theme of his irresistibility to women was something of a stretch. As a heartthrob, Lon Chaney Jr. was never a threat to Tyrone Power, but the Inner Sanctum films at least proved that he had more arrows in his acting quiver than just monsters, cowboys, and Average Joes.

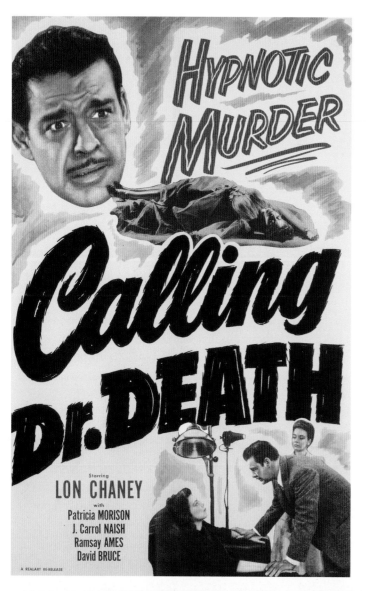

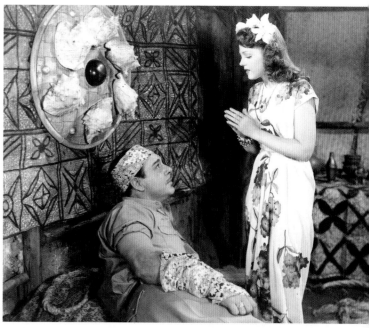

Calling Dr. Death *was the first, and the most stylish, of the "Inner Sanctum" mysteries.*

Anne Gwynne as "Paula" (the exotic women in Universal Horror tended to be named Paula) tries to get Professor Norman Reed (Lon Chaney Jr.) to go native in Weird Woman.

Tala Birell, Milburn Stone, and Lon Chaney Jr. examine sculptor Martin Kosleck's wax handiwork in The Frozen Ghost.

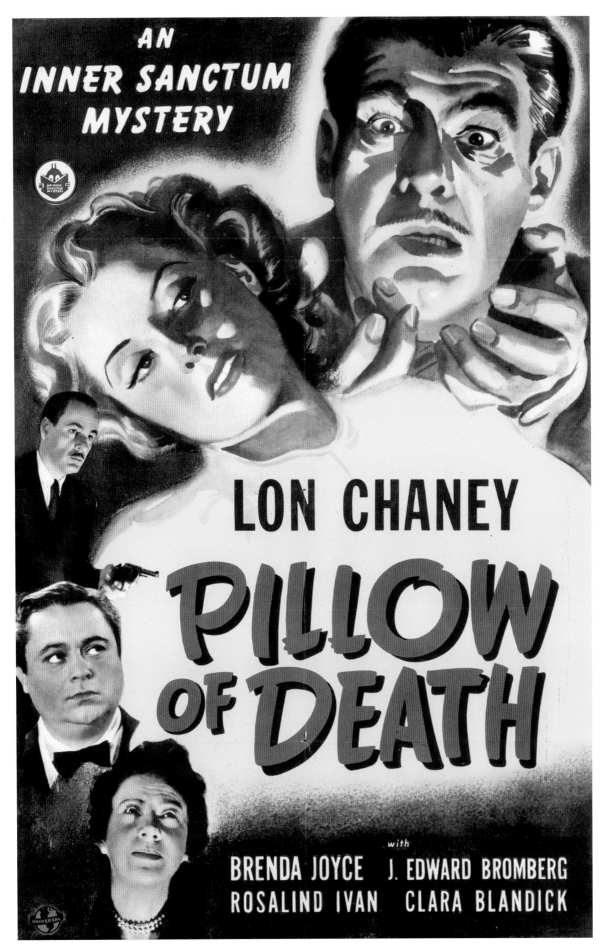

AN **INNER SANCTUM MYSTERY**

LON CHANEY

PILLOW OF DEATH

with

**BRENDA JOYCE   J. EDWARD BROMBERG
ROSALIND IVAN   CLARA BLANDICK**

16 SPOTLIGHT:
DWIGHT FRYE

Bela Lugosi, Boris Karloff, and Lon Chaney Jr. were not the only actors who were forced to wrestle with the problem of typecasting as a result of their successes in the horror film genre. There was also Dwight Frye, the diminutive, distinctive actor who had once been a Broadway ingénue, but who—until the arrival of Peter Lorre in Hollywood—was the guy producers went to whenever they needed a wild-eyed lunatic, with or without a twisted back.

Frye was there from the beginning of Universal Horror, playing the fly-eating Renfield in *Dracula*, Fritz the hunchbacked lab assistant in *Frankenstein*, and Karl, the grumbling grave robber in *Bride of Frankenstein*. In between he took such roles as the hot-tempered gunman Wilmer Cook in the first version of *The Maltese Falcon* (1931) and the bat-obsessed imbecile Herman in the independently produced (but shot on the Universal lot) horror epic *The Vampire Bat* (1933).

Of that last role, Frye bemoaned, "If God is good, I will be able to play comedy, in which I was featured on Broadway for eight seasons and in which no producer of motion pictures will give me a chance! And please, God, may it be before I go screwy playing idiots, half-wits, and lunatics on the talking screen!" The good news is that Frye managed to continue his career without going screwy. The bad news is that his career, and his life, had only another decade to go.

Dwight Illif Frye was born in 1899 in Salinas, Kansas. A musical prodigy, his attentions turned more toward the theater in his teen years. By 1923 he was not only appearing on Broadway, but was being touted in the *New York Times* as one of the best performers of the season, alongside the likes of John Barrymore, Jane Cowl, and Jeannie Eagles. Earlier that season he appeared in the New York premiere of Pirandello's *Six Characters in Search of an Author*. Within a few short years, Frye was a bona fide toast of Broadway. All that would change upon coming to Hollywood. In Frye's first film, 1928's *The Night Bird*, he was merely an extra, playing a guest in a wedding scene, but it put him on the Universal lot for the first time. After

Dwight Frye's innocent looks could turn demonic in an instant. Frye (center) is flanked by Edward Van Sloan (left) and Charles Gerrard in Dracula.

playing a couple more inconsequential roles in films, he was given the part of Renfield in *Dracula*.

It is doubtful that Frye realized the impact he was going to make as Renfield, who begins the picture as a pleasant, if rather fey, businessman, and quickly devolves into a raving madman. The shot of Frye's maniacal Renfield in the hold of the doomed ship *Vesta*, his pale blue eyes glaring insanely into the camera lens, his unnerving sing-song laugh forced up through a death's head grimace, is the most tangibly terrifying image in the picture. His fate in Hollywood was sealed.

Beginning with *Frankenstein*, in which he played the dwarfed, hunchbacked, scarred, but somehow strangely amusing, assistant to Dr. Henry Frankenstein, Frye became part of James Whale's stock company of actors. Whale gave him a cameo in *The Invisible Man* (1933) and an equally small turn in *The Road Back* (1937), the sequel to Universal's 1930 hit *All Quiet on the Western Front*. Frye also turns up briefly in Whale's *The Man in the Iron Mask* (1939). What might have been their greatest collaboration, *Bride of Frankenstein*, turned out less satisfactorily, at least for Frye, whose role of Karl, Dr. Frankenstein's grave-robbing assistant, was severely truncated in the final print.

After *Bride of Frankenstein*, Frye's career went into a tailspin. His Broadway résumé was no help in finding him leading roles, in comedy, horror, or any other genre. While he continued to work, the parts were largely thankless, often uncredited, and sometimes identified by role descriptions rather than character names. Occasionally they were *numbered* role descriptions, such as "Villager #2" or "Second Mug." Frye began to turn up in short subjects and had a tiny bit in the 1940 Saturday matinee serial *The Drums of Fu Manchu*, and participation in such venues was a signal that an actor was either on the way up or on the way down. There is a persistent rumor that he fell so far as to play a clothed bit in a stag film, but this has never been confirmed.

The intense actor would make two more appearances in the *Frankenstein* series (not counting the scenes he apparently filmed for 1939's *Son of Frankenstein*, which were edited out). In 1942's *The Ghost of Frankenstein* he was a nameless villager, but in *Frankenstein Meets the Wolf Man*, released the next year, he had visibility, billing, an actual character name, "Rudi." He also had one of the most jaw-fracturing lines of dialogue in Universal Horror history: "As much as I'd like to kill the Monster, I'd hate to crawl around through those dark catacombs of Frankenstein's castle in the black of the night." Only an actor of Frye's experience could put that over.

During the war, Frye took a night job with Douglas Aircraft as a tool designer, to support his wife and son and also to aid the war effort. But he remained intensely frustrated with his floundering career. He began to experience heart problems, but as a practicing Christian Scientist, he simply ignored them. Finally a break came; he was cast as Newton D. Baker, President Woodrow Wilson's Secretary of War, in the 1944 biopic *Wilson*. It looked like the beginning of a comeback, but before he could start filming, Dwight Frye suffered a fatal heart attack. He was only 44 years old.

No matter how frustrated he became in his later years, Dwight Frye never lost hope that his career situation would someday improve. At least he left the world with the knowledge that it finally appeared to be so.

Dwight Frye as Renfield listens for his master's voice in Dracula.

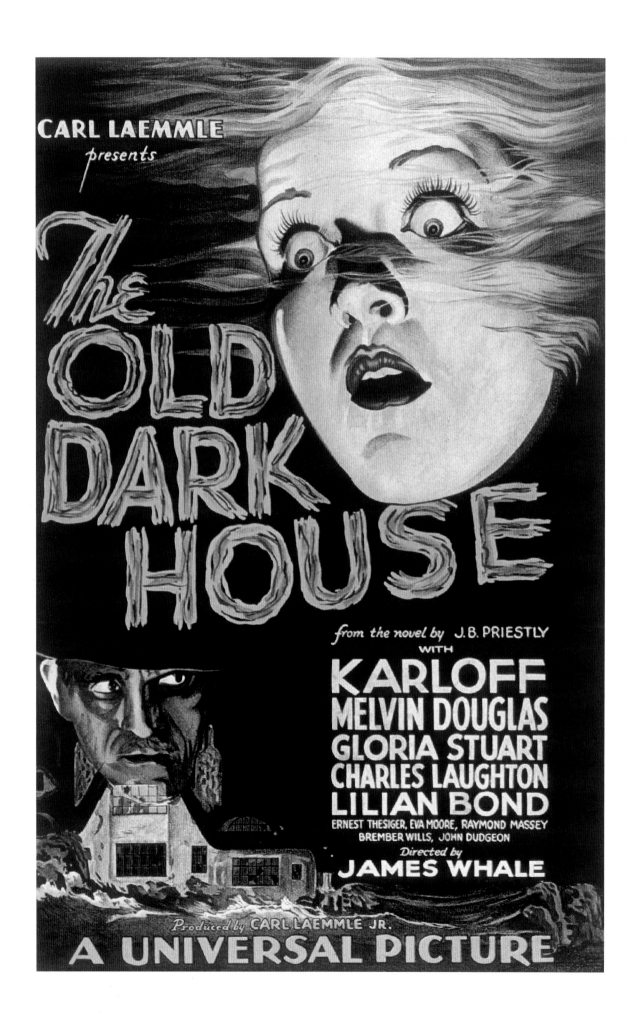

17
MONSTERS, MADMEN, AND FREAKS OF SCIENCE

Not every Universal Horror movie was part of a series. In between chapters in the sagas of the Frankenstein Monster, Dracula, the Mummy, the Wolf Man, and the like, were individual fright films made by the same studio creative teams, but with unique twists of their own. Many of these individual fright films have become classics on their own.

THE OLD DARK HOUSE (1932)

The Old Dark House was considered by Universal to be Boris Karloff's official follow-up to *Frankenstein*, which is why he received top billing over such luminaries as Charles Laughton, Raymond Massey, and Ernest Thesiger. Its story is as simple as its title: two separate groups of travelers (Massey, Melvyn Douglas, and Gloria Stuart in one and Laughton and Lillian Bond in the other) motoring through Wales are stranded by a horrific storm and forced to spend the night in the foreboding Femm mansion, inhabited by the strangest family in Britain. While eccentric Horace Femm (Thesiger) invites them in, his dour sister Rebecca (Eva Moore) tries to shoo them away. Adding to the surreal creepiness of the house is the bedridden presence of the family's 102-year-old patriarch Sir Roderick (who is actually the sanest one of the bunch), and another brother, the deviously insane pyromaniac Saul (Brember Wills), who is kept locked in his room.

There is also Morgan the butler, a huge, hulking grotesquely scarred, violent mute (Karloff). While the dangerous-when-drunk Morgan is the one the reluctant visitors all fear, it is the escaped Saul who causes the most trouble, nearly killing the hero Roger Penderel (Douglas), who the next morning escapes the house—barely—with the show girl Gladys (Bond) on his arm, in a troublingly happy ending.

It was exactly that troublingly happy ending that director James Whale was shooting for. In fact, *The Old Dark House* plays like something

Boris Karloff's success from Frankenstein *accorded him top billing over a distinguished cast in* The Old Dark House *(though this poster manages to misspell the names of both Melvyn Douglas and Lillian Bond).*

of a prolonged shaggy-dog joke: after a night of horror, the visitors leave on a bright, sunny, dry morning, to Horace cheerfully bidding them goodbye. Another of Whale's jokes is the billing for the player taking the part of the ancient Sir Roderick Femm. Credited as "John Dudgeon," it was actually 60-year-old actress Elspeth Dudgeon.

Filming of *The Old Dark House* began with Karloff in a more or less straight makeup, with curly hair. But ever eager to promote the actor's horror image, producer Carl Laemmle Jr. stepped in and stopped production, instructing Jack Pierce to remake Morgan as monstrous as possible. The film carried a precredit announcement that, lest there be doubt, the Karloff mentioned in the cast was the same actor who had played the Monster in *Frankenstein*, which seems redundant since in terms of movement, gesture, physical bulk, and inarticulateness, Morgan is quite reminiscent of the Monster (and for the record, the character's grunts are dubbed by an actor other than Karloff).

Thought to be lost for decades, a print of *The Old Dark House* was finally unearthed from the Universal Studios vaults around 1970.

MURDERS IN THE RUE MORGUE (1932)

Long accepted as the consolation prize for both director Robert Florey and Bela Lugosi for having lost *Frankenstein* (a few sets from which are reused), *Murders in the Rue Morgue* is actually a far better fit for their respective talents, with Lugosi allowed to craft an evilly driven character that is nothing like Dracula and Florey given reign to indulge in his beloved visual expressionism.

To the world at large, Dr. Mirakle (Bela Lugosi) is a side-show charlatan in mid-19th-century Paris, exhibiting a gorilla named "Erik" with which he claims to communicate, while expounding the theory of evolution—predating Darwin, as it turns out. Carnival audiences scorn him. But secretly, he is conducting experiments to mutate the simian and human race. He specializes in young women, who he injects with gorilla blood, but the experiments are never a success and the bodies of the victims are deposited into the Seine. Young medical student Dupin (Leon Waycoff), who has autopsied the bodies of several murder victims, discovers that each victim has traces of gorilla blood in her—and the only man in Paris with a gorilla is Dr. Mirakle. Unfortunately, Mirakle has by now discovered that Dupin's love, Camille (Sidney Fox), has the exact right kind of blood to mix with a gorilla's. But beauty, as they say, hath charm to soothe the savage beast, so when Mirakle begins to experiment on Camille, the smitten Erik breaks loose and kills him, then takes the girl and climbs with her to the rooftops of Paris, where Erik is killed by Dupin.

Ostensibly based on the story by Edgar Allan Poe, the only real connection between *Murders in the Rue Morgue* and its eponymous source is a sequence in which tenants in a boarding house hear a strange language being spoken and attribute it to every tongue in Europe, without realizing it is really fluent gorilla.

Sidney Fox, who received top billing over Lugosi, was an attractive ingénue with an oddly shrill voice. Having enjoyed a very brief career, she died in 1942 from an overdose of sleeping pills. Leon Waycoff, making his movie debut, would have a much longer career, lasting into the 1980s, under the name Leon Ames. Outside of the extravagantly coiffed,

Gloria Stuart and Boris Karloff (in revised, more horrible makeup) from The Old Dark House. *Stuart would garner an Oscar nomination as Best Supporting Actress for* Titanic *66 years later!*

Settling a dispute in The Old Dark House. *From left to right: Raymond Massey (on floor), Lillian Bond, Gloria Stuart, Melvyn Douglas, Boris Karloff, Charles Laughton, and Eva Moore.*

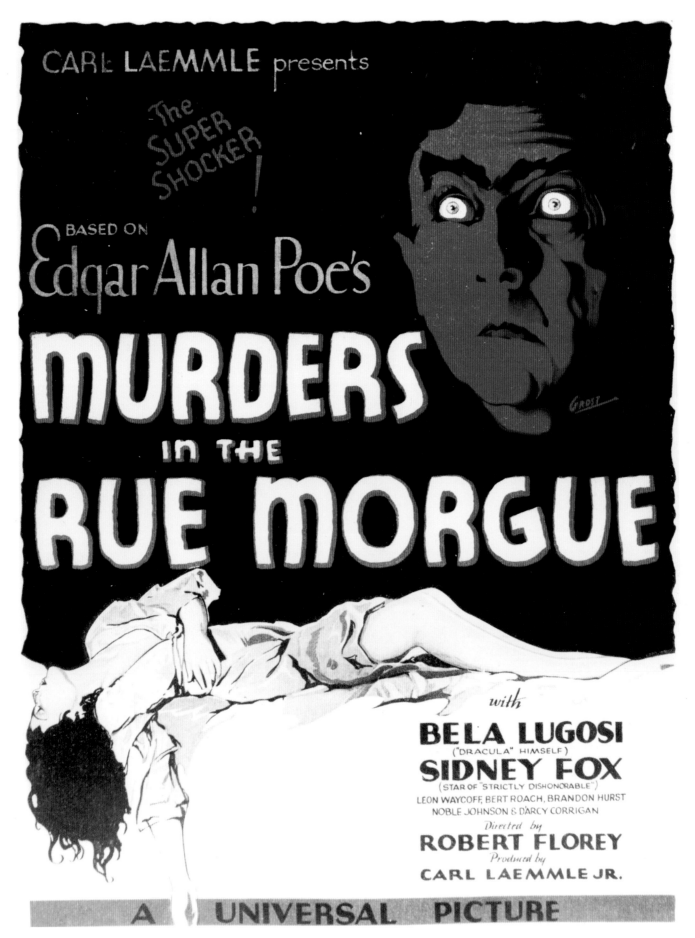

The poster for Murders in the Rue Morgue *was as stylized as the film (in the credits of which Sidney Fox gets top billing over Bela Lugosi).*

Curly-haired Bela Lugosi as Dr. Mirakle in Murders in the Rue Morgue. *The man in the gorilla suit is Charles Gemora, who specialized in playing apes from the silent era to the mid-1950s.*

Dr. Mirakle (Bela Lugosi) with one of the subjects of his unsuccessful experiments (Arlene Francis, who would later become renowned as a panelist on television game shows).

unibrowed Lugosi, the real star of the film is Erik the gorilla, played in stationary shots by gorilla specialist Charlie Gemora (who had a secondary career as a makeup artist), in action shots by strongman-turned-stuntman Joe Bonomo, and in close-ups by an actual chimpanzee.

THE BLACK CAT (1934)

The Black Cat, which has even less to do with Edgar Allan Poe than did *Murders in the Rue Morgue*, was the first teaming of Boris Karloff and Bela Lugosi. It is probably the most memorable of their eight films together.

Lugosi plays Dr. Vitus Werdegast, a haunted ex-soldier recently released from a World War I prison camp, who is traveling on the Orient Express to visit an old "friend," Hjalmar Poelzig (Boris Karloff), the man responsible for putting him there. He shares a compartment with young American honeymooners Peter and Joan Allison (David Manners and Jacqueline Wells), who are heading in his direction. After detraining, they all end up on the same bus, which crashes in a violent thunderstorm, killing the driver, injuring Joan, and forcing them to take refuge in the only available shelter: the Bauhaus-influenced mansion belonging to Poelzig.

The house has been erected on top of a battleground that Poelzig, as commander of a keep, surrendered, resulting in thousands of deaths and Werdegast's capture. Unfortunately the Allisons are now in the way of Werdegast's revenge and the satanic Poelzig (who actually leads a devil worship cult) views Joan's freedom as a pawn in the literal and metaphoric chess game he is playing with Werdegast. The doctor plays along until he discovers, to his horror, that not only had Poelzig killed his wife, keeping her body embalmed in the cellar, but he has taken Werdegast's daughter as his own wife. Once Werdegast has managed to ensure the Allison's release, he overcomes Poelzig and insanely tortures him by skinning him alive! Then he destroys the house through one of those Frankenstein laboratory levers ("It's the red switch, isn't it, Hjalmar?"), which is connected to dynamite under the structure.

Upon seeing this film, the *New York Times* termed Karloff "that jovial madman" and Lugosi "that suave fiend" and both descriptions are apt. Karloff is befitted with Jack Pierce's most severe widow's peak to date, but he plays the evil Poelzig (who was named for legendary German art director Hans Poelzig) in a casual fashion. Lugosi's performance, meanwhile, is perfectly straight, almost heroic, though no one was paying attention to his diction; when Werdegast first enters Poelzig's house, Lugosi is virtually unintelligible.

Universal's second teaming of Boris Karloff (left) and Bela Lugosi was for 1934's Gift of Gab, *in which they had cameos in a comedy sketch.*

One scene involving a Satanic black mass was pretty strong stuff for 1934, but signs that the Breen Office, Hollywood's censorship board, was involved can be detected by listening very carefully to Karloff's Latin invocation. It is largely nonsense, comprised of phrases like *cave canum* ("beware of dog"), *in vino veritas* ("in wine is truth") and most pertinently, *cum grano salis* ("with a grain of salt"). Among the Satanic revelers in this scene is a young, mustachioed John Carradine, then acting under the name "Peter Richmond."

The Black Cat—whose title is justified solely by having Lugosi's character possess a morbid fear of cats—was shot in 19 days on a very modest budget of $96,000, and yet it became Universal's top grosser for 1934. Why, then, was its director and scenarist Edgar G. Ulmer not

Boris Karloff (upper center) leads the black mass in The Black Cat.

A deadly game of chess from The Black Cat. *Bela Lugosi and Boris Karloff later spoofed this scene for a promotional short subject.*

The Black Cat *(1934) was probably Karloff and Lugosi's best teaming. The man depicted in the center of the poster is ubiquitous Universal contractee Harry Cording, enjoying the best publicity exposure of his career.*

Boris Karloff (left) is deliberately disfigured by crazed surgeon Bela Lugosi and forced into servitude in The Raven.

Bela Lugosi as the Poe-obsessed Dr. Vollin in The Raven.

elevated to the studio's directorial A-list? Because during the shoot Ulmer fell in love with a woman named Shirley Alexander, who happened to be the wife of Max Alexander, who happened to be Uncle Carl Laemmle's favorite nephew. Instead of receiving a star contract, Ulmer was banished from the lot.

Universal remade *The Black Cat* in title only in 1941, as a comedy/mystery, which featured Bela Lugosi in a small role.

THE RAVEN (1935)

Universal's third Poe-inspired film, *The Raven*, at least pays homage to the writer. Bela Lugosi plays Dr. Richard Vollin, a brilliant but bonkers surgeon who is so obsessed with the works of Poe that he has constructed replicas of the various torture devises described in Poe's stories in his basement. Vollin finds his "Lenore" in Jean Thatcher (Irene Ware), a young woman seriously injured in a car crash, whose life Vollin saves. But Jean's father, Judge Thatcher (Samuel S. Hinds), finds the middle-aged megalomaniac's attentions to his youthful daughter alarming.

Meanwhile a brutal criminal named Edmond Bateman (Boris Karloff) shows up at Vollin's house, begging him for a new face. It is not simply to escape detection; the scruffy, bearded Bateman believes that his antisocial actions are the result of his having been called "ugly" his entire life. The diabolical Vollin, seeing an opportunity to use the murderer to his own ends, gives Bateman a new face, but it is a shockingly disfigured one. Vollin then forces the criminal to do his bidding if he ever wants a normal face again. This includes abducting Judge Thatcher and strapping him to a table underneath a swinging pendulum. Now completely insane, Vollin threatens Jean as well, but Bateman has had enough. He releases the prisoners and is shot by Vollin for it, but still manages to thrust the mad doctor into one of his own Poe-etic torture devices before dying from the bullet wound.

Director Louis Friedlander (later Lew Landers) drew a Bogart-like, American-accented performance out of Karloff as the pre-operation Bateman, but after he's been turned into a human monster, Karloff goes into full *Frankenstein* mode, growling and gesturing like the Monster at his mirror reflection. Lugosi, meanwhile, was provided free reign to give the most maniacal performance of his career. And for once the two actors were accorded parity in above-the-title billing: "*Carl Laemmle presents Karloff and Lugosi.*" (The pair's next teaming, 1936's *The Invisible Ray*, was a stew of horror imagery, science fiction themes, and jungle adventure in which Karloff played the antisocial, megalomaniac scientist, while Lugosi took the role of his coolly rational nemesis.)

The grisliness of *The Raven* certainly frightened the British board of censors, which reacted by banning any kind of horror movies for a while.

BLACK FRIDAY (1940)

Black Friday is essentially a crime thriller with science fiction overtones. Boris Karloff (outfitted with an obvious wig, since his hair had not grown back after being shaved off for 1939's *Tower of London*) plays Dr. Ernest Sovac, who manages to save the life of his friend, Professor Kingsley (Stanley Ridges), by illegally transplanting the brain of a gangster named Red Canon into his head. Both men were seriously injured in the same

Stanley Ridges (left) plays kindly Professor Kingsley, who turns into the dangerous gangster Red Cannon, in Black Friday. *Originally, Boris Karloff (right) was supposed to play the dual role; why he did not remains unclear to this day.*

Despite his billing, Bela Lugosi played a small supporting role in Black Friday.

auto accident, which was caused by Cannon's gang, led by Eric Marney (Bela Lugosi), who wants to rub Cannon out and find his hidden stash of a half-million dollars. Sovac knows about the money, so when Cannon's consciousness and personality begin to emerge in the body of Kingsley, Sovac sees it as an opportunity to find out where the cash is hidden. But Cannon is more interested in extracting revenge on Marney and the gang. Kingsley/Cannon ends up dying by the hand of the man who "created" them, Sovac, who in turn goes to the electric chair for his actions.

Even though Karloff and Lugosi are top-billed, *Black Friday* belongs to Stanley Ridges, who expertly delineates the characters of the kindly, absent-minded Professor Kingsley, the cruel Red Cannon, and the uneasy combination of the two. But it was *Karloff* who had originally been cast as Kingsley, with Lugosi set to play Dr. Sovac. Why the switch? Curt Siodmak, who wrote the script with Eric Taylor, would later claim that Karloff felt he did not have the acting chops for the challenging role, but that rings a bit hollow. If anything, trying to twist his cultured accent around the tough-talking gangster's lines might have been the problem. For whatever reason, Karloff was shifted to the doctor role, and Lugosi moved down to the next largest part, which was the ambitious gang lieutenant, Marney, for which he was not well suited.

One long-standing legend is that Lugosi was actually hypnotized on the set by occultist Manly P. Hall, so that he really believed he was suffocating for a scene in which Marney is locked inside a closet. It's an intriguing story, but *Black Friday*'s director Arthur Lubin later acknowledged that it was nothing more than a publicity stunt.

Black Friday represented the last time Universal teamed Karloff and Lugosi (they would work together two more times for RKO Pictures). Over the years, a wealth of speculation has arisen concerning how well Karloff and Lugosi actually got along…if at all. The truth is while they were never close friends, they worked together amicably and demonstrated a professional regard for one another. They each had pet peeves about each other—Lugosi was annoyed when filming stopped precisely at four o'clock for Karloff's tea breaks, and Karloff had little patience for Lugosi's fears that he would try to upstage him—but they also had several things in common. Both men were passionate advocates of the fledgling Screen Actors Guild at a time when unionism was a risky cause for any actor in Hollywood to champion, and both became first-time fathers in their fifties, when their children were born only ten months apart in 1938. While in later years Lugosi would privately vent resentment toward Karloff's more viable career, when they were together, they were nothing less than pros.

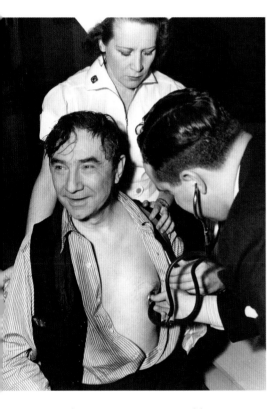

Bela Lugosi is examined by a doctor and an RN after being "hypnotized" for a scene in Black Friday*. It was really nothing more than a publicity stunt, probably to make up for Lugosi's relegation to a minor role.*

MAN MADE MONSTER (1941)

When a bus crashes into an electrical tower, only one man, Dan McCormick (Lon Chaney Jr.), survives. Dr. John Lawrence (Samuel S. Hinds) is puzzled until he learns that McCormick is "Dynamo Dan," a carnival performer who shoots voltage through his body as part of his act. Dan claims his act is largely faked but Dr. Lawrence believes he might actually be immune to electricity. He asks the young man if he can perform some tests on him.

Unfortunately for Dan, Lawrence's associate, Dr. Paul Rigas (Lionel Atwill) suffers from delusions of grandeur, believing that he can join the pantheon of great scientists by creating a race of electro-atomic super humans. Realizing Dan is the perfect subject, he secretly begins to bombard him with maximum doses of electricity until Dan becomes a glowing, obedient monster. Rigas instructs Dan to kill Dr. Lawrence and then take the rap for it. But when the state tries to execute him in the chair, all they do is create an unstoppable juggernaut! Dan breaks out of prison and kills Rigas (who is then attempting to kill Lawrence's niece, who had discovered Rigas's perfidy), and then dies by "shorting out" on a fence wire.

Man Made Monster grew out of a treatment called The Electric Man by Harry Essex, Sid Schwartz, and Len Golos, which was first put forth as another joint vehicle for Karloff and Lugosi. Instead it was tailored specifically for Lon Chaney Jr., to the point of making Dynamo Dan a more intelligent version of Chaney's Lennie character (in one scene, Dan asks about the fate of a lab rabbit—rabbits, of course, being Lennie's obsession in Of Mice and Men). Filmed very cheaply, the picture was also a test to see if Chaney warranted a studio contract, and in that regard, its success was obvious, so much so that the working title, The Mysterious Dr. R, was changed so as to throw the emphasis onto Chaney's character, not Atwill's.

HORROR ISLAND (1941)

Short, fast, and taking no prisoners, Horror Island is a comedic haunted house murder mystery, featuring a mysterious caped figure called "The Phantom," with a Ten Little Indians–style subplot and a pirate treasure hunt thrown in for good measure. Had it run longer than an hour, producer Ben Pivar and director George Waggner probably would have found a place for a musical number.

The film begins dockside, where struggling entrepreneur Bill Martin (Dick Foran) and his dopey sidekick Stuff Oliver (Roscoe Ates) spend most of their time dodging creditors. Suddenly people start showing interest in an old deserted island that Bill inherited from his grandfather, on which sits an allegedly haunted castle. When a garrulous peg-legged sailor called Skipper (Leo Carrillo) appears with half of a map purporting to show where the treasure of Sir Henry Morgan is buried on the island, Bill decides it's time for a visit, particularly since the other half is owned by The Phantom.

Along with a diverse group of treasure-hunting clients, Bill, Stuff, and Skipper head out for the island. Unfortunately, the Phantom beats them there, and once the group is settled in the eerie "haunted" castle, he begins killing the guests one by one. That's bad enough, but when the Phantom himself turns up murdered (he's really an old shipmate of Skipper's named "Panama Pete"), Bill and his remaining guests realize that the real murderer is one of them! Ultimately, the killer is detected and caught, and is foiled by one of Captain Morgan's booby traps.

Horror Island's production values far exceeded its actual budget, thanks to its borrowing the elaborate castle sets built for 1939's Tower of London, Universal's horror-coated treatment of the Richard III story. If nothing else, Horror Island might hold a Hollywood speed record: filming began on March 3, 1941, and the finished picture was in theaters as part of a double bill with Man Made Monster on March 28, less than four weeks later.

Lon Chaney Jr. (left) gets a charge out of mad doctor Lionel Atwill's lab in Man Made Monster.

Leo Carrillo encounters "The Phantom" in the comedy/horror/mystery Horror Island.

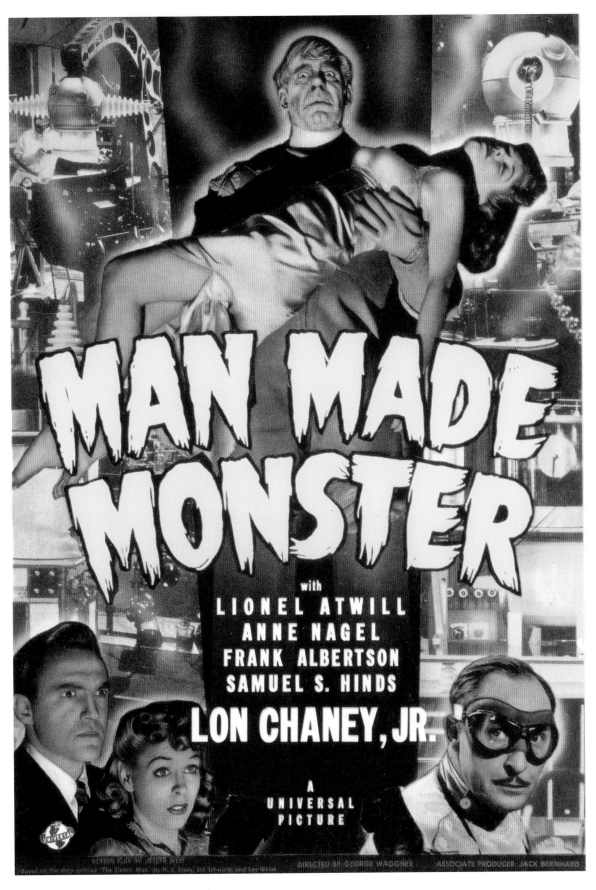

Man Made Monster *was Lon Chaney Jr.'s test film for a star contract with Universal, and also one of the last times he was billed as "Jr." (Compare this poster with the nearly identical one for* The Mummy's Hand *on page 112).*

The Phantom (not of the Opera, though they clearly use the same haberdasher) terrorizes Peggy Moran in Horror Island.

Mad doctor George Zucco (standing) gets zombified assistant David Bruce to do his bidding in The Mad Ghoul.

NIGHT MONSTER (1942)

Essentially an old dark house mystery with an eerie otherworldly twist, *Night Monster* concerns wealthy paraplegic Kurt Ingston (Ralph Morgan), who has holed himself up in a sinister mansion called The Towers with an eccentric assembly of people that includes Ingston's unstable sister Margaret (Fay Helm), a female psychiatrist, Dr. Lynne Harper (Irene Hervey), and the mystical Agor Singh (Nils Asther), who has been teaching old Kurt in the Eastern philosophy of mind-over-matter. To demonstrate his mental powers, Singh telepathically conjures up the ghastly image of a bleeding skeleton in the drawing room!

Also present (along with mysterious butler Rolf, played by Bela Lugosi) are three doctors who treated, but could not cure, Ingston. When the doctors turn up murdered, each one's face twisted in an expression of horror and lying next to a fresh blood stain, there is no shortage of suspects. Amateur sleuth Dick Baldwin (Don Porter) believes the killer is Ingston, suspecting that the recluse is merely faking his paralysis. But Ingston is not simply paralyzed, his legs have been amputated. How could he be the horrible, caped figure with the twisted, bleeding limbs, who is spotted prowling the property? How *indeed*?

Bela Lugosi gets top billing in *Night Monster* (which was originally titled *House of Mystery*), though his role as the butler is very much a thankless supporting one. Second-billed Lionel Atwill's part, as one of the three doctors who are quickly dispatched, is not much better. Why Lugosi was not cast as the sinister Agor Singh, instead of the bland Nils Asther, is the film's *real* mystery.

THE MAD GHOUL (1943)

While Lionel Atwill tended to have a lock on mad scientist roles at Universal, it was not an exclusive one: there was also George Zucco. In *The Mad Ghoul*, Zucco stars as science professor Dr. Alfred Morris whose research into the ancient Mayans has led him to conclude they created a kind of gas that turned their enemies into zombies. Morris asks bright medical student Ted Allison (David Bruce) to assist him with his research, and Ted agrees, not realizing that Morris is going to expose him to the gas, which turns him into a wizened slave with no mind of his own.

Having discovered that the antidote for zombification is fluid from the human heart—which is why the Mayans had a penchant for removing the hearts from their victims during ritual sacrifice—Morris instructs Ted to obtain hearts, either through grave robbing or murder. Police begin to realize that these killings, dubbed by the press the "Mad Ghoul murders," take place in every town in which singer Isobel Lewis (Evelyn Ankers) is performing, and theorize that the killer is someone she knows. The truth is even more disturbing: both Morris and Ted are obsessed with the singer, but she is really in love with her accompanist Eric (Turhan Bey). Isobel suspects that Ted is the killer, since he has enough skill with a scalpel to surgically remove a heart.

Mad Dr. Morris now orders Ted to kill Eric and then himself, thus taking the entire blame for the killings. But in his last rational moment, Ted sets it up so that Morris is exposed to the gas. He then coerces the police to shoot him before he can harm Eric, and leaves a letter for Isobel explaining everything.

A special kind of gas turned David Bruce into a shriveled zombie in The Mad Ghoul. *He unshrivelled when the gas wore off.*

Evelyn Ankers had at one time been a radio singer, but had never sung on film. She was hoping to do so in *The Mad Ghoul*, but the brevity of production—two-and-a-half weeks—left no time for her to prerecord the songs, leaving her to lip-synch to existing recordings. David Bruce, who spent much of the film shriveled by Jack Pierce's cotton-and-spirit-gum mask, was an appealing leading man whose career never gelled. By the mid-1950s he was out of Hollywood altogether and died in 1976 at the age of 62. Bruce was the father of actress/chanteuse Amanda McBroom.

THE STRANGE DOOR (1951) and **THE BLACK CASTLE** (1952)
Boris Karloff returned to Universal-International in the early 1950s for two gothic period melodramas that stand as the last traditional horror films (or at least *horrific* films, since there are no supernatural elements) the studio ever produced. First was *The Strange Door*, based on the Robert Louis Stevenson story "The Sire de Maletroit's Door," in which Charles Laughton plays the mad, bad, and dangerous-to-know Sire, who has dedicated his life to ruining the existence of his brother, whom he believes betrayed him, and his niece, who is the daughter of the woman he loved. Karloff, reunited with Laughton for the first time since *The Old Dark House*, plays a sympathetic servant named Voltan. Replete with shadowy passageways, creepy graveyards, murder, torture, and debauchery, as well as the spectacle of Laughton at his absolute hammiest (which is saying a *lot*), *The Strange Door* competes with *The Old Dark House* in terms of pure, ripe melodrama, though without the intentional humor.

Boris Karloff (left) and Charles Laughton in The Strange Door, *based on a Robert Louis Stevenson story. Laughton made only two Universal Horror appearances (this film and* The Old Dark House*), though his wife, Elsa Lanchester, gained immortality as the Bride of Frankenstein.*

The Black Castle* features both Karloff and Lon Chaney Jr., but neither is the main attraction: that is the sadistic, one-eyed hunter Count von Bruno, played by Stephen McNally, who engages in a deadly cat-and-mouse game with swashbuckling hero Sir Ronald Burton (Richard Greene), after Burton journeys to von Bruno's castle to find out why two of his old friends have disappeared there. Karloff plays a sinister court physician named Dr. Meissen and Chaney takes the role of a hulking, mute, murderous thug named Gargon, who comes to a particularly nasty end in a pit of starving alligators.

Fans of Universal's 1940's horror cycle will recognize the Tower of London façade, which was used for the exteriors of the castles in both films, and also many of Frank Skinner's and Hans J. Salter's musical motifs, reused to good effect.

TARANTULA (1955)
With its gargantuan, marauding arachnid scuttling across the Arizona desert, *Tarantula* falls more into the science fiction monster category that producer William Alland and director Jack Arnold established at Universal in the mid-1950s, and would continue throughout the decade with such films as *The Deadly Mantis* (1957). Even so, it has enough elements of classic Universal Horror—man-made monsters created by a scientists tampering with the unknown—to be considered something of a sci-fi/horror hybrid.

Dr. Deemer, played by Leo G. Carroll, is not exactly mad, but he is a bit careless. His quest for a radioactive growth nutrient ends up creating not just the title creature, but when ingested by humans results in immediate deformation through a rapidly advancing case of the glandular

Giant bugs were the
monsters of note in
the 1950s.

Leo G. Carroll,
depicted in the
advanced stages of
acromegalia, with
Mara Corday in
Tarantula.

Eddie Parker as the diseased Dr. Lund in Tarantula. *The mask Parker is wearing is the same one he wore while playing Mr. Hyde in* Abbott and Costello Meet Dr. Jekyll and Mr. Hyde, *two years earlier.*

affliction acromegalia. Deemers' two colleagues at the lab, Dr. Jacobs and Dr. Lund, are both turned into human monsters because of this, as ultimately is Deemer himself. What really ties *Tarantula* into Universal Horror, though, is the grim fact that acromegalia (also called acromegaly) was the disease suffered in real life by Rondo Hatton.

Stuntman Eddie Parker played the nonspeaking roles of Dr. Jacobs and Dr. Lund, wearing a different rubber mask for each. Parker became known as "The Universal Monster" because he had at one time or other appeared as every one of the studio's golden age horror icons. He doubled both Lon Chaney Jr. and Bela Lugosi as the Frankenstein Monster, and Chaney as the Wolf Man and the Mummy, and often turned up in bit parts of his own (he played a Nazi soldier in *Invisible Agent*). Parker had started at Universal in the 1930s, during which time he doubled Buster Crabbe in the *Flash Gordon* serials, and remained active virtually right up to his death in 1960 at the age of 59.

Eddie Parker was not the only actor unrecognizable in *Tarantula*; there was a young studio contractee playing the leader of a jet squadron, whose face was obscured by his helmet. You can't tell, but it's Clint Eastwood.

THE MOLE PEOPLE (1956)

"I think if you'll study this picture and think about it when it's over, you'll realize this is something more than just a story told; it's a fable with a meaning and a significance for you and for me in the Twentieth Century."

The above exhortation—as spoken in a prologue by Dr. Frank Baxter, a University of Southern California professor who appeared in a series of educational films in the late 1950s—would indicate that this is a monster movie with a message. And looking past the obvious thrills of the story, which involves the discovery of a lost race of people descended from the ancient Sumerians who are now living in the center of the earth, a meaning does indeed emerge.

When an archaeological team led by Dr. Roger Bentley (John Agar) discovers the ruins of a Sumerian temple to Ishtar atop Mount Kuhitara, they subsequently learn that a long-lost race descended from the Sumerians is living far underneath the surface of the earth, so hidden from the sun's rays that they have become albinos, intolerant to light. With them is a secondary race: hideous, hunchbacked, bug-eyed creatures that the neo-Sumerians call "beasts of the dark" and use as slaves. Particularly of interest to Bentley is the beautiful Adal (Cynthia Patrick), who is also treated like a slave because she is "marked," being a different shade than the ultra-white-skinned race. Since she is not harmed by the sun, Bentley takes her with him when he escapes, only to lose her again when she is killed by falling debris from a sudden earthquake.

Cut off the prologue and *The Mole People* is a pretty straightforward monster film, with some good, creepy creatures whose ability to emerge from and disappear into sand pits is highly effective. But with the prologue and its promise of a message, one can only interpret the film as a condemnation of racism. Every character in the netherworld is marked by their color: the neo-Sumerians are so white they glow in the dark, while the enslaved mole people (who are never identified as such outside of the title) are dark-skinned. In between is Adal (whose name in the script and credits is "Adad"), neither white nor dark-skinned, but dark enough to be shunned.

The Mole People are among the most memorable
creations to come from Bud Westmore's tenure as
head of makeup for Universal. Here a mole person
(probably Eddie Parker) carries Cynthia Patrick.

1830-25

Seeing the star of The Deadly Mantis *was enough to make anyone pray.*

Even though they come up from and go into holes in the ground, the hideous title creatures of The Mole People *are never actually referred to as "mole people" in the film.*

Lazlo Gorog's script originally had Bentley pull Adal/Adad to safety during the earthquake. Why the ending was changed so that she was killed as soon as she reached the surface of the earth remains a mystery (another message, perhaps?).

Far easier to explain is why the walls of the underground Sumerian palace are decorated with Egyptian hieroglyphics: *The Mole People* was shot on leftover tomb sets from *Abbott and Costello Meet the Mummy*.

MONSTER ON THE CAMPUS (1958)

At least marginally, *Monster on the Campus* is Universal's nod to the then-hot trend for teen-themed horror pictures. Dunsfield University paleontology professor Dr. Donald Blake (Arthur Franz) has just scored a scientific coup by obtaining the body of a coelacanth, a throwback to a prehistoric fish, once thought extinct. But its bacteria, which has been super-charged with gamma radiation, is still very much alive. Blake accidentally infects himself by cutting his hand on the fish's teeth and regresses into a brutally vicious Neanderthal man that goes on a murder spree. The ever-vigilant press dubs the mystery killer "The Beast of Dunsfield," and since the killings always seem to revolve around Blake's whereabouts, the police believe someone is trying to frame him for the murders. With time, however, Blake comes to realize that *he* is the beast, turning into the ape man whenever he comes into contact with the bacteria. Having obtained photographic proof that he is the killer, he deliberately transforms in front of the police, knowing they will kill him.

Eddie Parker once again played the monster in a rubber mask and body padding, but the mask itself, created by Bud Westmore's makeup department, was nowhere near as convincing as the ape woman makeup for the Paula Dupree films 15 years earlier. In one close-up, the bottom of the mask is painfully obvious, its edge moving independently of Parker's hair-covered neck. The final transformation scene of ape man back to human doctor was carefully shot, but Arthur Franz himself was involved in only the last few transitional stages. The rest were done with gradations of makeup applied to a cast of his face.

A variation on the Wolf Man theme, *Monster on the Campus* was the penultimate monster movie produced by Universal in the black-and-white era. *The Leech Woman*, released in 1960, would be the official swan song, but by then the horror had shifted to television, primarily through "Thriller," an NBC anthology hosted by Boris Karloff, co-produced by Revue Studios, Universal's television arm.

Stuntman Eddie Parker filled in for star Arthur Franz as the Neanderthal man in Monster on the Campus. *The catch-of-the-day this time is Joanna Moore.*

The mutant from This Island Earth *(1955) represented the full melding of horror and science fiction.*

Colleen Gray in The Leech Woman, *unofficially the last film of the golden age of Universal Horror.*

Bacteria from the coelacanth fish causes every creature to regress to prehistoric proportions, even a dragonfly, in Monster on the Campus.

18 SPOTLIGHT:
JAMES WHALE

If any one man can be said to have established the pattern for Universal Horror throughout the 1930s, it is British-born director James Whale. Tod Browning may have gotten there first with *Dracula*, but it was Whale's themes, motifs, and quirky vision that other filmmakers tried to duplicate in their own work.

James Whale was born in 1889 to a working class family in Dudley, England. An artistic child with a sense of destiny, he contemplated a career as an art teacher before hearing the siren song of the theater. After serving in World War I (part of which time was spent as a prisoner-of-war), he entered the professional theater as an actor, designer, and director. His breakout success came through his direction of a 1928 London production of R. C. Sherriff's intense war drama *Journey's End*, which went on to spawn a larger production that become a major West End hit.

Whale came to Hollywood in 1929, where his first notable success was directing the dialogue sequences for the talkie version of Howard Hughes's 1930 blockbuster *Hell's Angels.* He followed that with the film version of *Journey's End* starring Colin Clive, before directing another drama with a wartime setting, *Waterloo Bridge* for Universal, which was a hit in 1931. Whale's reputation as director was firmly established, and he was now on the Universal lot, all ingredients that led to his next project, the one for which he would be forever known, *Frankenstein.*

Jumping into a project and a genre that was so far removed from the war dramas, for which he had become known, probably seemed to Whale like a way to break any potential typecasting. He approached the project in a straightforward manner, rarely indulging himself in the bits of bizarre humor that would increasingly fill his later horror films and as a re-sult created not only a huge commercial hit for the studio at the time, but an enduring classic.

Whale followed up *Frankenstein* with *The Old Dark House*, a send-up of the "stranded-for-the-night-in-a-spooky-house" genre that even then was becoming pretty threadbare. It was also the first film in which Whale seemed to feel comfortable enough to reveal his strange sense of humor and character. *The Invisible Man* (1933) continued in this vein (though not quite so blatantly) and through it Whale would introduce several stock

James Whale takes advice from Boris Karloff's lighting stand-in (made from a lighting stand), on the set of Bride of Frankenstein.

*James Whale and old friend
Ernest Thesiger take tea on
the crypt set from* Bride
of Frankenstein.

characters that would eventually become archetypes within the world of Universal Horror, chiefly inept, broadly played cockney policemen, and eccentric, shrieking women.

It would take 1935's *Bride of Frankenstein* to give full reign to Whale's sense of melodrama, comedy, sentimentality, and irony—sometimes all at the same time—iced by a heavy layer of camp.

On a personal level, Whale never felt the need to closet himself when it came to his homosexuality, and one does not have to dig too deeply to find traces of gay sensibility in his films. Some latter-day film historians have argued that Frankenstein's Monster, particularly how the innocent creature is abused by society, is a projection of Whale's feelings about his homosexuality, and that he himself identified with the Monster.

In truth, however, Whale seems to have identified more with Dr. Frankenstein than with his creation. That sense of greatness that Whale felt as a young man never left him—it only increased. During the shooting of *Frankenstein* Whale seemed to regard Boris Karloff as his own "creation," having pulled him from obscurity and delivered to him the role of a lifetime. Once the film was released and Karloff suddenly became the center of attention, Whale reacted with jealousy. Just as Dr. Frankenstein had lost all control of his creation, Whale's felt his "creation" was now supplanting him in terms of credit for the picture's success. Although the director and actor worked amicably for two more pictures, Whale rarely missed an opportunity to disparage Karloff, dismissing him as "a truck driver" who had suddenly become overly taken with himself (a judgment shared by no one else who worked with the actor).

After *Bride of Frankenstein* Whale was asked to develop the script for *Dracula's Daughter* with his old colleague R. C. Sherriff, though the unacceptable script turned in by the two may have been an example of self-sabotage to get out of the project. Radically shifting direction again, he took on a remake of the Broadway musical *Show Boat*. Whale managed to announce his presence through some bizarre, expressionistic touches, particularly during the *Ol' Man River* montage sequence.

For a variety of reasons, James Whale's career fell apart as rapidly as it had risen. He would go on to make only a few more films, including 1939's *The Man in the Iron Mask* and the unintentionally hilarious jungle film *Green Hell* the following year, before disappearing from Hollywood completely. He occasionally returned to the theater, but spent most of his later years painting and throwing parties. Some have sought to characterize his decline as an example of ostracism by the film industry because of his lifestyle, but one also has to take into account his vision of himself as an *artiste* in a commercial town. Whale thought himself above studio interference and direction, which resulted in a reputation for being difficult and financially profligate. Neither did his autocratic manner engender love amongst his casts. "Away from the set he was charming and relaxed, but back on the set, the next morning, it was 'Ach-tung' time," actress Gloria Stuart said of him.

James Whale was found dead, fully dressed, in his swimming pool on May 29, 1957. For decades it was a true Hollywood mystery: had it been suicide? Murder? A tragic accident? The mystery was solved 30 years later when Whale's suicide note was finally made public. It revealed a depressed, ailing man who was fearful of what the future held.

Abbott and Costello met the Monster (Glenn Strange), Dracula (Bela Lugosi), and the Wolf Man (Lon Chaney Jr.), but no one actually named "Frankenstein" in Abbott and Costello Meet Frankenstein.

19

ABBOTT AND COSTELLO

For most the 1940s, Hollywood's biggest attractions were not virile, toothy leading men, nor glamorous leading ladies, nor even monsters. The Kings of Hollywood for wartime audiences were a fast-talking slicker named Bud Abbott and a baby-faced clown named Lou Costello.

Bud Abbott and Lou Costello were already experienced burlesque performers in 1936 when they decided to team up, with Abbott as the straight man and Costello as the comic. They quickly moved out of burlesque and into nightclubs and radio, becoming stars through appearances on *The Kate Smith Show*, where they introduced their signature routine, "Who's On First?," and even onto the Broadway stage.

Arriving at Universal City in 1940, Abbott and Costello appeared in supporting roles in the romantic comedy *One Night in the Tropics*, which led to their first starring vehicle, *Buck Privates* (1941), today a cinematic time capsule, but a blockbuster back then. The team started turning out films so quickly that the one-liner of the time was, "It's slow in Hollywood…Abbott and Costello haven't made a picture all day." They applied their trademark fast-talking nonsense to every genre from Westerns to gangster films to horror. Among the latter was 1946's *The Time of Their Lives*, a haunted house comedy involving genuine ghosts (one of which was played by Costello), which incongruously featured one of the eeriest séance scenes ever put on film.

As bright as their stars shone, by the war's end they were in danger of burning out through overexposure and changing public tastes. Then in 1948 Universal-International (a merger that had occurred two years before) hit on the idea of teaming the pair with its classic monsters, who had themselves been on hiatus for years, and everything changed. The result, *Abbott and Costello Meet Frankenstein*, is generally considered Abbott and Costello's all-time best film (though ironically, Costello initially fought the idea, thinking it wasn't funny).

Caring not a whit for continuity under the circumstances, the studio brought back Lon Chaney Jr. to reprise his signature role as the doomed Larry Talbot, Glenn Strange as the Monster, and Bela Lugosi to take on the role of Dracula for the first time in 17 years, and only the second time on film. A female Dr. Frankenstein of sorts was introduced in the person of Dr. Sandra Mornay, played by Yugoslavian actress Lenore Aubert, who, within the context of the film, is working with Dracula to restore the Monster back to strength to make him the vampire's slave. But part of the deal is to replace his brain (presumably still Ygor's) with one more easily controllable, namely that of Wilbur Grey (Costello).

Larry Talbot enters the picture as a result of having tracked Dracula from Europe. He informs Wilbur—who has *no* idea what is going on—and his friend Chick Young (Abbott) that the mysterious European calling himself "Dr. Lahos" is really Dracula, and his intentions are not good. Of course, neither of them realizes that Talbot has problems of his own every cycle of the full moon. Before Wilbur's brain can be transplanted into the Monster, though, Dracula and the Wolf Man battle to the death, and the escaped Monster is destroyed by fire (again). Now free of monsters, Wilbur and Chick breathe a sigh of relief, only to be greeted by the Invisible Man (the voice of Vincent Price) who regrets missing all the fun!

Directed by Charles T. Barton and shot by Charles Van Enger, who had filmed the original *The Phantom of the Opera, Abbott and Costello Meet Frankenstein* revitalized the careers of the comedy team, and reminded audiences that the classic monsters were still viable. The comedy plays against the backdrop of a classic horror film so well because at no point are the monsters themselves open to ridicule. In fact, the scene of Dracula, in extreme close-up, telepathically calling for Wilbur, backed by eerie music, is as effective as any Bela Lugosi ever played. (Barton and Van Enger were responsible for one major flub, though, showing Dracula reflected in a mirror as he attacks Sandra.)

By the time Chaney, Lugosi, and Strange reported back for duty at Universal's makeup room, Jack P. Pierce was gone, having been replaced by Hamilton "Bud" Westmore, a scion of the movie capital's first family of makeup. From the 1930s through the 1950s, just about every major studio had a Westmore brother on staff. Bud Westmore and his assistant Jack Kevan instituted more modern techniques using foam rubber appliances, which saved hours in makeup preparation. That proved to be a good thing for *Abbott and Costello Meets Frankenstein*, since Lon Chaney Jr. was pressed into double duty in the film to play the Monster after Glenn Strange broke his ankle in one scene—the shot in which the Monster hurls Sandra through the window. This was not the only Monster-related injury: for the scene in which the Monster's massive fist crashes through a door and hits Wibur in the face, Costello stood too close and really took the punch as the cameras rolled. His resultant split lip can clearly be seen in his tête-à-tête with Lenore Aubert, which occurs earlier in the picture.

The success of *Abbott and Costello Meet Frankenstein* convinced Universal that it was onto something, so they looked around for more potential meetings with monsters. In 1949, Abbott and Costello encountered Boris Karloff in the clumsily and inaccurately titled *Abbott and Costello Meet the Killer Boris Karloff*, which was not so much a horror

Abbott and Costello Meet Frankenstein not only brought the monsters back to Universal, it revitalized the comedy team's career as well.

Universal makeup man Jack Kevan can barely reach the neck of Glenn Strange (who stood 6'4" when not in costume).

In the context of the story of Abbott and Costello Meet Frankenstein, *Dracula (Bela Lugosi) is in control of the Monster (Glenn Strange).*

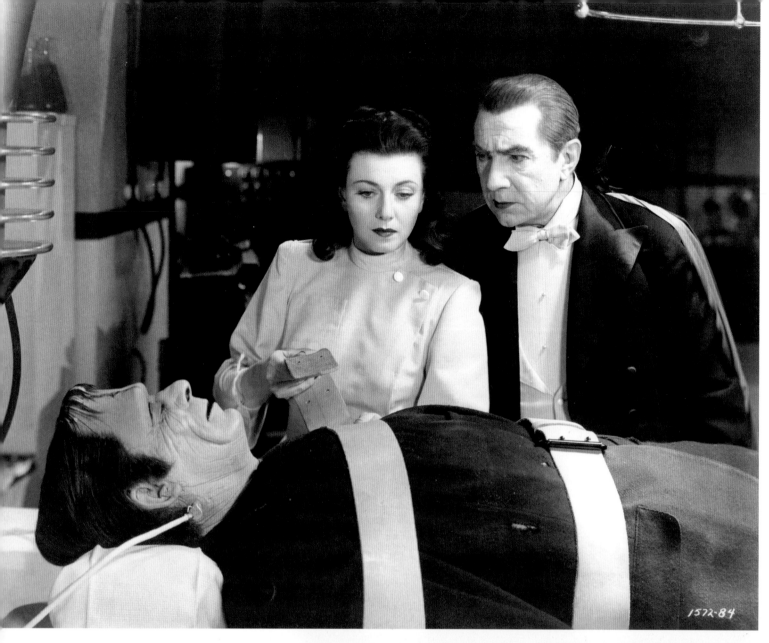

*"No more transformations!" Lon
Chaney Jr. (right) "gets tough"
with Charles T. Barton, the
director of* Abbott and Costello
Meet Frankenstein.

For the first time in the Frankenstein saga, the mad doctor of Abbott and Costello Meet Frankenstein *is a woman: Dr. Sandra Mornay (Lenore Aubert), shown between the Monster (Glenn Strange) and Dracula (Bela Lugosi).*

picture as a send-up of noirish mysteries. Then in 1951, the team struck gold again with *Abbott and Costello Meet the Invisible Man*.

The invisible one in this film is not any of the previous ones, rather it is Tommy Nelson (Arthur Franz), a boxer who ends up taking the rap for the murder of his manager, and uses the dangerous invisibility formula as a way of eluding the police. Fledgling detectives Bud Alexander and Lou Francis (Abbott and Costello—*Bud Alexander* and *Lou Francis* being the comics' actual first and middle names) are trying to help Tommy clear himself, but everyone runs afoul of a gangster named Morgan (Sheldon Leonard), who is the real killer. Complicating the process is the fact that, as before, the effects of the invisibility serum are causing Tommy to suffer from megalomania.

In the kind of plot contrivance that can only exist in comedies of this time, Costello, with the invisible Tommy's help, becomes an overnight prizefight sensation called "Louie the Looper" as part of the plan to trap Morgan and reveal him as the murderer.

The film's excellent special effects were handled by David S. Horsley, who had been John P. Fulton's assistant going all the way back to *Bride of Frankenstein* (Horsley had also worked on some clever invisibility "ghost" gags in *The Time of Their Lives*). In once scene where Abbott, Costello, and Tommy go into a nightclub, Costello frantically has to cover for the fact that a plate of spaghetti is being eaten by no one visible.

Abbott and Costello's next excursion into horror utilized a classic character that had never before been exploited by Universal, at least under his own name—Dr. Jekyll. Both *Black Friday* and *House of Dracula* had played on the basic theme of the duality of man—good and evil—as had every werewolf movie, but in a more extreme way. But Robert Louis Stevenson's character had not appeared as himself until Boris Karloff donned the Victorian cape and top hat for 1953's *Abbott and Costello Meet Dr. Jekyll and Mr. Hyde*. Karloff, however, only played the Jekyll half, and the usually beneficent character had a decidedly sinister twist; outwardly respected by London society, Karloff's Jekyll is more of a mad doctor who secretly harbors an unhealthy desire for his beautiful young ward, played by Helen Westcott.

Boris Karloff played a sinister swami in the noirish comedy mystery Abbott and Costello Meet the Killer Boris Karloff (the unwieldy title is taken from the credits, which run Karloff's billing into the title itself).

Karloff's participation in the dual role ended with the transformation scenes, which were accomplished in Wolf Man fashion, through a progressive series of makeup stages that were optically dissolved from one to the next. But once Hyde was in his full, hideous glory (in a hairy rubber mask that looked like an ape man), he was played by the ubiquitous Eddie Parker. The mask Parker wore as Mr. Hyde, incidentally, was reused for his role as the deformed, dying scientist Eric Jacobs in 1955's *Tarantula*.

Two more classic monsters appear in *Abbott and Costello Meet Dr. Jekyll and Mr. Hyde*, albeit briefly: the Frankenstein Monster and Dracula. They show up as wax figures in a museum, though when Costello (who with Abbott is playing an American policeman in London), accidentally electrifies them, they begin to move. Both monsters were played by unidentified extras, though the Dracula figure faintly resembles a mustachioed Bela Lugosi.

Bud and Lou got even more wrapped up in their work in 1955's *Abbott and Costello Meet the Mummy*. This time, though, the Mummy is not Im-Ho-Tep or Kharis, but *Klaris*. Abbott and Costello (whose names in

Lon Chaney Jr. and Glenn Strange clown around on the set of Abbott and Costello Meet Frankenstein. *While the monsters were played straight in the film, off-camera was a different story.*

Since invisibility cannot be photographed on the set, the Universal publicity department faked the stills for the Invisible Man films, sometimes using preexisting photos of actors not in the picture. This transparent figure promoting Abbott and Costello Meet the Invisible Man *looks like a double exposure of David Bruce from* The Mad Ghoul!

The only official appearance of Robert Louis Stevenson's famous dual act in Universal Horror was Abbott and Costello Meet Dr. Jekyll and Mr. Hyde.

Bandaged Arthur Franz is flanked by Bud and Lou in Abbott and Costello Meet the Invisible Man.

the script and credits are "Pete Patterson" and "Freddie Franklin" respectively, but who are simply "Bud" and "Lou" on the soundtrack) are broke and stuck in Egypt—not unlike Steve Banning and Babe Jenson in *The Mummy's Hand*—and in the process of trying to get back to the United States end up as the chief suspects for the murder of archaeologist Dr. Zoomer (Kurt Katch). If that isn't bad enough, they fall into the clutches of a cult that is keeping Klaris (Eddie Parker, here billed as "Edwin") alive to guard a hidden treasure in the mummy's tomb, and a team of crooks led by sexy Madame Rontru (Marie Windsor) who is out to find the treasure for herself.

Eddie Parker's Klaris seems like a combination of all the monsters he had played at one time or other rolled into one. He has all the physical trappings of a mummy, but he also stalks like the Frankenstein Monster and growls like the Wolf Man. His backward-leaning stance with his hands held up in front of him makes his mummy look like he's a bandaged biker riding an invisible chopper. Still, Parker was provided exactly what the film needed: a threatening presence off which Abbott and Costello could do terrified takes.

As directed by Charles Lamont (who had also helmed *Abbott and Costello Meet the Invisible Man* and *Abbott and Costello Meet Dr. Jekyll and Mr. Hyde*), *Abbott and Costello Meet the Mummy* contains all the inherent logic of a burlesque sketch, a format that the team had been reviving for the last few years on the television show *The Colgate Comedy Hour*, onto which they brought several of the old monsters. In one memorable 1951 episode, Lon Chaney Jr. donned the Frankenstein Monster costume to dance a jitterbug with Costello during a spoof of Bizet's *Carmen* (it made sense in context, sort of). In a 1954 episode, Costello encountered not only the Monster, this time played by Glenn Strange, but also the Creature From the Black Lagoon, in his very first public appearance.

Abbott and Costello Meet the Mummy garnered good reviews, but did not deliver much voltage into Bud and Lou's faltering careers. It would be the last film they made for Universal, and also the last film to feature a golden age monster in any variation from the studio. Abbott and Costello split up in 1957. Lou Costello enjoyed a very brief solo career before dying in 1959 at the age of 53. Bud Abbott worked only occasionally after his partner's death, passing away in 1974 at age 78.

Abbott and Costello were not the only Universal comedy team to encounter a classic monster, though: the no-holds-barred comedy team of Ole Olsen and Chic Johnson managed to include the Frankenstein Monster in the 1941 film version of their legendary Broadway revue *Hellzapoppin'*. Fulfilling the promise made in the film's theme song that "Anything can happen, and it probably will!" the Monster, in the person of stuntman Dale Van Sickel (Eddie Parker must have been busy that day) shows up for a gag cameo.

Near the end of his life, Lon Chaney Jr. groused that Abbott and Costello had ruined horror films and some over the years have agreed. But one can argue equally well that neither Bud and Lou nor Universal should be blamed for following the changing taste of the audience, presenting the old monsters in a way that postwar moviegoers—whose willingness to suspend disbelief was being relegated to the realm of comedy—could appreciate.

Eddie Parker (left) as Mr. Hyde and Boris Karloff (right) as Dr. Jekyll in Abbott and Costello Meet Dr. Jekyll and Mr. Hyde.

Monsters were not exclusively reserved for Abbott and Costello at Universal: the studio's other 1940s comedy team, Chic Johnson (left) and Ole Olsen (right) are stalked by a Mummy in 1944's Ghost Catchers. *Even though Lon Chaney Jr. was in the cast, this Mummy is actor Leo Carrillo.*

Universal's new makeup chief Bud Westmore (right) shows the Mr. Hyde mask to Boris Karloff on the set of Abbott and Costello Meet Dr. Jekyll and Mr. Hyde. *Karloff would only appear as Hyde at the end of the transformation sequences, after which Eddie Parker took over the role.*

The Monster and Dracula make cameo appearances as wax figures (but played by actors) in Abbott and Costello Meet Dr. Jekyll and Mr. Hyde. *The identities of the actors are unknown, though the man in the Monster makeup might be stuntman Dale Van Sickel.*

Having met Dracula, the Wolf Man, Frankenstein's Monster, the Invisible Man, and Dr. Jekyll and Mr.Hyde, you'd think that Lou Costello would stop looking in coffins. Here he encounters Klaris (Eddie Parker) in Abbott and Costello Meet the Mummy.

20 SPOTLIGHT:
ROGUE'S GALLERY

While Universal Pictures never had an official stock company for its horror films, its repeated use of familiar faces, some of whom were on the studio's roster of contract players (meaning those small part actors who were on full-time salary and who were likely to pop up fleetingly in virtually any film the studio made), elevated the films to a kind of repertory status. Below are some of the most frequently seen actors in the realm of Universal Horror.

EDWARD VAN SLOAN (1881–1964)
Edward Van Sloan always managed to project a European air, even though he was born in Minnesota, and always seemed old, even before he really was. He was most often cast as the scholarly nemesis of the monster, such

as Professor Van Helsing (a role he had played on Broadway, opposite Bela Lugosi) in *Dracula* and *Dracula's Daughter*, Dr. Waldman in *Frankenstein*, and Dr. Muller in *The Mummy*. The actor also appeared in bit roles in Universal's *The Man Who Reclaimed His Head* (1935) and the serial *The Phantom Creeps* (1939). He retired from films in 1950.

LIONEL ATWILL (1885–1946)

British-born Lionel Atwill had established himself in the horror genre in the early 1930s as the star of such non-Universal films as *The Mystery of the Wax Museum, Doctor X*, and *Murders at the Zoo*. At Universal City he was most often cast either as a mad doctor, a policeman, or village official. A crisp and incisive (if occasionally baroque) actor, Atwill's most memorable role was as Inspector Krogh in *Son of Frankenstein*, though he also appeared in *Man Made Monster, The Ghost of Frankenstein, Frankenstein Meets the Wolf Man, House of Frankenstein, House of Dracula*, and three quasi-horrific mysteries made in 1942, *The Mad Doctor of Market Street, The Strange Case of Dr. Rx*, and *Night Monster*.

GEORGE ZUCCO (1886–1960)

Born in Manchester, England, George Zucco began his acting career in Canada in 1908. He came to the United States a few years later, but returned to his homeland at the outbreak of World War I and did not return to America until 1935 to appear in the Broadway production of *Victoria Regina*, which starred the very young Vincent Price as Prince Albert. Given his dripping voice and dark eyes, which had the ability to radiate evil, he quickly found himself in villainous roles. He played Andoheb, the High Priest of Karnak/Arkam, in *The Mummy's Hand, The Mummy's Tomb*, and *The Mummy's Ghost*, and also appeared in *The Mad Ghoul* and *House of Frankenstein*. Renowned for his professionalism, Zucco suffered a stroke on the set of the 1951 film *The Desert Fox*, after which he never made another film.

JOHN CARRADINE (1906–1988)
One of Hollywood's most successful portrayers of villains, John Carradine always thought of himself as a stage actor—despite the fact he claimed to have appeared in more than 450 movies. (Only 350 can be documented, but still...) Carradine's saturnine looks and rich voice kept him in constant demand throughout his 60-year career. For Universal he played Dracula in *House of Frankenstein* and *House of Dracula*, and appeared in bit parts in *The Invisible Man* and *The Black Cat*, and took more substantial roles in *Captive Wild Woman*, *The Invisible Man's Revenge,* and *The Mummy's Ghost*. Carradine suffered from crippling arthritis in later years, but nonetheless continued to work right up to his death.

FRANK REICHER (1875–1965)
Scion of a theatrical family from Germany, Munich-born Frank Reicher was already appearing on Broadway before the turn of the 20th century. He first landed in Hollywood in 1915, but left again, returning at the dawn of the sound era to find work as an actor, writer, director, and acting coach. He often appeared as a no-nonsense professor, doctor, or other professional man, though his best-known role is that of Captain Englehorn in *King Kong* (1933). His contributions to Universal Horror include *The Invisible Ray, Night Monster, The Mummy's Tomb, The Mummy's Ghost*, and *House of Frankenstein*, the latter as Ullman, whose brain is earmarked for transplantation into the Monster.

MICHAEL MARK (1886–1975)

Short, bald, mustachioed Michael Mark most often turned up in Universal Horror as a villager or town elder. Born in Russia, he immigrated to the United States in 1910, but did not enter films until 1928. Mark's most notable role for Universal was as Ludwig, the father of the doomed Little Maria, in *Frankenstein*. He also appeared in *The Black Cat* (as a devil worshiper), *Son of Frankenstein*, *Tower of London*, *The Mummy's Hand*, *Ghost of Frankenstein*, and *House of Frankenstein*. Mark also had a role in Universal's 1940s science fiction serial *Flash Gordon Conquers the Universe*. His last film was 1969's *Hello, Dolly!*

LAWRENCE GRANT (1870–1952)

British-born Lawrence Grant's earlier Hollywood career playing European rulers, notably Kaiser Wilhelm, stood him well in later years when he was seen as a village official in *Son of Frankenstein* and *Ghost of Frankenstein*. He was also seen as the lawyer Crosby in *The Cat Creeps*, and Sir Thomas Forsythe in *Werewolf of London*. An indication of his standing within the Hollywood community can be gauged by the fact that he hosted the 1931 Academy Awards ceremony.

HARRY CORDING (1891–1954)

While the vast majority of his roles were bits, thickset, stern-faced Harry Cording is probably the most ubiquitous presence in all of Universal Horror. His showiest role was that of Bela Lugosi's servant "Thamal" in *The Black Cat*. He subsequently appeared in *Son of Frankenstein*, *Tower of London*, *The Invisible Man Returns*, *The Wolf Man*, *The Ghost of Frankenstein*, *The Mummy's Tomb*, *The Pearl of Death* (as well as six other films in Universal's Sherlock Holmes series), *The Strange Door*, and *Abbott and Costello Meet Dr. Jekyll and Mr. Hyde*. Anytime a dour, bluff, British presence was required anywhere in Hollywood, chances are Cording was there.

LIONEL BELMORE (1867–1953)

Plump, white-haired, and authoritative, London-born Lionel Belmore was in Hollywood practically from its beginnings, working as an actor, writer, and director as early as 1914. He was also there at the beginning of Universal Horror, playing Herr Vogel, the Burgomaster in *Frankenstein*, and returning for *Son of Frankenstein*, *Tower of London*, and *Ghost of Frankenstein*. In addition, he can be spotted in *The Mummy's Tomb* in stock mob footage cribbed from *Frankenstein*.

21 SPOTLIGHT:
JACK P. PIERCE

In 1957, Universal's makeup artist supreme Jack P. Pierce was enlisted by television's *This is Your Life!* to be a surprise guest of honor paying tribute to Boris Karloff, the man Pierce had turned into a monster time and time again. Right on cue, Pierce strode onstage, but before he could say anything, Karloff turned the tables on him, declaring, "The best makeup man in the world...I owe him a lot."

Pierce was born Janus Piccoulas in Greece in 1889, and with his family, immigrated to America right after the turn of the century. As a young man he played semi-professional baseball, but upon settling in Los Angeles, he began working a string of odd jobs, in and around the film industry. He landed at Universal in 1914, working, among other things, as an assistant cameraman and even an actor. As time went on, though, he drifted into the field of makeup, finding his true calling.

For the 1927 Fox film *The Monkey Talks*, Pierce devised an amazingly realistic chimpanzee disguise to be worn by actor Jacques Lerner. Because of that film, Pierce was invited back to Universal City to take over the makeup department. His first job was to devise the startling permanent grin for Conrad Veidt in 1928's *The Man Who Laughs*.

Pierce quickly and proudly became the lord of his domain, approaching his work in a scholarly fashion, carefully thinking out his designs and then achieving them with trial-and-error experimentation. His methods were time consuming: to build up a surface on the face, he used layers of cotton, sealed and hardened with collodion, and hair was applied one tuft at a time, which were painstakingly singed at the ends to create a more realistic layered look. It took hours and hours for Pierce to create his effects.

In Karloff, Pierce's favorite actor, he found his perfect working partner, someone with equal patience, dedication, and willingness to ignore the

Jack P. Pierce was almost never seen outside of his white makeup smock.

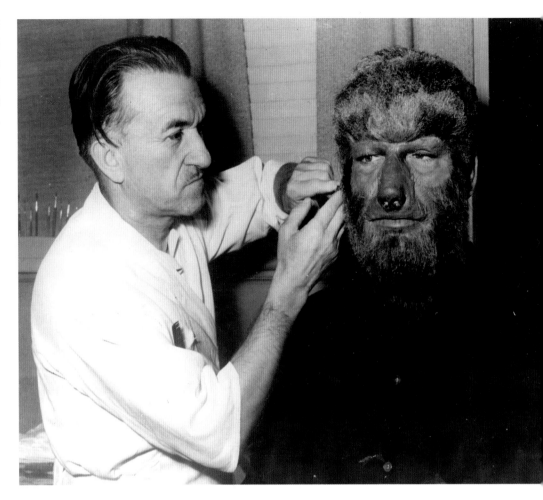

If the Wolf Man (Lon Chaney Jr.) looked slightly less hairy than usual in House of Dracula, *it was because Jack P. Pierce ran out of yak hair; his usual suppliers were ravaged by the war in Europe.*

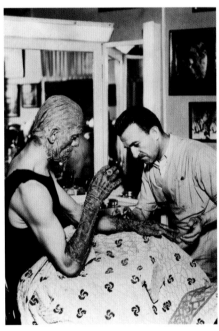

Jack P. Pierce puts finishing touches on the mummified hands of Boris Karloff for The Mummy.

discomfort. Not everyone had the same regard for his painstaking—and often painful—procedures, particularly in the makeup removal process. Nor did many appreciate Pierce's dismissal of their complaints. When Tom Tyler complained that the removal of his cotton-and-spirit-gum casing in *The Mummy's Hand* hurt like the devil, Pierce shrugged it off, saying, "Just stings a little is all." Lon Chaney Jr. summed up the scores of hours spent in Pierce's makeup chair by grumbling, "He leaves *some* of the skin on my face." Stuntman George de Normand, who doubled Karloff in *Bride of Frankenstein*, recalled that the actor invited him to his dressing room and handed him a stiff drink, saying, "You're going to need this," before sending him off to have his headpiece and collodion scars wrenched off.

While Pierce was able to modernize his techniques somewhat as time went on, particularly through the use of rubber Monster headpieces and Mummy masks, many younger makeup artists were making far more advancements (and were less autocratic on the job). In 1947 he was given his pink slip from Universal, and settled into a life of freelancing. Occasionally there would be a special makeup job—he was hired by Samuel Goldwyn to once again transform Karloff into the Monster for the 1947 film *The Secret Life of Walter Mitty*, but the gag sequence was cut from the final version—but most of his post-Universal assignments were conventional. His last regular gig was on the television show *Mr. Ed*. Jack P. Pierce died in 1968.

Hans J. Salter, the man responsible
for much of the signature sound
of Universal Horror.

22 SPOTLIGHT:
HANS SALTER

One of the most prolific artists in all of Universal Horror never appeared on camera, never wrote a script, and never directed a picture, yet his contribution to the horror film was monumental: he was composer and musical arranger Hans J. Salter.

Salter was born in Vienna in 1896 and received his musical training at the Vienna Academy of Music, where he studied composition with the likes of Franz Schreker and Alban Berg. Relocating to Germany, he became Music Director for the State Opera of Berlin and broke into film composing at the Universum Film AG studio (UFA), which in the late 1910s and 20s had pioneered the movement of film expressionism. But during the 1930s, UFA fell increasingly under the control of Hitler's Nazi Party, using the studio as a propaganda machine. Salter was one of the many who chose to leave rather than stay and glorify the Third Reich.

The composer immigrated to America in 1937 and the next year was hired by Universal as a composer, conductor, and arranger of other composers' music. His first foray into classic horror came through arranging the musical themes composed by Frank Skinner for *Son of Frankenstein*. By 1939 Salter had become Universal's musical director, a position that entailed taking existing musical tracks from the studio's stock library, the work of several composers, and reworking them into a score for any given film. The job meant working on a lot of films—42 of them in 1940 alone—and not all horror or thriller pictures, but everything from Westerns to serials to Ritz Brothers comedies. But it is his themes and motifs backing the studio's nightmare squad for which he is best known.

Salter's greatest gift was his versatility. He could write darkly romantic passages—the love theme from *The Invisible Man Returns*, for instance, which was reused to underscore the unhappy ending of *Son of Dracula*—or be in your face (or at least your ears), as with the flutter-

tongued trumpet blares that punctuate *Black Friday*. He could also be whimsical, as in his syncopated, tonal "Ice Cavern" theme heard in both *Frankenstein Meets the Wolf Man* and *House of Frankenstein*.

Salter's best known, and most frequently reused, motif was the driving three-note, half-tone ascension that accompanied just about every shot of a monster reaching for a victim or lurching toward the camera. His familiar monster themes extended beyond the careers of the Wolf Man and the Mummy, and can be heard in *Creature From the Black Lagoon*.

Hans Salter was nominated four times for an Academy Award (none for his horror films) but never won. He continued in films and television into the late 1960s, and then retired. He died in 1994 at the age of 98, living long enough to see younger generations treating the music he wrote for Universal's horror pictures with the kind of respect and appreciation afforded to classical composers in all areas of musical composition.

The Gill Man was played on land (and in shallow water) by Ben Chapman.

23
THE GILL MAN

Being a monster means never having to ask permission to come aboard. From Creature From the Black Lagoon.

The last great monster series produced by Universal Pictures had a uniquely interesting genesis: it was borne of an idea planted in the mind of a struggling actor working on no less a cinematic project than *Citizen Kane*. How on earth did Orson Welles's legendary production seed the beginnings of *Creature From the Black Lagoon*, 12 years later?

As a young man, producer William Alland was a member of Welles's Mercury Theatre company, usually playing small roles. In *Citizen Kane* he received the best part of his career as the reporter Thompson, who looks into the past of Charles Foster Kane. While the picture was being shot, its cinematographer Gregg Toland was not only mentoring first-time film director Welles, but also a young Mexican cameraman named Gabriel Figueroa. It was Figueroa who told Alland an old South American legend concerning a race of fish-men living on the Amazon River. The idea stuck with Alland, who eventually quit acting in order to go behind the camera. In the early 1950s when Alland teamed up with director Jack Arnold at Universal to oversee the studio's last wave of monster films—all of which had an emphasis on science fiction instead of gothic horror—he remembered the fish-men idea.

The Gill Man was born.

CREATURE FROM THE BLACK LAGOON (1954)

When the fossilized claw of an unknown creature is discovered in the Amazon jungle by Dr. Carl Maia (Antonio Moreno), he believes it to be a great scientific discovery. What Maia does not realize is that an even greater scientific discovery—a living version of the unknown creature—is only steps away. His discovery attracts the attention of evolutionist Dr. David Reed (Richard Carlson), his fiancée Kay Lawrence (Julia Adams), and the head of the institute for whom they work, Mark Williams (Richard Denning), a wealthy, if not entirely scientifically minded, entrepreneur.

Upon seeing the claw, Williams agrees to sponsor an expedition to find the rest of the fossilized skeleton, in return for credit for its discovery.

Having chartered the rattletrap steamer *Rita,* which is skippered by the colorful Captain Lucas (Nestor Paiva), the party chugs up the Amazon to continue their search in a body of water at the end of a tributary called the Black Lagoon, renowned as a paradise from which no one has ever returned. When they reach the primeval lagoon, Kay—for whose attentions Reed and Williams have become rivals—goes off for a swim, and attracts yet another caller: the Gill Man. The creature swims underneath her in a spontaneous underwater ballet.

Following Kay back to the boat, the Gill Man gets caught in the *Rita*'s netting, and nearly sinks the boat before finally ripping his way out. He leaves a claw, as evidence of his presence. They continue their efforts to catch the creature using a powerful drug called rodenal, which eventually works, rendering the Gill Man unconscious. The crew capture and cage him on the boat, but not for long. After mauling one of the party, Dr. Thompson (Whit Bissell), the Gill Man not only escapes, but he goes on the offensive, using a fallen log to block the only exit from the lagoon. The expedition is now stuck there.

The first attempt to move the log by winching it up fails, so Reed and Williams dive down to secure the cable around it. The Gill Man is waiting for them, and drags Williams down, killing him. Then he climbs on board the boat and abducts Kay, dragging her down to his underwater grotto. Reed dives down to follow while Maia and Lucas search for the land entrance to the cave like lair, which they manage to find just in time to shoot the marauding Gill Man, saving both Kay and Reed. The injured creature staggers back into the sea and sinks to the bottom.

Scripted by Harry Essex and Arthur Ross, from Maurice Zimm's story treatment of Alland's fish story, and filmed in the then-hot 3-D format by Jack Arnold, *Creature From the Black Lagoon* represents something of a hybrid between traditional Universal Horror film elements—the monster, the dedicated scientist, the love triangle—and newer trends for science fiction themes. In fact, the roles played by Julia Adams, Richard Carlson, and Richard Denning could have been filmed verbatim a dozen years earlier with Evelyn Ankers, Patric Knowles, and Ralph Bellamy. (Richard Denning, by the way, was Evelyn Ankers husband in real life.)

Antonio Moreno had been a major star of the silent era and was nearing the end of his long film career (which began in 1912) when *Creature From the Black Lagoon* was filmed. Ex-Monster Glenn Strange was first offered the role of the Gill Man, but he did not care for the thought of being submerged in a restrictive costume; perhaps he was remembering having been suited up head-to-toe as a monster called "The Gocko" in the 1936 serial *Flash Gordon.*

Two separate film units, operating simultaneously, worked on the picture, one at Universal City, whose backlot pond was transformed into the vast Black Lagoon through skillful camera angles and cutting, and the other on location at Wakulla Springs, Florida, where all underwater scenes were filmed. Alland and Arnold chose a young, 6'5" ex-Marine named Ben Chapman to play the Gill Man above ground in the scenes filmed in Hollywood, but a swimming specialist was required for the underwater shots. Arnold found just the right swimmer almost by accident.

Creature From the Black Lagoon *carried on the Universal Horror tradition of leading ladies being carted away by the monster. Here Ben Chapman (as the Gill Man) offers a lift to Julia Adams.*

Julia Adams was Universal's most popular leading lady of the 1950s. After Creature From the Black Lagoon *she would be known as "Julie" instead of "Julia."*

Universal's last great classic monster was the Gill Man introduced in Creature From the Black Lagoon.

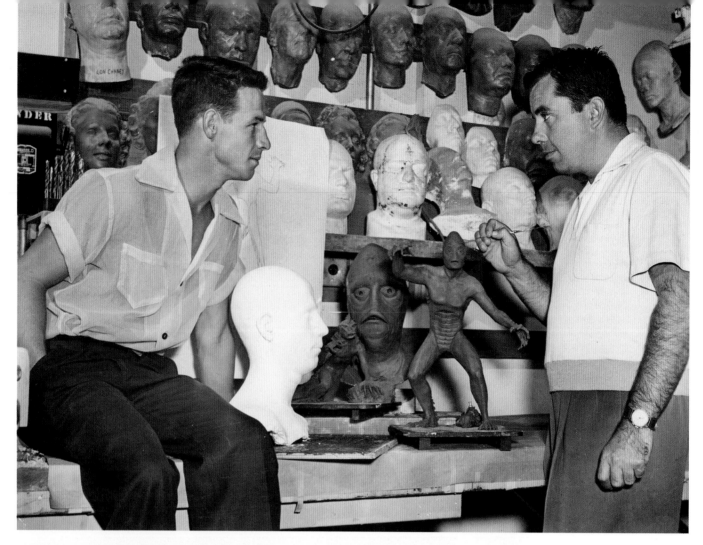

The underwater sequences for Creature From the Black Lagoon *were filmed separately in Florida and featured swimmer Ricou Browning as the Gill Man.*

Ricou Browning (left) is shown the alien-like, streamlined design for Creature From the Black Lagoon's *Gill Man by makeup department head Bud Westmore. The design was not used.*

Ricou Browning as the underwater Gill Man.

A 23-year-old Florida State University student named Ricou Browning had been recruited by the manager of Wakulla Springs to transport Arnold and a location scouting crew out to the site. Once there, they asked the young man to swim for some test footage, in order to gauge the perspective of the Springs on camera. After returning them to the airport, Browning thought little about it until he received a phone call from the director the next week. "He asked me if I wanted to play the monster," Browning recalls. "I said, 'Play the monster what?' He said, 'We're doing a film underwater about a creature and we like the way you swim. Would you like to do it?' I said, 'Yeah!'"

Journeying to Universal, Browning's body was cast by makeup artists Bud Westmore and Jack Kevan, and a suit made of latex rubber was readied, but it was not the one seen in the film. Studio head Edward Muhl wanted a more streamlined monster, one reminiscent of the Oscar statue. A suit reflecting that version was built and tested in the backlot water tank, but it looked more alien than amphibian and so was also rejected. The final version of the creature was designed by artist Millicent Patrick, who had earlier conceptualized the Mr. Hyde mask in *Abbott and Costello Meet Dr. Jekyll and Mr. Hyde*. Two complete suits were required in slightly different sizes, one for Browning and one for Chapman, who was five inches taller.

It has been asserted that Browning was able to hold his breath for five minutes, facilitating the length of the underwater shots, but even he dispels that rumor. "I can hold my breath for a fairly long time," he says, "but if you're fighting and moving and swimming fast, you're using up your oxygen. I had four safety men, each with an air hose. I'd do my scene, holding my breath, and then I'd go to one of the safety men for more air. I was always moving my hands or my head or swimming, so if I went totally limp that was my signal to the safety men that I needed air."

For the underwater "ballet" between Kay and the creature, Browning's dance partner was swimmer Ginger Stanley, who doubled Julia (later Julie) Adams. The strikingly beautiful Adams was at that time Universal's primary leading lady, and as such had appeared opposite James Stewart, Glenn Ford, Tyrone Power, and Rock Hudson, stars who may not have been as tall as her newest leading man, but who were nowhere near as scaly. Initially, the new assignment was a bit of a shock.

"At first I thought, 'The Creature from *what*?'" Julie Adams says today. "Then I read through it and thought, 'What the hey? It might be fun.' And it was a lot of fun. We had a good time making that picture, we all laughed a lot. In the morning, I would pat Ben [Chapman] on his rubbery cheek and say, 'Good morning, beastie!'" One incident on the set was slightly more serious: Chapman had difficulty seeing through the Gill Man mask, and while filming the scene of the creature carrying Kay through cave set, he bonked her head into the rocks.

While Adams did not perform in any scenes with Browning, she did meet him during his costume tests at Universal, and ended up getting aqualung instruction from him and underwater cinematographer Scotty Welbourne. "We went over to Catalina and I got to go aqualunging in those clear waters, so I had an adventure before we started shooting," she says. They might have had an even greater adventure had they followed through on a gag involving a tour boat running at night to look for flying fish. "Those boats shone lights on the water, and the three of us said, 'We'll

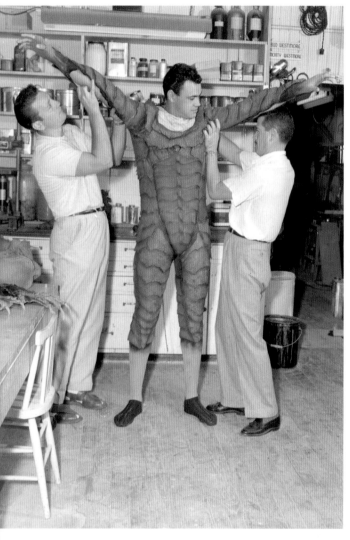

Ben Chapman being suited up for his role as the Gill Man in Creature From the Black Lagoon.

Julia Adams meets Ricou Browning, who was at Universal Studios to film tests in the "alien" version of the Gill Man suit that was ultimately rejected.

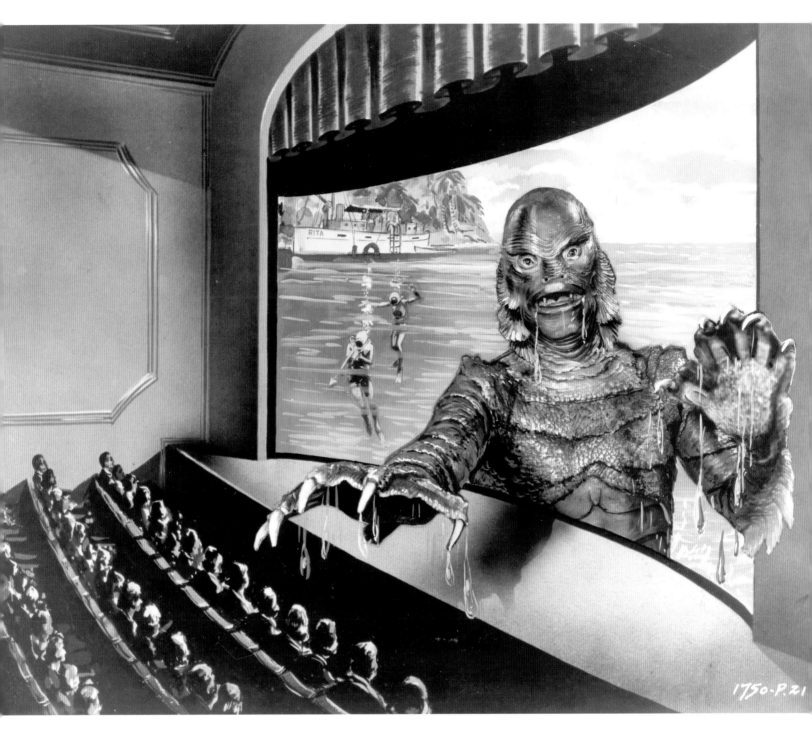

The 1950s craze of 3-D was a big selling point in marketing Creature From the Black Lagoon—*but the film became a classic even without it.*

get the Creature outfit and when they shine the lights, Ricou can come up!' We never did it, of course, but we had a lot of laughs thinking about it."

Even before *Creature From the Black Lagoon* went into general release in March of 1954, television audiences got their first glimpse of the Gill Man the preceding February through a gag appearance on *The Colgate Comedy Hour*, in which he menaced Lou Costello.

REVENGE OF THE CREATURE (1955)

Anticipating great success, Universal put a sequel to *Creature From the Black Lagoon* into production almost immediately after the first picture's release. *Revenge of the Creature* brought director Jack Arnold back to the Black Lagoon, and Charles S. "Scotty" Welbourne, who shot the Florida unit's footage for *Creature*, was the film's sole cinematographer this time. Martin Berkeley's script was crafted from a story by producer William Alland. Except for Nestor Paiva as Captain Lucas, however, none of the principal non-monster cast returned from the first film.

Lucas, whose new boat is the *Rita II*, is once more piloting an expedition up the Amazon to look for the Gill Man, this time at the behest of George Johnson (Robert Williams) and Joe Hayes (John Bromfield), who are hoping to capture the creature and take him back to Ocean Harbor aquarium and water park in Florida. The Gill Man proves as difficult to capture as ever, though they manage to take him by shocking him comatose through the use of dynamite. University professor Clete Ferguson (John Agar) and a grad student named Helen Dobson (Lori Nelson) join the research team at Ocean Park.

The Gill Man (Tom Hennessy) rebels against being chained in Revenge of the Creature.

Revived and subdued (at least temporarily), the Gill Man becomes the park's biggest attraction. Clete and Helen work with the chained creature, trying to teach him to respond to Helen's magnified voice, while prodding him with electricity. The creature proves to be a remarkably fast learner, and upon conducting further research, it is discovered that his blood is biologically closer to human blood than fish blood. He also begins to take an interest in Helen, who he gazes at through a window in his tank.

Part of being human, though, is losing one's temper, and the Gill Man decides he has just about had enough of both Clete's underwater cattle prod and being shackled to the bottom of the tank. He snaps the chain and escapes, drowning Hayes in the process, and escaping into the ocean. Now at large, the Navy sets about looking for him, but the creature is closer than most people think: he's actually stalking Helen! When Helen and Clete go to a waterfront nightclub and restaurant one evening, the Gill Man follows them in, grabs her, and then leaps back into the ocean.

Since the creature can stay on land for only so long, he has to periodically leave the unconscious Helen on the beach while refreshing himself in the surf. During one of these rest stops, Helen's prone body is spotted by two unfortunate college boys, who attempt to help, but are killed by the creature. But the subsequent discovery of their bodies puts Clete, the Navy, and the police on the Gill Man's trail. Leading an armed mob, Clete tracks down the Gill Man on the beach and saves Helen, while the police open fire on the creature, apparently killing him.

Like its predecessor *Revenge of the Creature* was released in stereoscopic 3-D, the last Hollywood film of the 1950s to be made in that format. This time the entire picture was filmed in Florida, chiefly at Marineland

TERROR IS LOOSE IN THE CITY!

REVENGE OF THE CREATURE

ALL NEW
THRILLS!
SHOCK!
SUSPENSE!

starring **JOHN AGAR · LORI NELSON · JOHN BROMFIELD**

with NESTOR PAIVA · Directed by JACK ARNOLD · Screenplay by MARTIN BERKELEY · Produced by WILLIAM ALLAND · A UNIVERSAL-INTERNATIONAL PICTURE

Even more so than the original, Revenge of the Creature *had a Beauty-and-the-Beast theme to it.*

The Gill Man mask (here worn by Tom Hennessy) was slightly altered for Revenge of the Creature.

Studios and Silver Springs, and its story revolved around yet another love triangle, only this time the third angle of it was the Gill Man himself. He and Helen develop a Beauty and the Beast–style fascination for each other, to the point where her command to "Stop!" actually prevents the creature from killing someone. Stuntman Tom Hennessy played the land-bound Gill Man, whose design was changed slightly to include larger, more fish-like eyes. Since the creature's intolerance of air breathing was more of a plot point this time, his gills were seen to expand and contract more frequently, like he was gasping, an effect achieved by building air bladders into the head mask.

For the underwater creature scenes, a swimmer named John Wayan was hired and costumed, but not long afterward, Ricou Browning got another call from Jack Arnold. "The guy they hired apparently wasn't used to swimming the way I swam or hose breathing, and he was having trouble underwater, so they weren't getting the footage they wanted," Browning says. He took over for the rest of the shoot, in a hastily altered costume.

Revenge of the Creature contains one throwback to the classic Universal monster films: the mob that chases the monster across the landscape at the picture's climax, but given the modern, realistic setting, they now wield flashlights instead of torches. The film has also become renowned as the very first appearance by a then-green, $75-a-week contract player named Clint Eastwood.

THE CREATURE WALKS AMONG US (1955)

Director John Sherwood took over from Jack Arnold for the third film of the series, *The Creature Walks Among Us*, which was written by Arthur Ross. The picture effectively exploits the theme of tampering with biological evolution that had run through the first two Gill Man films, and transforms the Creature into a whole new kind of monster. But in doing so, it also brings the series around full circle to the very beginnings of Universal Horror, because that hybrid monster, while different, also seems very familiar.

Yet another expedition is setting out to find the Gill Man, only this one is concentrating on the area of Florida in which he was last seen. The man behind this expedition is the wealthy, brilliant, but unstable surgeon Dr. William Barton (Jeff Morrow), who wants to leapfrog the evolutionary process and create a new race of beings. With him on board the high-tech yacht *Vagabondia III* are geneticist Dr. Tom Morgan (Rex Reason), diver Jed Grant (Gregg Palmer), scientists Dr. Borg (Maurice Manson) and Dr. Johnson (James Rawley), and Barton's adventurous but bored trophy wife Marcia (Leigh Snowden). While the doctors want to research the Gill Man for themselves, they frankly think Barton's plans are more than a little cracked. Meanwhile, Grant is far less concerned with a six-and-a-half-foot fish as he is with the seemingly vague Marcia Barton.

The party tracks the Gill Man into an isolated lagoon, the waters of which they infuse with a powerful sedative. But the creature fights back, attacking their boat. During the fight he ends up doused with gasoline and set afire. The combination of his third-degree burns and the sedative knocks him out and enables Barton's group to capture him.

Back in the ship's laboratory, they bandage the Creature like a mummy and begin to study his biology, discovering that he has a dormant

The Gill Man (Tom Hennessy) doesn't like anyone messing with his girl (Lori Nelson), particularly teenaged boys, from Revenge of the Creature.

More so than any other classic Universal Monster, the Gill Man, seen here after humanizing plastic surgery in The Creature Walks Among Us *(played by 6'6" Don Megowan), had a genuine fascination for women (in this case, Leigh Snowden).*

The humanized Gill Man (Don Megowan) as depicted in The Creature Walks Among Us *demonstrated very similar characteristics to the Frankenstein Monster—particularly when it came to demolishing a room.*

lung and human skin underneath his burnt-away scales (and since the scales provided protection for his sensitive derma, they are now forced to make a suit of clothes for him out of sail material). Barton believes that he has facilitated the creation of a transitional being, but the more rational Morgan argues that they have simply discovered a complex life form that already existed. As for the Creature, he's more confused than anyone. Not realizing his gills are gone, he leaps overboard and nearly drowns. Morgan has to rescue him.

The group heads for Barton's seaside compound in Sausalito, California, where they house the Creature in an electrified pen, from where he gazes longingly at the nearby water. Meanwhile a bigger problem for the increasingly disturbed Barton is the attention that Grant is showing his wife, who proves to be not as shallow as she first appears. Barton confronts Grant and in a rage, beats him to death. Then he drags the body to the Creature's pen, hoping to frame the creature for the murder! But in the process of turning off the juice to the fence, he enables the Creature to escape. Suddenly enraged, the monster chases Barton to the house and destroys the place, killing Barton in the process. Leaving Barton and Morgan's bodies alone, the monster staggers back to the shore of the ocean, preparing to go home.

The ending of *The Creature Walks Among Us* is ambiguous. We never really find out the fate of the transformed Creature. It appears that he is going to walk back into the ocean, and since he no longer possesses gills, he would be walking to his death. Yet the Creature up to this point has been a quick learner, which means he might realize that the ocean means destruction. Could it be that the evolutionary call of the water is stronger than the will to live, thereby completely eradicating Barton's theories?

Ricou Browning returned once more as the Gill Man for his few underwater scenes early in the film. After this picture, Browning would turn away from acting in favor of writing, producing, and directing, becoming one of the key creative forces on the 1960s film and television series *Flipper*, and staging underwater sequences for the James Bond film *Thunderball*, among others. The humanized version of the Creature was played by 6'6" actor Don Megowan. Given his redesigned makeup, which looks like a fishy golem, and his loose-fitting, whip-stitched costume, this monster is definitely rendered in the fashion of the Frankenstein Monster. This is emphasized at the film's climax when he goes on the rampage and destroys Barton's home, much the way the Monster has destroyed so many laboratories. Reinforcing this return to the basics is the character of Dr. Barton, whose zeal to prove his unorthodox convictions is positively Frankensteinian. Megowan would officially play the Monster three years later in a television pilot called "Tales of Frankenstein," which was directed by Curt Siodmak and produced by Revue Studios, Universal's television division.

24 SPOTLIGHT:
SCREAM SIRENS

Among the most valuable assets for a leading lady in Universal Horror films were beauty, talent, and a powerful shriek. Here are some of the best.

GLORIA STUART (1910–
Blonde leading lady Gloria Stuart was discovered by Hollywood at the prestigious Pasadena Playhouse and was signed by Universal in 1932. She immediately was taken under the wing of director James Whale, who cast the newcomer opposite a throng of experienced British actors in *The Old Dark House*, and then paired her opposite Claude Rains in *The Invisible*

Man. Stuart remained active in Hollywood until the 1940s and then dropped out for three decades, returning in the mid-1970s to play character roles in television and films. In 1997, she made one of the most spectacular comebacks in Hollywood history playing the 100-year-old Rose in *Titanic*, which garnered her an Oscar nomination. She has long had a secondary career as an artist.

VALERIE HOBSON (1917–1998)

Even though she appeared as the wife of middle-aged Henry Hull in *Werewolf of London* and as Baroness Frankenstein opposite Colin Clive in *Bride of Frankenstein*, this elegant, dark-haired Irish actress was only 17 years old when she made those films. A couple years later Hobson left America for England, where she appeared in some of Britain's earliest television programs before resuming her film career. Upon marrying British politician John Profumo in 1954, she retired from acting, but not headlines: in 1963 Profumo, then minister for war, was caught up in a messy sex scandal that was credited for bringing down Britain's Conservative government. Nevertheless, Hobson remained with Profumo until her death, though she never resumed her acting career.

EVELYN ANKERS (1918–1985)
The undisputed scream queen of Universal Horror, Evelyn Ankers was born in Chile to British parents, and began acting in films by the age of 18. An appearance on Broadway in 1940 led to attention from Hollywood, and ultimately a contract with Universal, where she became the most popular leading lady in the horror unit. After starring in *The Wolf Man* (which utilized her scream to full advantage), she appeared in *Ghost of Frankenstein, Captive Wild Woman, Son of Dracula, The Mad Ghoul, Weird Woman, Jungle Woman, The Invisible Man's Revenge,* and *The Frozen Ghost,* as well as 20 other non-horror Universal pictures. She retired from acting in 1960.

ELENA VERDUGO (1925–
A native Los Angelino, pert and naturally blonde Elena Verdugo entered films as a teenaged dancer, a talent that she displayed as Ilonka in *House of Frankenstein* (along with a healthy scream). She also appeared in *The Frozen Ghost.* Much of her career was spent in television, most notably in the 1970s series *Marcus Welby, M.D.,* in which she had a regular role as Nurse Lopez. She is a descendant of the Verdugo family who, in California's Spanish period in the 1700s, owned a good portion of what is now the San Fernando Valley, including the site of Universal City.

ANNE GWYNNE (1918–2003)

A former beauty queen and swimsuit model, Texan Anne Gwynne was signed by Universal after what was publicized as the shortest interview in history, 45 seconds. Dubbed "The T.N.T Girl" (Trim, Neat, Terrific) by the Universal publicity department, she bounced back and forth between horror films, comedies, Westerns, and serials, never quite achieving stardom. Gwynne screamed her way through *Black Friday,* the 1941 version of *The Black Cat, The Strange Case of Dr. Rx, House of Frankenstein,* and *Weird Woman.* Outside of the studio, the redheaded actress was one of the most popular pin-ups for soldiers fighting in World War II. Gwynne remained active as an actress through the 1950s.

ILONA MASSEY (1910–1974)
Born Ilona von Hajmassey in
Hungary, this coolly stylish blonde
was primarily an opera singer—at
one time she was promoted in
Hollywood as "The Singing
Garbo"—but since Universal also
had operatic Susanna Foster under
contract, Massey became a horror
heroine. Similarly likened to
Marlene Dietrich (like whom she
sounded), she gave European
credibility to the part of double
agent Maria Sorensen in *Invisible
Agent* and Elsa Frankenstein in
Frankenstein Meets the Wolf Man.
Returning to music after her stint
with monsters, Massey hosted her
own musical television series in
the 1950s

ACQUANETTA (1921–2004)
Burnu Acquanetta was born in
1921 on an Arapaho Indian reser-
vation in Wyoming and was raised
under the name Mildred Davenport
by a foster family in Pennsylvania.
Moving to New York as a teenager,
she was taken under the wing of
graphic designer Lucian Bernhard
who, in *Laura*-like fashion, molded
her into a socialite and model.
Signed by Universal shortly after
coming to Hollywood, she starred
as Paula Dupree in *Captive Wild
Woman* and *Jungle Woman*, and
also appeared in the "Inner
Sanctum" mystery *Dead Man's
Eyes.* Her career was over by the
early 1950s, though in later years
she became a local television
celebrity in Arizona, where she
made her home.

MARTHA VICKERS (1925–1971)
While never a lead actress at Universal, the smoldering beauty of Martha Vickers (a.k.a. Martha MacVicar) still managed to draw attention in small roles. In *Frankenstein Meets the Wolf Man*, she played the serving girl who first encounters Larry Talbot in the inn, and later becomes the Wolf Man's victim. In *Captive Wild Woman* she is the donor of the gland that transforms Cheela the gorilla into Paula Dupree. In *The Mummy's Ghost* she has a one-line bit as a college student, yet the camera lingers on her as though reluctant to let her go. One of Mickey Rooney's many ex-wives, she retired from acting in 1960, and died of cancer 11 years later.

MARY GORDON (1882–1963)
Short, matronly, white-haired, and blessed with a thick Scottish accent, Mary Gordon possesses one of the most familiar faces and voices in all of Universal Horror. She can be seen in *Frankenstein*, *The Invisible Man*, *Bride of Frankenstein* (in which she's thrown into the ruined mill by the Monster), *The Invisible Man Returns*, *The Invisible Woman*, *The Mummy's Tomb* (in which she is strangled by Kharis), and *Strange Confession*. She is perhaps best known as Mrs. Hudson, the landlady at 221b Baker Street, in Universal's Sherlock Holmes films.

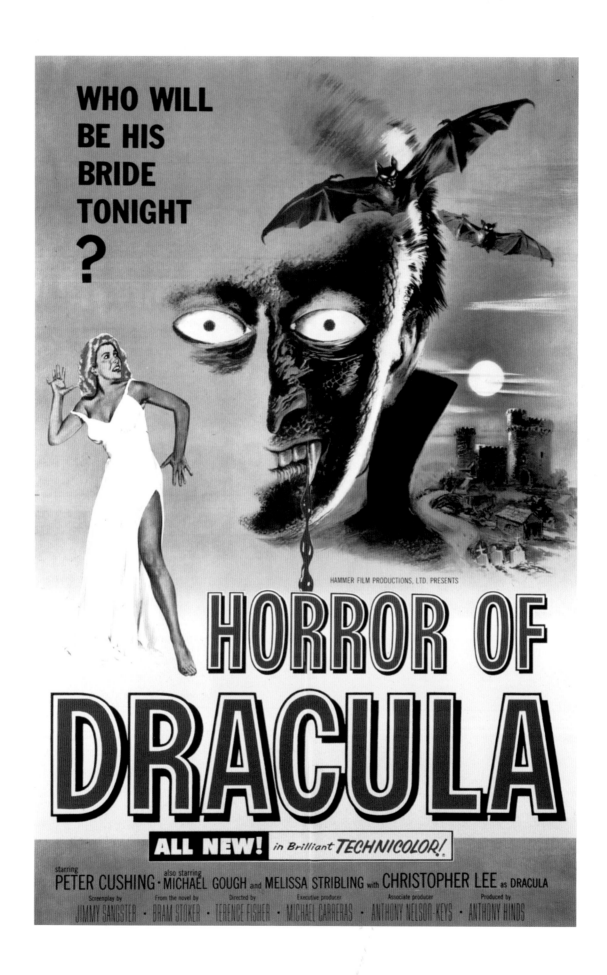

Hammer Films' Horror of Dracula, *which launched British actor Christopher Lee as the Dracula of his generation, was distributed by Universal-International in the United States.*

25

MONSTERS WALK AMONG US

John Zacherle, a.k.a. "Zackerly," was the most famous of all the regional hosts of "Shock Theatre!" a package of Universal Horror films released to television in the late 1950s.

By the mid-1950s, the realm of horror had changed for Universal Pictures. The classic monsters were largely memories, and even the cycle of science fiction–based monsters, such as the aliens of *This Island Earth* (1955), or the giant bug menaces of *Tarantula* or *The Deadly Mantis*, was starting to wind down. In 1957, however, television changed everything. That year, 52 of Universal's horror films were offered to television stations through Screen Gems, which owned the TV rights to the films, as part of the syndicated package "Shock Theater" (or simply "Shock!"). The films were scheduled for airing late in the evening and presented in each market by that city's own "horror host," a local television personality decked out in a suitably ghoulish persona. The "Shock Theater" package scored immediate success in stations across the country and served to introduce an entirely new generation of viewers to the vintage monsters.

The monsters were simultaneously being presented in a new venue, Warren Publishing's magazine *Famous Monsters of Filmland*, which was launched in 1958 and edited by science fiction and horror authority Forrest J Ackerman. While it was not devoted exclusively to Universal Horror, the monthly publication prominently featured the monsters and their portrayers. In the era before home video and DVDs, when old movies were generally unavailable unless they popped up on television, *Famous Monsters* was the primary place for young readers to learn about them. Among those who have acknowledged being influenced by *Famous Monsters* when they were kids are Steven Spielberg, Stephen King, directors Joe Dante and John Landis, and Oscar-winning makeup artist Rick Baker (and, for the record, the author of this book).

With something of a monster renaissance already underway in 1958, Universal-International forged a deal with the studio that was then the leading horror film producer in the world, Britain's Hammer Films, which had been producing low-budget thrillers and crime dramas since the 1930s. But in 1957, the small company had exploded into the public

If this lobby card from Dracula looks a bit sensationalized, it's because it is from the 1951 Realart Pictures rerelease. Universal-International sold theatrical distribution rights to many of its pictures, including most of its horror films, to Realart, which sent them back into theaters in the early 1950s.

Oliver Reed's werewolf makeup in Hammer's Curse of the Werewolf was somewhat reminiscent of Henry Hull's in Werewolf of London.

Herbert Lom's burn makeup in Hammer Film's remake of The Phantom of the Opera *was similar to Claude Rains's in the 1943 Universal version.*

Christopher Lee as Kharis in Hammer Films The Mummy, *which borrowed character names and plot elements from Universal's* The Mummy *and* The Mummy's Tomb.

consciousness with *The Curse of Frankenstein*, a gruesome, color retelling of the classic story directed by Terrence Fisher, and starring Peter Cushing and Christopher Lee. Because Universal had copyrighted Jack P. Pierce's makeup design for the Monster, an entirely different look had to be devised for Lee—which the actor has accurately described as looking like the victim of a car crash.

Soon, though, Universal became a bigger part of the equation by forging a U.S. distribution deal with Hammer, beginning with 1958's *Horror of Dracula* and followed by a string of semi-remakes of Universal films, notably *The Mummy* (1959), *Brides of Dracula* (1960), which like *Dracula's Daughter* did not actually feature the count, *Curse of the Werewolf* (1961), for which Oliver Reed wore a werewolf makeup reminiscent of Henry Hull's in *Werewolf of London*, and *The Phantom of the Opera* (1962). The latter featured Herbert Lom as a rather sympathetic Phantom, whose face was destroyed by fire, and transplanted the action from Paris to London.

In 1962 Universal-International was acquired by MCA, dropping its "U-I" designation and becoming simply "Universal" once more. For 1964's *The Evil of Frankenstein*, Universal's involvement with Hammer meant that the copyrighted Monster could now be replicated, though British makeup artist Roy Ashton's interpretation of it rendered it largely unrecognizable anyway. Kiwi Kingston, a professional wrestler from New Zealand, stomped around with a gray, boxlike head as the Monster, wearing a suit that looked like a hand-me-down from Don Megowan's humanized Gill Man in *The Creature Walks Among Us*. One direct echo from Universal's classic Frankenstein series was the discovery of the monster encased in a block of ice, ala *Frankenstein Meets the Wolf Man*.

That same year saw Universal simultaneously spoofing its classic horror figures and sitcoms in general in *The Munsters*, a half-hour comedy set in a house of genial monsters. John Carradine was first offered the role of Herman Munster, the goofy head of the household, but he turned it down, though he would appear in a few episodes as Herman's boss Mr. Graves, an undertaker. Producers instead chose towering Fred Gwynne to play the Frankenstein Monster who was wired for laughs instead of terror. Herman was married to Lily (Yvonne de Carlo, who had been a leading lady at Universal in the 1940s), whose father, known as "Grandpa" (Al Lewis) was really Count Dracula. Herman and Lily's son Eddie looked like a fledgling werewolf, and played with a wolf man doll, while their niece Marilyn was incongruously gorgeous. Incidental characters included Lily's lycanthropic brother Lester and Uncle Gilbert, the Gill Man. *The Munsters* ran for two seasons and spawned a feature film, 1966's *Munster Go Home* (which featured John Carradine in a different role), and a slate of revivals.

The growing army of fans for Universal Horror in the mid-1960s could even play Dr. Frankenstein at home by building the monsters for themselves. Frankenstein's Monster, Dracula, the Wolf Man, the Mummy, the Phantom, the Gill Man, the Bride of Frankenstein, and even the Munsters, could all be obtained in the form of model kits from the Aurora Company. At their peak, most Aurora monster kits sold for under a dollar. Today, if one can find one unopened and unbuilt, the collector's value can be in the hundreds of dollars. The model kits, though, were just the beginning: over the last five decades literally countless dolls, toys, rubber

Hammer's Brides of Dracula *had the brides, but no Dracula. Universal-International also distributed Hammer's Dracula-less 1963 film* Kiss of the Vampire.

Launched in 1958, Famous Monsters of Filmland *magazine introduced the classic monsters to readers not yet born during the Golden Age of Universal Horror.*

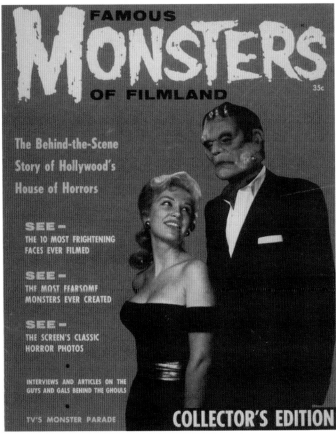

Wrestler Kiwi Kingston's Monster makeup in The Evil of Frankenstein *was supposed to resemble the copyrighted Jack P. Pierce Monster design, but Hammer Films' makeup artist Roy Ashton didn't quite get it right. Even so, the Universal tradition of monsters toting leading ladies (here Katy Wild) was adhered to.*

Science fiction writer, editor, and fan Forrest J Ackerman, the driving force behind Famous Monsters of Film-land *magazine, and the monster renaissance of the late 1950s.*

masks, books and collectables have been created in the likenesses of the great monsters, and the great monster stars.

In 1997 the United States Postal Service afforded a singular honor to the Universal Monsters by putting their images, and those of their portrayers, Boris Karloff, Bela Lugosi, and the Chaneys, on commemorative postage stamps depicting the Frankenstein Monster, the Mummy, Dracula, the Phantom and the Wolf Man. Karloff appeared on yet another stamp in 2003, one that celebrated the craft of movie makeup. Outside of a handful of U.S. Presidents, Boris Karloff is the only person to have appeared on three postage stamps: that is an incredible achievement for a man who at one time struggled mightily for a day's work, and the promise of eating the next day.

Fire, sulfur, explosions, swamps, stakes, sunlight, and bullets (silver or otherwise) could never stop the Universal Monsters for very long, and neither can time. The heroes and heroines of our nightmares—The Phantom of the Opera, Dracula, Frankenstein's Monster, the Bride of Frankenstein, the Wolf Man, the Mummy, the Invisible Man, the Gill Man, the Ape Woman, the Creeper, and all the others crafted by the artists, artisans and technicians of Universal Studios—are, and will remain, truly immortal.

Television's The Munsters *brought back many of the classic monsters through a comedic lens. From left to right: Butch Patrick as "Eddie," Yvonne de Carlo as "Lily," Fred Gwynne as "Herman Munster," Beverly Owen as "Marilyn" and Al Lewis as "Grandpa" (actually a mellowed-out Count Dracula).*

Artist Afua Richardson's reimagining of Count Dracula emphasizes the bestial side of his nature.

26 THE LEGACY CONTINUES

Ninety years have passed since Dracula, in the form of Bela Lugosi, and Frankenstein's Monster, unforgettably portrayed by Boris Karloff, first strode across movie screens and frightened people out of their wits. It has been eighty years since Larry Talbot, in the personage of Lon Chaney Jr., first suffered the tortures of the full moon and became the Wolf Man. For the better part of a century, these iconic characters—as well as the Mummy, the Bride of Frankenstein, and the Creature from the Black Lagoon—have haunted our dreams. But age, as they say, is simply a number, and the task of these timeless characters is not yet over. They remain as popular today as they ever did and will continue to appear in a variety of new media incarnations for years to come.

MONSTERS REBORN

With the release of the eerie, spine-chilling *The Invisible Man* in 2020, Universal Pictures launched the first of what promises to be a new, revitalized series of films based on the classic monster characters. As written and directed by Leigh Whannell, *The Invisible Man* was not a remake of the H. G. Wells story, but rather an ingenious reinterpretation of it as a paranoia thriller. "I thought that was the best way to do it in a modern context," Whannell said. "I didn't want to make anything retro. I didn't want the fog-machine-and-wolves-baying-at-the-moon version of the film."

The picture centers on a young woman, Cecilia Kass, played by Emmy and SAG Award winner Elisabeth Moss, who is suffering through a toxic relationship with Adrian Griffin, a brilliant but abusive scientist (played by Oliver Jackson-Cohen). In one sense, Cecilia is relieved when she gets word that Griffin has committed suicide and left his wealth to her, but then strange occurrences begin to leave her feeling as if she's being stalked and tormented by an unseen force. Cecilia eventually suspects that her former partner is not dead after all, but has somehow found a way to render himself invisible. She's right, of course—Griffin has developed an

*Elisabeth Moss as Cecilia Kass
increasingly finds herself standing
alone against an invisible menace in
Leigh Whannell's paranoia thriller*
The Invisible Man *(2020).*

invisibility suit—but no one believes the increasingly harried woman, not even her own sister, Emily (Harriet Dyer).

Shot mostly in Australia, with a few sequences filmed in Canada, *The Invisible Man* features highly effective yet often very simple special effects. Shots of doors moving from an unseen force, for instance, were achieved simply by using hidden strings. In the sequence where Cecilia is being attacked by an invisible force, Moss was rigged with ropes and wires so crew members could move her around, making it appear as if her bad boyfriend (a stuntman in a digitally erasable green suit) was interacting with her. Even simpler was Whannell's strategy of composing shots involving one actor as though these were two shots (framing two actors), psychologically implying an unseen person standing in the empty space.

Produced by Jason Blum's Blumhouse Productions, which has a distribution deal with Universal, *The Invisible Man* was a critical and commercial hit. It was also the first of a prospective line of modernized Universal Monster films. "We will absolutely be making monster movies with a modern sensibility," says Holly Goline, vice president in charge of Universal Monsters. She adds that a common thread among future projects will be telling the stories of outsiders and misfits. "We are all seeking to be heard, to be seen, and to be understood," Goline says. "Our monsters have a unique way of embodying that narrative, so they will always be timeless. Being an outsider never goes out of style, and there is always a story to be told around helping people feel less alone in their pain."

MONSTERS AMONG US

Motion pictures are not the only medium through which these venerable characters thrill and chill us. Over the years, the monsters' participation in the studio's theme parks in the United States and later Japan has been prominent. A live stage show called *Castle Dracula* ran from 1980 to 1983, while *Beetlejuice's Graveyard Review* was a perennial hit between 1995 and 2016. In addition, Universal's annual Halloween Horror Nights attractions have become enormously popular since being introduced in the Orlando, Florida, theme park in 1991. Universal Studios Hollywood launched their own Halloween Horror Nights event in 2006, and Universal Studios Singapore and Universal Studios Japan both followed suit in 2011. In 2018 Halloween Horror Nights at Universal Studios Hollywood featured a classic monsters walk-through attraction that brought many of the revered characters up close and personal for guests. Universal Orlando Resort created their own version of this attraction called Universal Monsters house in 2019. While there were slight differences between the Hollywood and Orlando Classic Monsters maze attractions, both succeeded in delivering the chills. Also in 2019 Universal Studios Hollywood produced an elaborate maze attraction based on *Frankenstein Meets the Wolf Man*, a haunted-house style walking tour led patrons through a dark, creepy gypsy's house, a haunted graveyard, Dr. Frankenstein's sparking, shocking laboratory, and a recreation of the "Ice Cavern" sequence from the 1943 film of *Frankenstein Meets the Wolf Man*. Multiple actors (dubbed "scareactors") played the title monsters, poised and ready to scare the pants off of guests in each of the different settings. The Hollywood production also featured an original music score by Slash, lead guitarist for Guns N' Roses.

In 2020, the Bride of Frankenstein became the star of her own Halloween Experience attraction called "The Bride of Frankenstein Lives."

Even the Frankenstein Monster gets into the spirit of dress-up for Universal's Halloween Horror Nights.

This creepy image of the handprint on the shower does not actually appear in the film The Invisible Man (2020) *but became an iconic promotional image.*

The classic monsters redesigned for modern audiences in Universal's Halloween Horror Nights events.

"It was actually a sequel to the movie as a maze," says Mike Aiello, Senior Director of Entertainment Creative Development at Universal Orlando. "The Bride's quest was trying to revive Frankenstein's Monster using the blood of Dracula's vampire brides. We really enjoy taking these characters and creating real stories around them." Aiello takes particular pleasure in using the attractions to introduce a new generation of park-goers to the characters. "A lot of people know these classic monsters very well, but for younger people it might be their first engagement with the characters," he says. "This is a way for them to learn about the characters and grow to love them."

The overall goal, of course, is to give everyone, including die-hard fans of the films, a fresh, fully immersive experience. "People have never had a chance to walk through Frankenstein's lab or Dracula's crypt, and I feel the architecture is just as much of a character as the characters themselves," says TJ Mannarino, Vice President, Entertainment Art & Design for Universal Orlando. The strategically designed sets in the walk-through maze attractions not only provide chills—they also control the movement of the crowd. "Most of the scares happen in the peripheral view," Mannarino says, "because if it comes in front of you, most people will retreat. If it comes from the right or left, you're going to move forward. You might catch a glimpse of Dracula three feet in front of you, but what you don't realize is that maybe on the other side is another scare, maybe Dracula's bride. The performers really know how to work the crowd so they don't always scare the same way."

While some modern tweaks are made in the sets and character designs, a few effects that were pioneered for the films ninety years ago still hold up fine, according to John Murdy, Creative Director/Executive Producer of Halloween Horror Nights at Universal Studios Hollywood. "For *The Invisible Man* [theme park walk-through] in 2018, we used almost the exact same approach as they did in the original movie," he says. "We had him against an all-black background, and the articles of clothing we wanted to be visible were treated to stand out under a black light. Through the use of a black light and controlling its focus, we could make him completely disappear while the clothing items we wanted to appear remained visible."

While this was startlingly convincing, Murdy admits that the effect works only by establishing a specific audience point-of-view. "It was one of our fans' favorite elements, but if you had to do it for every scene throughout the maze, it would be hard to pull off," he says.

THE EVOLVING LOOK OF HORROR
The challenge of redesigning the venerable characters for modern audiences is embraced by creature designer Mark "Crash" McCreery, who has spent more than thirty years as a top visual effects artist for motion pictures. "Depending on the story or the 'take,' there is plenty of room to get creative with the designs so long as you don't disrespect the original and change the design solely for the purpose of doing something different," McCreery says. "You want the characters to feel real and grounded, and reflect the technological and societal advances of today," he says, "but at the same time depict them in a way that doesn't disrespect the iconography of the Universal monsters that fans hold so dear. In the case of Leigh Whannell's *The Invisible Man*, we had a very modern design element, the Invisi-Suit, that justified the invisibility of the antagonist. The designs should reflect the needs of the story, and if you can't justify the design decisions within the story you are telling, you're going to disappoint a lot of people."

Eerie, spectacular environments are as crucial as the character appearances in Universal's Halloween Horror Nights.

Fine Artist and Muralist Tristan Eaton used up to forty cans of spray paint each day while creating his monumental Classic Monster murals at Universal Studios Hollywood.

Among the updated monster designs used in theme park events is a version of Dracula that emphasizes his blood and veins. "Dracula is like an addict," says John Murdy. "With an addict, you see the penalty of their addiction on their face, so we had the blood show on Dracula's face in the veins underneath the surface of the skin."

The classic monsters have also been heralded in a unique way at Universal Studios Hollywood, through a massive artwork collection created by noted street muralist Tristan Eaton. Created in 2019, the fifty-by-two-hundred-foot mural was spray-painted on the side of a soundstage at the edge of the backlot. Working from a boom lift that elevated him some twenty-five feet into the air, Eaton pressed through about forty cans of spray paint every working day to create the mural, which depicts Dracula, Frankenstein's Monster, the Bride of Frankenstein, the Wolf Man, and the Creature from the Black Lagoon.

For inspiration in designing the project, Tristan visited the NBCUniversal Archives & Collections facility, where historical artifacts from Universal motion pictures, television productions, and theme parks are stored, from posters and photographs to costumes and props to the minutes from Universal Film Manufacturing Company's first-ever board of directors meeting in 1912!

"We provided Tristan with a lot of stills and movie posters and lobby cards in digital format so he could look through them and incorporate content into the murals," says Jeff Pirtle, director of the archives. Eaton included a 1930 conceptual art design for *Frankenstein*, back when Bela Lugosi was announced as the film's star, in the Frankenstein panel of his mural. "The illustration shows the Monster the size of King Kong with lasers coming out of his eyes," Pirtle says. "What's interesting is that specific illustration, from before the movie was launched, came from the imagination of the artist who created it, and what he thought Frankenstein looked like. One of the things I love about the classic monsters is how they continue to be reimagined and reinterpreted throughout the years."

UNDYING MONSTERS

Terrified villagers and burgomasters might try staking them, burning them, or shooting them with a silver bullet, but ninety years' worth of audiences know better: you can't really kill the classic monsters of Universal Studios. They will always be back, ready to thrill and delight a new generation of moviegoers or theme-park patrons, unaffected by the passage of decades, continuing to come back ever stronger—and, in many ways, scarier.

Overleaf: Artist Matt Taylor's Frankenstein *poster (left) captures the lonely bewilderment of the Monster as characterized by Boris Karloff in the 1931 film. Artist Yuko Shimizu's striking image (right) of the Wolf Man evokes other European folklore, such as the Hand of Glory, the Green Man, and of course the omen of doom appearing in the palm of one's hand.*

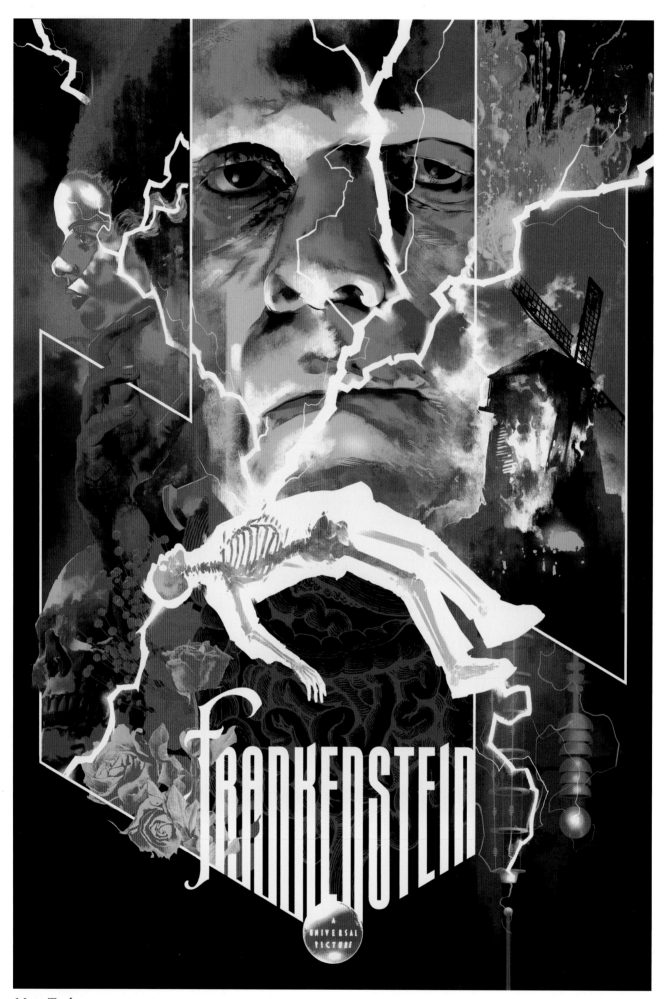

Matt Taylor

Yuko Shimizu

Page numbers in *italics* refer to photographs.

Abbott, Bud, *202*, 203, 207, *209*, 210
Abbott, Norman, *62*
Abbott and Costello Meet Dr. Jekyll and Mr. Hyde (1953), 207, *209–211*, 210, 216, 227
Abbott and Costello Meet Frankenstein (1948), *62*, 63, *202*, 203–204, *205*, *206*, 207, *208*
Abbott and Costello Meet the Invisible Man (1951), 207, *208*, *209*, 210
Abbott and Costello Meet the Killer Boris Karloff (1949), 204, *207*
Abbott and Costello Meet the Mummy (1955), 207, 210, *211*
Ackerman, Forrest J., *249*, 249
Acquanetta, *154*, 155, 157, *158*, 161, 166, *240*, 240
Adams, Jane "Poni," 57, *59*, 165
Adams, Julia (Julie), 223, 224, *225*, 227, *228*, 230
Agar, John, 193
Alland, William, 19, 190, 223, 224
Allbritton, Louise, *55*, 56, *56*
Ames, Leon, 14, 176
Ames, Ramsey, 120
Ankers, Evelyn, 56, 78, *80*, 91, *94*, 128, 144, 155, 157, 189, 190, 224, *238*, 238
Arliss, George, 85
Arnold, Jack, 19, 190, 223, 224, 227, 233
Arozamena, Eduardo, *50*
Ashton, Roy, 246, 248
Asther, Nils, 189
Ates, Roscoe, 186
Atwill, Lionel, *74*, 76, *77*, 78, *80*, 185, *186*, 189, 213, *213*
Aubert, Lenore, 204, *206*, 207
Avalos, Enrique Tovar, *50*

Baclanova, Olga, 34, 35, *37*
Baker, Rich, 243
Balderston, John L., 73, 110
Barrymore, John, 138, *138*, 141
Barton, Charles T., 204, *206*
Baxter, Frank, 193
Beast With Five Fingers, The (1946), 107
Beatty, Clyde, 157
Bellamy, Ralph, 78, 224
Belmore, Lionel, 217, *217*
Bey, Turhan, *117*, 119
Big Cage, The (1933), 157
Birell, Tala, *168*
Bissell, Whit, 224
Black Castle, The (1952), 190
Black Cat, The (1934), 180, *181–182*, 183, 214–216
Black Cat, The (1941), 14, *62*, 85, 239
Black Friday (1940), 106, 183, *184*, *185*, 185, 207, 221, 239
Boles, John, *68*, 69
Bond, Lillian, 175, 176, *177*
Bonomo, Joe, 25
Bricker, George, 165
Bride of Frankenstein (1935), 11, 12, 54, 70, *70–73*, 73, 85, 148–149, *151*, 170, 173, *200*, 201, 207, 219, 237, 241
Bride of the Gorilla (1951), 107
Brides of Dracula (1960), 246, *247*
Bromberg, J. Edward, 56, 141, *143*, 144
Bromfield, Louis, 45
Brown, Phil, 157, 161

Browning, Ricou, *226–229*, 227, 233, *233*, 235
Browning, Tod, 8, 45, *48*, 49, 198
Bruce, David, *188*, *189*, 190, 208
Bruce, Virginia, 138, *139*, 165
Brute Man, The (1946), *164*, 165–166
Bunton, Herbert, 45
Byron, Arthur, 109

Cabanne, Christy, 116
Cabinet of Dr. Caligari, The (1919), 21, 34
Calling Dr. Death (1943), 166, *168*
Captive Wild Woman (1943), *154*, 155, *156*, 157, 214, 238, 240, 241
Carewe, Arthur Edmund, 26
Carlson, Richard, 223, 224
Carradine, John, 56, 58, *58*, 59, 67, 100, 120, 144, *146*, *147*, 147, 155, *156*, 157, 180, *214*, 214
Carrillo, Leo, *186*, 186, *210*
Carroll, Leo G., 190, *191*
Cat and the Canary, The (1927), *31*, *32*, 33
Cat Creeps, The (1930), 33, 51, 216
Cat Creeps, The (1946), 33
Chandler, Helen, *44*, 45, *48*
Chaney, Lon, 19, *22–25*, 26, *26*, 28, *28*, *30*, 34, 38, *38–40*, 41, 45, 49, 60, 82, 100, 119, 126, 128, 129, 249
Chaney, Lon, Jr., 19, 41, *54*, *56*, 56, 58, 59, 78, *78*, *79–81*, 81, *91*, 91, *93–95*, 95, *97*, 97, *98*, *100–102*, 103, *104*, 104, *116–118*, 119–120, *121*, *122*, 123, *124*, *125*, 126, *127–129*, 128–129, *166*, 166, *167*, 167, *168*, 170, 185, 186, *186*, *187*, 190, 193, *202*, 204, *206*, *208*, 210, *219*, *219*, 249
Chaney, Patsy, *122*
Chapman, Ben, *222*, 223, 224, *225*, 227, *228*
Christine, Virginia, 123, *123–125*, 125
Churchill, Margueritte, 54
Clark, Mae, *68*, 69, 70
Climax, The, 106
Clive, Colin, *68*, 69, 70, 73, 132, 198, 237
Cobra Woman, 129
Cody, Buffalo Bill, 14, *14*
Coe, Peter, 123, *124*
Collier, Lois, 157
Coltin, John, 90
Corday, Mara, *191*
Cording, Harry, *182*, 216, *216*
Corrigan, Lloyd, 105
Corrigan, Ray "Crash," 157
Costello, Lou, *202*, 203, 207, *209*, 210, *211*, 230
Cowdin, J. Cheever, 19
Craven, Frank, 56
Crawford, Joan, 41
Creature From the Black Lagoon, The (1954), 19, *221*, *223*, 223–224, *225–229*, 230
Creature Walks Among Us, The (1955), 106, *232*, 233, *234*, 235, *235*
Creighton, Cleva, 41
Curse of Frankenstein, The, 246
Curse of the Werewolf (1961), *244*, 246
Curtis, Alan, 144
Curucu, Beast of the Amazon, 107
Cushing, Peter, 125, 246

Dade, Frances, 45
Dante, Joe, 243
Darling, W. Scott, 81
Davis, Bette, 49

Davis, Richard, 157
De Brulier, Nigel, 25
De Carlo, Yvonne, 246, *249*
Dead Man's Eyes (1944), *166*, 167, 240
Deadly Mantis, The (1957), 190, *195*, 243
Deane, Hamilton, 60, 65
Denning, Richard, 223, 224
Dmytryk, Edward, 157
Douglas, Melvyn, 176, *177*
Dracula (1931), 14, 19, 43, *44*, 45, *46–48*, 49, 170, *172*, 173, 198, 213
Dracula (1951), *244*
Drácula (Spanish Version-1931), 49, *50–51*, 51
Dracula's Daughter (1936), 51, *52–53*, 54, 201, 213, 246
"Dracula's Guest" (Stoker), 54
Dudgeon, Elspeth, 176
Dudley, Robert, *56*
Dunagan, Donnie, 76, *77*
Dvorak, Geraldine, *46*

Eastwood, Clint, 193, 233
Errol, Leon, 147
Essex, Harry, *186*, 224
Evil of Frankenstein (1964), 246, *248*

Famous Monsters of Filmland magazine, 246, *247*
Faragoh, Francis Edwards, 67
Farnum, William, *124*
Figueroa, Gabriel, 223
Finlayson, Jimmy, 105
Fisher, Terrence, 246
Fletcher, Bramwell, 109
Florey, Robert, 65, 67, 176
Foran, Dick, 113, *114*, 116, 186
Ford, John, 85
Ford, Wallace, 113, 120
Fort, Garrett, 45, 54
Fox, Sidney, 176, 178
Francis, Arlene, *179*
Frankenstein (1931), 14, 19, *64*, 65, *66–69*, 67, 69–70, 85, 119, 170, 173, 175, 176, 198, 201, 213, 215, 217, 241
Frankenstein, or the Modern Prometheus (Shelley), 65, 70
Frankenstein Meets the Wolf Man (1943), 73, 81, 95, *96–99*, 97, 100, 106, 161, 173, 213, 221, 240, 241, 246
Frankenstein (Webling), 65
Franz, Arthur, 196, 207, *209*
Freund, Karl, 49, 110, *113*, 113
Friedlander, Louis (Lew Landers), 183
Frozen Ghost, The (1944), 167, *168*, 238
Frye, Dwight, 43, *44*, 46, 65, *67*, 68, 69, 73, 170, *171–172*, 173
Fulton, John P., 131, 138, 141, 152–153, *153*, 207

Gable, Clark, 128
Gallow, Janet Ann, 78, *79*, *80*
Gemora, Charles, *179*
Gerrard, Charles, *172*, 173
Ghost Catchers (1944), 210
Ghost of Frankenstein, The (1942), 12, 59, 78, *78–81*, 81, 95, 97, 173, 213, 215–217, 238
Gift of Gab (1934), *180*
Golos, Len, 186
Goodwins, Leslie, 123, *125*
Gordon, Gavin, 70, *72*

Gordon, Mary, 116, 241, *241*
Gorog, Lazlo, 196
Grant, Lawrence, 216, *216*
Gravina, Cesare, 34
Gray, Colleen, *197*
Greene, Richard, 190
Grey, Nan, 51, *53*, 135, *136*, 138
Griffies, Ethel, *88*
Gwynne, Anne, *58*, 100, *166*, 166, *168*, 239, *239*
Gwynne, Fred, 246, *249*

Hale, Creighton, *32*, 33
Hall, Jon, 141, *142*, *143*, 144, *145–147*
Hall, Manly P., 185
Harding, Kay, 123, *124*, *125*
Hardwicke, Sir Cedric, 78, *80*, 135, *137*, 138, 141, *142*, *143*, 144
Harker, Mina, *44*
Harrigan, William, 132
Harris, Marilyn, *68*, *69*, 69
Hatton, Rondo, 157, 161, *161–165*, 165, 166
Hayden, Sara, 105
He Who Gets Slapped (1924), 60
Heggie, O. P., 70, *71*
Hell Harbor (1930), 161
Hellzapoppin' (1941), 210
Helm, Fay, *156*, 157, 189
Hennessy, Tom, *230*, *231*, 233, *234*
Hervey, Irene, 189
Hillyer, Lambert, 54
Hinds, Samuel S., 183, 185
Hobson, Valerie, 70, 90, *237*, 237
Hoey, Dennis, 95
Hoffman, David, 166
Holden, Gloria, 51, *52*, *53*, 54
Homolka, Oscar, 138
Horror Island (1941), 186, *186*, *188*
Horror of Dracula (1958), *242*, 243, 246
Horsley, David S., 207
House of Dracula (1945), 56, *57*, 58–59, *59*, 81, 207, 213, 214, *219*
House of Frankenstein (1944), 56, 58, 59, 81, 100, *100–103*, 104, 106, 213–215, 221, 238, 239
House of Horrors (1946), *163*, *164*, 165
House of Rothschild (1934), 85
Howard, John, 138, *138*
Howard, Shemp, 141
Hubbard, John, 116
Hugo, Victor, 25, 33
Hull, Henry, *86*, 87, *88*, *89*, 90, 244, 246
Hunchback of Notre Dame, The (1923), 12, 21, *22–24*, 25–26, 38, 100
Huntley, Raymond, 48
Hurlburt, William, 73
Hurst, Brandon, *24*, 25, 33, *36*
Hutchinson, Josephine, 76
Hyans, Edward, *158*

"Inner Sanctum Mysteries," 166–169
Invisible Agent (1942), 106, 131, *140*, 141, *142–143*, 144, 193, 240
Invisible Man, The (1933), 14, *130*, 131–132, *132*, *133*, 135, 148, *150*, 152, 153, 173, 198, 214, 236–237, 241
Invisible Man Returns, The (1940), 106, 120, 131, *134*, 135, *136–137*, 138, 216, 220, 241
Invisible Man's Revenge, The (1944), 144, *145–147*, 214, 238
Invisible Ray, The (1936), 183, 214

Invisible Woman, The (1941), 106, 131, 138, *139*, 140, 241
Irving, George, *54*

Jass, Mel, 8
Jay, Griffin, 116, 120
Johann, Zita, 110, *113*, 113
Johnson, Chic, *210*, 210
Julian, Rupert, 26, 28, *29*
Jungle Captive, The (1945), 157, *159*, *160*, 161
Jungle Woman (1944), 157, *158*, 238, 240

Karloff, Boris, 8, 11–12, *15*, *18*, 19, 34, 41, 49, 63, *64*, 65, 67, *67*, *68*, 69, 70, *73*, 73, *75–77*, 76, 78, 81, 82, *83–85*, 85, 100, *101*, 103, 104, *108–110*, 109, 110, 113, 116, 119, 132, 143, *151*, 170, 175, 176, *177*, 180, *180–182*, 183, *184*, 185, 186, 190, *190*, 196, 201, 207, *207*, *210*, *211*, 218, *219*, 219, 249
Katch, Kurt, 210
Kellaway, Cecil, *113*, 113, 135
Kenton, Erle C., 19, 81, 104
Kerry, Norman, 25, 26, *30*
Kevan, Jack, *204*, 204, 227
King, Stephen, 243
Kingston, Kiwi, 246, *248*
Kiss of the Vampire (1963), 246
Knowles, Patric, 95, *99*, 224
Knox, Elyse, 116, *118*, 119
Kohner, Paul, 49, 51
Kosleck, Martin, 123, 164–166
Kruger, Otto, 51, *53*, 157, *160*

La Plante, Laura, *31*, *32*, 33
Laemmle, Carl, 12, *13*, 14, *15*, 49, 67, 69
Laemmle, Carl, Jr. (Julius), 14, *17*, *19*, 45, 54, 65, 67, 132, 176
Lamont, Charles, 210
Lanchester, Elsa, 70, *70*, *72*, 190
Landis, John, 243
Lane, Charles, 138, *139*
Lane, Vicky, *159*, *160*, 161
Lang, Fritz, 106
Laughton, Charles, 175, 176, *177*, 190, *190*
Le Borg, Reginald, 19, *122*, 128, 157
Lee, Christopher, 125, 243, *245*, 246
Lee, Rowland V., 76, 78
Leech Woman, The (1960), 196, *197*
Lees, Robert, 138
Leni, Paul, 33, 34, *37*
Leonard, Sheldon, 207
Leroux, Gaston, 26, 28
Lewis, Al, 246, *249*
Lewis, David, 67
Liveright, Horace, *48*
Livingston, Robert, 69
Lockhart, June, 105
Loftin, Carey, *103*
Lom, Herbert, *245*, 246
Lorre, Peter, 141, *142*, 144, 170
Lost Patrol, The (1934), 85
Lowery, Robert, 120
Lubin, Arthur, 185
Lugosi, Bela, 11–12, *18*, 19, 34, *42*, 43, *44*, 45, *46–48*, 49, 51, 54, 56, 60, *61–63*, 63, 65, *75*, 76, *77*, 78, 91, 95, 97, *97–99*, 170, 176, 178, *179*, 180, *180–183*, 183, *184*, *185*, 185, 186, 189, 193, *202*, 204, *205*, *206*, 207, 249
Lukas, Paul, 63

Mad Ghoul, The (1943), *188*, 189–190, 208, 213, 238
Maltese Falcon, The (1931), 170
Malvern, Paul, 19
Man Made Monster (1941), *126*, 128, 185–186, 186, *187*, 213
Man Who Laughs, The (1928), 33–34, *34–37*, 218
Man Who Reclaimed His Head, The (1935), 167, 213
Mander, Miles, 161, *162*
Manners, David, *44*, 45, 110, 180
Manson, Maurice, 233
Marin, Edward L., 141
Mark, Michael, *215*, 215
Marshall, Tully, *31*, 33
Massey, Ilona, 95, 97, *99*, 141, *143*, 144, *240*, 240
Massey, Raymond, 175, 176, *177*
Matinee Movie, 8
Matthews, Lester, 90, 144, *146*
May, Joe, 106, 138
Maynard, Ken, *15*
McNally, Stephen, 190
Megowan, Don, 106, *107*, *234*, *235*, 235
Melford, George, 51
Méliès, Georges, 21
Melody of Love, 35
Miller, Patsy Ruth, *24*, 25, 100
Millhauser, Bertram, 147
Miracle Man, The (1919), 41
Mole People, The (1956), 19, *192*, 193, *194–195*, 196
Monkey Talks, The (1927), 218
Monster on the Campus (1958), 19, 196, *197*
Montez, Maria, *129*, 141
Moore, Dennis, 123, *124*, *125*
Moore, Eva, 175, 176, *177*
Moran, Peggy, *115*, 116, *188*
Moreno, Antonio, 223, 224
Morgan, Ralph, 189
Morris, Chester, 49
Morrow, Jeff, 233
Muhl, Edward, 227
Mummy, The (1932), 8, 14, 84, 85, *108–111*, 109–110, *113*, 113, 119, 213, *219*, 245
Mummy, The (1959), 125, *245*, 246
Mummy's Curse, The (1944), 123, *123–125*, 125
Mummy's Ghost, The (1944), 120, *121*, *122*, 125, 213, 214, 241
Mummy's Hand, The (1940), *112*, 113, *113–115*, 116, 119, 125, 210, 213, 215, 219
Mummy's Tomb, The (1942), 116, *116*, *116–118*, 119, 120, 125, 213, 214, 216, 217, 241, 245
Muni, Paul, 49
Munster Go Home (1966), 246
Munsters, The, 246, *249*
Murders in the Rue Morgue (1932), 14, 176, *178–179*, 180
Murphy, Dudley, 45, *48*

Naish, J. Carrol, 100, 157, *167*
Naked City, The (1948), 104
Napier, Alan, 135, *136*, *137*, 165
Nash, Ogden, 14
Neal, Tom, 165
Neill, Roy William, 161
Nelson, Lori, *234*
Newhard, Robert, *20*, 21